El Libro del conoscimiento
de todos los reinos

(The Book of Knowledge of All Kingdoms)

MEDIEVAL AND RENAISSANCE

TEXTS AND STUDIES

VOLUME 198

El Libro del conoscimiento
de todos los reinos

(The Book of Knowledge of All Kingdoms)

Edition, Translation, and Study

by

NANCY F. MARINO

Arizona Center for Medieval and Renaissance Studies

Tempe, Arizona

1999

A generous grant from The Program for Cultural Cooperation Between Spain's Ministry of Culture and United States' Universities has assisted in meeting the publication costs of this volume.

Library of Congress Cataloging-in-Publication Data

El libro del conoscimiento de todos los reinos = The book of knowledge of all kingdoms / edition, translation and study by Nancy F. Marino.
     p. cm. — (Medieval & Renaissance texts & studies ; v. 198)
Includes bibliographical references and index.
ISBN 0-86698-240-X (alk. paper)
    1. Voyages and travels. 2. Flags. I. Marino, Nancy F., 1951– . II. Title: Book of knowledge of all kingdoms. III. Series: Medieval & Renaissance Texts & Studies (Series) ; v. 198.
G370.L5 1999
910.4–dc21   99–13118
                                                        CIP

This book is made to last.
It is set in Bembo,
smythe-sewn and printed on acid-free paper
to library specifications.

Printed in the United States of America

For Frank

To the memory of Jules Piccus

"Men travel about to wonder at the heights of mountains, the wide sweep of rivers, the circuit of the oceans, and the revolutions of the stars, but themselves they consider not."

St. Augustine

Table of Contents

Foreword

When Marcos Jiménez de la Espada first wrote about the *Libro del conoscimiento de todos los reinos* in 1874, he was enthusiastic about his plans to edit for the first time what he considered a historical account of the travels that an anonymous Franciscan missionary had made throughout Europe, Asia, and Africa in the fourteenth century. Before his edition was finally published in 1877, Jiménez de la Espada's confidence in the text met with the ridicule of Alfred Morel-Fatio, Manuel Serrano y Sanz and others, who quickly recognized the apocryphal nature of the book: the voyage was too long, too extensive, and much too fantastic in parts to be accepted so readily as a true story. Despite Jiménez de la Espada's conviction in the veracity of this travel book, nineteenth- and twentieth-century evidence suggests otherwise.

Probably composed in the last quarter of the fourteenth century, the *Libro del conoscimiento* is an anonymous work of some 20,000 words. It is doubtful that its author was a Franciscan friar, as the book's first editor imagined him. Jiménez de la Espada had at his disposal three manuscripts of the text from which to render his edition. However, it is not entirely reliable because he modified the text without justification or explanation. In addition to this shortcoming, Jiménez de la Espada's introductory study is based upon his undemonstrable assumptions about the historicity of the book and its supposed Franciscan authorship. In 1912 Clements R. Markham translated into English the text that Jiménez de la Espada provided in his edition.

The need to re-edit the *Conoscimiento* has become even more pressing with the recent reappearance of a fourth manuscript, whose inclusion in the study of the present work reaffirms some opinions about the other three codices and helps establish a reliable text that is probably very close to the original. In addition, our knowledge about medieval travel books, geography, maps, and the state of exploration in the fourteenth century has increased enormously since the work's first modern appearance in 1877. This information has been indispensable not only for the purposes of editing the

text, but also for the reconsideration of many aspects of the book (author-ship, sources, date of composition, etc.). In addition, it provides the modern reader with useful annotations.

The present edition is the result of my participation in the ADMYTE project, for which I provided a paleographic edition of the *Conoscimiento*. When I agreed to undertake the editing of this text, I had little idea of what the book was about, and no concept of how suggestive a work it is; over the past few years, I have become obsessed with medieval maps, heraldic devices, and travel books in general.

My thanks to Charles Faulhaber for suggesting that I edit this text for ADMYTE. I should also like to express my gratitude to Sir Peter Russell, who has written several times on the *Conoscimiento*, examined the fourth manuscript before it was sold at Sotheby's and disappeared again for a time, and has been most encouraging about my edition of the text; and to Pedro M. Cátedra, who helped me locate some materials that concern this work. The University of Salamanca, the Biblioteca Nacional (Madrid), and the Bayerische Staatsbibliothek (Munich) were most cooperative in sending me microfilms of the manuscripts, as was the library staff of the University of Arkansas, who provided me a photocopy of a facsimile of the Catalan Atlas of 1375.

Introduction

THE MANUSCRIPT SOURCES

Until 1993 scholars had available to them three manuscript witnesses of the *Libro del conoscimiento*; a fourth codex, missing since the seventeenth century, finally surfaced and was sold at Sotheby's in 1978, then disappeared into an unnamed "German state library," rendering it unaccessible for fifteen years. Its recent location in the Bayerische Staatsbibliothek in Munich makes it possible to complete for the first time an edition of the work with all known extant manuscripts. All of the existing texts were copied in the mid- to late-fifteenth century and, as we shall see, there probably were at least two (and perhaps more) earlier exemplars of the *Conoscimiento* from which these four were reproduced.

The complete text of the *Conoscimiento* is found in MS. 1997 of the Biblioteca Nacional (Madrid), and is commonly referred to by the *siglum* *S*.[1] In addition to its completeness, *S* is also the most artistically rendered of the four codices. Its forty-nine folios (numbered in modern times) are written on excellent vellum in a careful Gothic hand. The flexible parchment binding is relatively modern as well, perhaps dating from the eighteenth century, and on its spine is written *Viaje del mundo con las Armas de todos sus Reynos* [*A Trip around the World with the Arms of all its Kingdoms*]. Folio 1r has an initial capital E of eleven lines that contains an exquisite miniature of a gentleman seated at a writing table, on the lower shelf of which there are two jugs, painted in grey tones to simulate silver. He wears blue and red clothing and a black cap in the late fifteenth-century style, and is in the act of writing: in his right hand is a pen, in the left, an inkwell. Behind him is a window through which one can see the countryside and the wall of the next building. On this wall is a type of cabinet which appears to

---

[1] This *siglum* was assigned to the manuscript by Marcos Jiménez de la Espada, in his edition of the *Libro del conoscimiento de todos los reinos* (Madrid, 1877; repr. Barcelona: El Albir, 1980) as were the *sigla* of the next two under consideration, *N* and *R*. I have found no reason to change them.

contain several other "silver" objects. The first folio also has an ornate and colorful border of flowers and other such decorative motifs. On the bottom of the page are two angels holding a red shield with the Hebrew letters that spell "Jeová." This last detail led nineteenth-century bibliographer Francisco González Vera to convince the work's first editor, Marcos Jiménez de la Espada, that the manuscript once belonged to the famed fifteenth-century poet and book-collector, Iñigo López de Mendoza, Marqués de Santillana: apparently all of his books were decorated similarly, but displayed *Ave Maria gratia plena* [Hail Mary, full of grace] instead of *Jeová* on the shield. González Vera believed that the manuscript probably had been adulterated by unscrupulous persons who mishandled the Marqués's library.[2] He also believed that the gentleman depicted in the miniature was Santillana himself, whose portrait normally adorned the initial of the first folio of the codices he owned. After comparing the miniature in *S* with other known likenesses of the Marqués, Jiménez de la Espada concluded that it was not the famous nobleman who was portrayed, rather it was the author of the *Conoscimiento*. This is probably an accurate assessment, given the activity of the individual in the miniature. Nevertheless, Jiménez de la Espada would go on to insist that the author was a Franciscan missionary, an incongruous idea considering the evident secular and indeed elegant fashion of the man's clothing.

The rest of manuscript *S* manifests the same quality of decoration. All of its initial letters are illuminated in red and blue, and the rendering of the 108 coats of arms it displays is the most exquisite of the four extant manuscripts. (There are also eight outlines of shields left blank.) There are no drawings of people or monuments, as there are in the other copies which we shall discuss below. The rich execution of the book probably means that it was destined for a serious and wealthy collector, the Marqués de Santillana or someone of like interests. Despite the great care taken for the appearance of this book, the copyist nonetheless had little idea of what he was writing; he made errors in reading the text from which he copied, especially with place-names unfamiliar to him. But we must agree with Jiménez de la Espada that *S* seems to be the codex that contains the smallest number of copyist mistakes and errors of omission; this, coupled with its completeness, make it the most satisfactory of the manuscripts for use as the basis of an edition. In this we follow the lead of Jiménez de la Espada, and

---

[2] Peter E. Russell, "La heráldica en el *Libro del conosçimiento*," in *Studia Riquer*, vol. 2 (Barcelona: Quaderns Crema, 1987), 688, is not convinced by this opinion. Mario Schiff does not count this work among those of the Marqués's library, studied in his *La bibliothèque du Marquis de Santillane* (Paris: Emile Bouillon, 1905).

have employed *S* as the foundation for our edition. It is probably not, however, the oldest of the four witnesses, as our predecessor would have it; but he had never seen the recently re-emerged text that appears to be the earliest known copy.

The Biblioteca Nacional owns a second manuscript of the *Libro del conoscimiento*, MS. 9055 (*siglum N*). It is, however, incomplete. Unlike *S*, which lacks a title, *N* prefaces the text with the rubric: "[E]ste es el libro del conosçimiento de todos los rregnos et tierras et señorios que son por el mundo et delas señales et armas que han en cada tierra et señorio por sy et delos rreys et señores que las proueyen" [This is the book of knowledge of all the kingdoms and lands and lordships that there are in the world, and of the emblems and arms that there are in each land and lordship itself, and of the kings and lords that rule them]. Written on paper, *N* is missing at least one folio at its end, and seven other folios interspersed throughout the text are unaccounted for as well. After its last existing folio (66v) there follow two blank pages, then the last half of the work entitled *La Donzella Teodor* [The Maiden Theodora] (fols. 69r–74r), and finally a list of some Visigothic and later kings of Spain (fols. 74v–78v). The entire manuscript was copied in one precise Gothic hand, perhaps by the "Rodericus de Gaton" who signed the last folio. At the foot of this page is written: "Año de mill et quatroçientos et çinquenta et quatro años a veynte et dos dias del mes de Julyo faleçio el rrey don John en Valladolit" [Year of one thousand and four hundred and fifty-four years, at twenty-two days of the month of July King Don Juan died in Valladolid]. The manuscript evidently was copied sometime following the death of Juan II of Castile.

The depiction of the coats of arms in *N*, while more than adequate, is not as well executed as in *S*. In addition to the 110 shields in this manuscript, there are eleven miniatures which portray unusual humans or famous places. As we have mentioned above, *S* contains no miniatures of this type. Besides some textual discrepancies, this is the aspect that most distinguishes *S* from *N* (and from the other two codices as well, as we shall see below). *N*'s non-armorial illuminations are generally prefaced by a short piece of text which is missing, logically, from *S*. This usually takes the form of "et esta es su figura" [and this is its image], probably a copyist's makeshift interpolation designed to introduce the drawing that follows. Important textual variants clearly demonstrate that *S* and *N* originated from distinct manuscript sources. These differences include both additions and omissions in *N* as well as variant use of lexical items.

The third codex, MS. 1890 of the University of Salamanca (*R*), was housed previously in the library of the Royal Palace in Madrid, and prior

to that in the Colegio Mayor de Cuenca. Like *S*, it offers a complete text
of the *Libro del Conoscimiento*. Like *N*, it was written on paper, and bears the
same title as in that manuscript. Less care was taken with the production of
this text than with *N* or *S*: the script is not as regular, for example, and the
coats of arms are represented the most primitively of all four codices. The
drawing and illuminating were done hastily in most cases. Some shields are
only half painted; some are not illuminated at all, but are simply outlined
roughly in pen; several have been obliterated, probably the result of discovered but uncorrected errors; from fol. 37v to the end of the text on fol.
41v, the coats of arms disappear altogether although space was left for them
by the copyist. The miniatures of monstrous humans and legendary places
are likewise rendered poorly.

R and *N* seem to have been copied from the same source, as Jiménez de
Espada also assumed.[3] Their texts are strikingly similar, and the discrepancies between them are not significant enough to suggest that they would
have originated from two different manuscripts. The copyist of *N*, for
example, sometimes omits a word or phrase, or sometimes inserts an incon-
sequential addition (especially when introducing a miniature) or makes a
relatively unimportant alteration (as in "rreynado" [reign] instead of "rreino"
[kingdom]); and there are the typical variant readings of names unfamiliar to
the copyists (Birona/Bixna, Liristol/Bristol, etc.). But Georges Pasch, in his
study of the coats of arms of the three manuscripts known to him (*S*, *R* and
N), concluded that the illustrators of these codices worked independently of
one another; at times the representations of the shields are different in small
ways, and sometimes there is nothing at all in common between them.[4]
Perhaps there is a simple, but unverifiable, explanation for this: once the
copying of the text had been accomplished, the new codex could have
passed on to an artist who worked from a description rather than a visual
image of the arms.

In his 1678 work entitled *Progressos de la historia en el reyno de Aragon, y
elogios de Geronimo Zurita* [*Progress of History in the Kingdom of Aragon and
praise for Geronimo Zurita*], Diego José Dormer described a book belonging
to the Count of San Clemente that had previously been in the possession of
the renowned Aragonese historian Zurita.[5] Dormer called it a "Viaje del
mundo, escrito en 1305 y tiene notas de Zurita" [Trip around the world,

---

[3] Jiménez de la Espada, *Conoscimiento*, xiii.

[4] "Les drapeaux des cartes-portolans: Drapeaux du *Libro de Conoscimiento*." *Vexillologia:
Bulletin de l'Association Française d'Etudes Internationales de Vexillologie* 2, nos. 1–2 (1969): 9.

[5] (Zaragoza, 1680), 268–69.

written in 1305, and it has notes by Zurita], surely a reference to a copy of the *Conoscimiento* mistaking the author's stated date of birth for the year of composition of the work. This is the last mention of this particular manuscript until 1978, when it resurfaced at Sotheby's. Sir Peter Russell was fortunate at that time to have the opportunity to examine the codex before it disappeared again, and baptized it with the *siglum Z* in honor of its previous owner. He recognized it as probably the oldest of the known texts, dating from the middle of the fifteenth century (rather than the latter half, when the others evidently had been produced) and noted its many Aragonese spellings which suggest that it was copied by an Aragonese amanuensis who was working from a Castilian text.[6]

Written on vellum, manuscript *Z* now consists of twenty folios and is incomplete at its end. It is bound in worn red leather and has the remains of four pairs of closing ties. Zurita's signature can be seen at the top of fol. 1v; he also added short annotations (generally just a place-name) to five folios, but none of these notes is particularly elucidative. The most interesting aspect of this codex is its frontispiece illumination, which depicts a man in lay dress presenting a book with a red binding to an unidentifiable King of Castile. Above, the arms of Castile and Leon are shown on either side of the arms of the Orden de la Banda [Order of the Garter], founded in 1330. Two men in court costume flank the king, who is seated, and behind whom can be seen the countryside. It is not far-fetched to imagine that the man offering the book is meant to represent the author. In this case, we may have two illuminations (the present one and the initial E of manuscript *S*) that depict a definitely secular author, and not a Franciscan friar as Jiménez de la Espada and others have believed he was.

Russell is correct in thinking that the reappearance of manuscript *Z* places into doubt Jiménez de la Espada's supposition that *S* was the oldest known codex. But Russell also casts doubt on Jiménez's opinion that *S* is the superior source of the *Conoscimiento* given that, like *N* and *R*, *Z* includes drawings of strange humans and legendary places that seem to coincide with the intentions of the author.[7] However, after comparing *Z* to the other three extant codices, it clearly cannot supersede *S* as the superior textual version. In the first place, *Z* is the most incomplete of the four texts, missing perhaps as many as three folios at its end (absent is the narrator's

---

[6] The language of all of the manuscripts is Castilian, and only MS. *Z* shows signs that its copyist was not Castilian. In this study we will not address any phonological or lexical issues of this text.

[7] Russell, "La heráldica," 689.

return to Spain from Persia). But even more important is the copyist's egregious carelessness in the execution of his task. Comparison of Z with N and R seems to confirm that it was copied from the same or a similar source, but there are striking discrepancies in Z that can only be attributed to the laxity of the person who reproduced it. The omissions are both numerous and important: often whole words, phrases, or sentences are absent, frequently to the detriment of the grammatical sense of a particular section. It is a characteristic of the author's style to mention a place-name more than once in a sentence or a paragraph; it is a characteristic of the copyist of Z to duplicate the text up to the first mention of a name, leave out any text found between it and the second mention, then continue to copy from that point. This is the obvious result of inattention to his work. But the consequences to the author's original composition of the book are dire. Besides this kind of common error of omission, the reader must also contend with the oversight and consequent elimination of entire passages that result in the total absence of information about certain kingdoms. The omission of text is compounded by the copyist's gratuitous (although relatively harmless) addition of the adverb *muy* [very] to adjectives such as *grande* [large] or *poblado* [populated]. The indifference of the amanuensis toward his work therefore taints the merit of Z, making it the least reliable of the four extant manuscripts.

A REAL OR IMAGINARY JOURNEY?

Scholars who most recently have considered the *Libro del conoscimiento* generally accept that it is a pseudo-travel book which does not describe an authentic voyage throughout the world as it was known in the mid-fourteenth century. Rather, it is instead a geographical "novel" composed probably with the aid of a portolan chart or mappamundi. The present disbelief in the likelihood of such travel is based on our current knowledge of geography, toponymy, navigation by land and sea, as well as the amount of time needed to accomplish this kind of extensive travel. In the fourteenth century, however, the credibility of the information in the *Conoscimiento* apparently was not questioned at all. As we are about to see, soon after the book was written some explorers employed it as an authority on geography, and it might even have served as a source of information for a section of a mid-fifteenth-century map. By the end of that century, however, recent discoveries and explorations probably improved on or disproved much of the geographical data presented in the book; its primary element of interest became its description and pictoral representation of the heraldic arms of

many nations, rather than its narrative of the long journey. Ironically, when the *Conoscimiento* was rediscovered and published in the nineteenth century, its editor and other scholars once again chose to believe that the anonymous author actually did undertake the virtually impossible voyage he described.

In early May 1402, an expedition left the seaport of La Rochelle with the intention of conquering the Canary Islands for the French crown. The campaign was headed by Jean de Béthencourt, a nobleman from Normandy who was assisted by Gadifer de la Salle, a minor noble who could be considered a soldier of fortune. Their unexpected reliance on Castilian assistance for materials and men for this expedition led Béthencourt to shift his allegiance to the Castilian monarchy and eventually to establish a Spanish colony in the Canaries. In addition to his expectation of conquest, he planned to sail the west coast of Africa south of Cape Boujdour (a navigational limit at the time) and locate the celebrated "River of Gold." Here he planned to take as much gold as he could find, convert to Christianity as many Guineans as possible, and travel to the kingdom of Prester John, which he also expected to find in Africa.[8] The chronicle of Béthencourt's actual and intended activities is entitled *Le Canarien*, composed by Pierre Bontier and Jean LeVerrier, both priests. In their discussion of the expedition's exploration of African territory, the authors wrote of the reliance on the *Conoscimiento* for geographical data:

> As M. de Béthencourt had a great desire to learn the true state and government of the land of the Saracens and their sea-ports ... we have here inserted sundry notes on this subject, extracted from a book by a mendicant friar who made the tour of this country and visited all the sea-ports, which he mentions by name. He went through all the countries, Christian, Pagan, and Saracen, of those parts, and names them all. He mentions the names of the provinces, and the arms of the kings and princes, which it would be tedious to describe. ... Finding his account correct of the countries they al-

---

[8] The River of Gold and Prester John were, of course, only attractive legends. Prester John was thought to be an extremely wealthy priest-king who lived in Ethiopia; belief in his existence was so strong that ambassadors were sent twice to find him. See C. F. Beckingham, "The Quest for Prester John," *Bulletin of the John Rylands Library of Manchester* 62 (1979–80): 290–304.

On the River of Gold, see E. G. R. Taylor, "Pactolus: River of Gold," *Scottish Geographical Magazine* 44 (1928): 129–44.

Felipe Fernández Armesto, in his *Before Columbus: Exploration and Civilization from the Mediterranean to the Atlantic, 1229–1492* (Philadelphia: University of Pennsylvania Press, 1987), 181, believes that Béthencourt drew his information about the location of the River of Gold from the *Libro del Conoscimiento*, then enhanced it with detail from legend as well as from his own imagination about the easy accessibility of gold there.

ready knew, they relied on his information with regard to all the other countries; they have therefore inserted in the sequel other extracts from his book, as they found occasion.[9]

It was this book's convincing description of a sailing venture south of Cape Boujdour (which provided accurate distances between sites and therefore seemed credible), its information about the location of the River of Gold, and its directions on how to reach Prester John's kingdom by sea, that gave the Béthencourt campaign confidence that they would accomplish their expeditionary goals. Jean Richard conjectures that, because of the many credible details concerning types of shipping vessels and travel by camel in this section of the book, the explorers did not realize that it might be a description of an imaginary journey. Buenaventura Bonnet and George Kimble consider the French nobleman's dependence on the *Conoscimiento* as evidence that the narrative was well-known throughout Europe at the time, and in fact was employed as a textbook, especially of the geography of Africa.[10]

The failure of the Béthencourt expedition to locate the River of Gold and Prester John did not dampen the hopes of other fifteenth-century explorers, notably Henry the Navigator, who in the 1420s proposed to undertake a journey whose objectives were essentially the same as those proposed by his French predecessors. Peter Russell reflects on the similarities between these two ventures and concludes that the Portuguese prince may have read a translation of *Le Canarien*, and decided to attempt the exploration of Africa based upon what he had learned.[11] This would mean, of course, that Henry would have been influenced at least in an indirect manner by the information from the *Libro del conoscimiento* contained in the French chronicle, and it is likely that he was familiar with the anonymous book itself. While there is no documented evidence of the specific work or works that Henry may have consulted to provide him with information on African exploration, Russell deduces from the similarity between the 1402 campaign and the Infante's intended journeys that the *Conoscimiento* may have played a significant role in these plans, and that *Le Canarien* probably gave

[9] Jean de Béthencourt, *The Canarien or Book of the Conquest and Conversion of the Canarians in the year 1402*, trans. Richard Henry Major (London, 1872), 96–97. It is evident that a copy of the *Conoscimiento* no longer extant was consulted by these explorers, because the four manuscripts we know today all date from the second half of the fifteenth century.

[10] Jean Richard, *Les récits de voyages et de pèlerinages* (Turnhout: Brepols, 1981), 35; Buenaventura Bonnet, "Las Canarias y el primer libro de Geografía medieval, escrito por un fraile español en 1350," *Revista de Historia* 67 (1944): 207; George H. T. Kimble, *Geography in the Middle Ages* (London: Methuen, 1938), 113.

[11] "The Infante Dom Henrique and the Libro del conoscimiento del mundo," in *In memoriam Ruben Andresen Leitão*, vol. 2 (Lisbon, 1981): 259–67.

him impetus to undertake his own exploration of the Atlantic coast of Africa. But the *Conoscimiento* misled its readers to believe that sailing south of Boujdour was not only a feasible but a common navigational feat as early as the mid-1300s; it deceived Béthencourt and probably the Infante as well.

Béthencourt's confidence in and utilization of the geographical material of the *Conoscimiento* convinced Marcos Jiménez de la Espada, the nineteenth-century editor of the book, that the author in fact did accomplish the voyage in question. For his conviction he was reproached strongly by some of his contemporaries and defended by others. His harshest critic was Alfred Morel-Fatio, who substantiated his own rejection of the validity of the book with corroboration from other scholars. The geographer Otto Peschel, for example, remarks that the book is so full of absurdities that it seems but a literary prank.[12] Morel-Fatio's own objections have to do in part with a disparaging comment about the veracity of the *Libro del conoscimiento* made in the 1630 publication of *Le Canarien*, edited by Pierre Bergeron. In the section which recounts the "mendicant friar's" stay in the city which was the supposed residence of Prester John, the 1630 version says: "He remained there several days, for he saw there a considerable number of marvelous things, of which at present we make no mention in this book, in order to hasten on to other matters, and for fear the reader might take them for lies."[13] The original edition apparently read: ". . . in order to hasten on to other matters, and our intention is, with the grace of God, to declare them more fully at another time."[14] According to Bonnet, Bergeron adulterated his version, omitting certain chapters, joining others together to form one, eliminating entire sentences, and modernizing the text.[15] Bonnet would vindicate Jiménez de la Espada because of the alteration of the quotation used by Morel-Fatio to discredit the *Conoscimiento*. However, this eliminates only one of his arguments against the authenticity of the book. Later we shall examine others. Manuel Serrano y Sanz is as rigorous as Morel-Fatio in his refusal to accept that the book reflects a true travel experience: "[S]olamente por un efecto de esas alucinaciones que á veces padecen los eruditos encariñados con un autor ó una obra, se puede explicar que sostuviese lo contrario un hombre de tan acertado criterio y vasta ilustración cual era el Sr. Jiménez de la Espada" [Only by the effect of these

---

[12] Alfred Morel-Fatio, review of *Andanças e viajes de Pero Tafur por diversas partes del mundo avidos, 1435–1439*, ed. Marcos Jiménez de la Espada, *Revue Critique d'Histoire et de Littérature* 9 (1875), 136–37; Otto Peschel, *Geschichte der Erdkunde* (Amsterdam: Meridian, 1961), 174.

[13] Béthencourt, *Le Canarien*, 101–02.

[14] Bonnet, "Las Canarias," 205–27. The translation from page 214 is mine.

[15] Bonnet, "Las Canarias," 213.

hallucinations that scholars enamored of an author or a work sometimes suffer, can one explain that a man of such good judgment and vast erudition, which Mr. Jiménez de la Espada was, might sustain the contrary].[16]

There is another navigational reference in the *Libro del conoscimiento* that has intrigued and probably misled its readers since the late Middle Ages: the fate of the Vivaldi expedition of 1291. In May of that year, Ugolino Vivaldi, his brother, two Franciscan friars and several other Genoese men outfitted two galleys and put to sea to find India by sailing through the Strait of Gibraltar. No one had ever before attempted this route to the East.[17] Whether the Vivaldis intended to circumnavigate the African continent or sail across the Atlantic Ocean is not made clear in the documents of the era that report the event. In any case, the galleys disappeared after passing a place called Gozora on the African coast. The author of the *Conoscimiento* claims to have been informed about the fate of the Vivaldi expedition during his trip through Africa. In the section of the work that deals with his presumed travels through Nubia and Ethiopia, the narrator stops at "Granҫiona" (Aksum, the capital of an ancient Ethiopian kingdom) where he had heard that one of the galleys had shipwrecked and its men had escaped. The other galley was never heard from again. He was told also that "Sorleonis," the son of one of the Genoese merchants, went in search of his father at a place called Magdasor. Although he was received with great honors, the Emperor did not allow him to cross Granҫiona in his search because of the dangers of the journey.

To his contemporaries, the narrator seems to speak with authority on the subject: Ugolino Vivaldi in fact did have a son named Sor Leone; the traveler knows the number and flag of the galleys, and so forth. But his mention of "Magdasor" is an ambiguous, although crucial reference. Did he mean Mogador, the Moroccan port on the Atlantic, or Mogadishu, the Somalian city on the other side of Africa on the Indian Ocean? Francis Rogers and Florentino Pérez Embid are convinced that the author intended to name a site on Africa's Atlantic coast, where he was "visiting" when he heard these remarks.[18] Gozora, where the Vivaldi expedition abruptly

---

[16] *Autobiografía y memorias* (Madrid: Bailly-Bailliére e hijos, 1925), xli.

[17] Among the many studies of the Vivaldi voyage is the useful article by Francis M. Rogers, "The Vivaldi Expedition," *Annual Report of the Dante Society of America* 73 (1955): 31–45.

[18] Rogers, "The Vivaldi Expedition," 42, and Pérez Embid, *Los descubrimientos en el Atlántico y la rivalidad castellano-portuguesa hasta el Tratado de Tordesillas* (Seville, 1948), 58. Carlo Conti Rossini, "Il *Libro del Conoscimiento* e le sue notizie sull'Etiopie," *Bollettino della Reale Società Geografica Italiana* Series 5, 6:9–10 (1917): 675, n.1, believes that it is Mogadishu, and says that this is the earliest, if not the absolute earliest, mention of this place in Western sources.

ended, is probably the ancient city of Gaetulia (Gazula in the *Conosc imie nto*), a place on the West African coast opposite the Canary Islands. Pérez Embid assumes that the Vivaldi brothers intended to find the route to India by sailing west into the Atlantic Ocean—therefore anticipating Columbus' voyage 200 years later—and that they were probably shipwrecked or fell victim to Berber pirates.[19] Fernández Armesto (and other readers both medieval and contemporary) believe that the Genoese galleys, ill-suited for either African or Atlantic waters, were headed around Africa in their search for a route to India when their vessels were destroyed.[20] In either case, readers of the *Conoscimiento* were led to believe that such expeditions had been attempted a century prior to the composition of the book, a supposition that could have led to other efforts to do the same.

The credibility given to the *Libro del conoscimiento* also might have led to its use in the production of the Este World Map, a work of Catalan origin dating from the mid-fifteenth century. Kimble believes that "the only part of the map which may be considered unmistakably moulded on the narrative is the west coast of Africa, south of Cape Verde. The delineation of a longitudinal gulf, doubtless intended for the Gulf of Guinea, with the nomenclature accompanying it recalls, in the most striking fashion, the Friar's Gulf."[21] All other Catalan maps, including the famous 1375 mappamundi, depict nothing south of the River of Gold. But the maker of the Este World Map does not refer to information found in the *Conoscimiento* when working on other parts of Africa, as the map legends and the details in the travel book do not coincide anywhere else. Based on this presumed reliance on the *Conoscimiento*, Kimble concludes, as others have, that the work was employed as a geography textbook in the early fifteenth century.

Today we have many good reasons to doubt that the author of the *Libro del conoscimiento* actually undertook the journey he narrates. The routes he proposes and the amount of time it would have taken in the fourteenth century to accomplish all of this make this extraordinary journey virtually inconceivable. The text is so replete with place-names as to make the supposed itinerary of the book difficult to follow. Because the author apparently employed a map to create his travel route, he frequently enumerates cities, rivers, and mountains where he does not claim to have been, complicating the task of differentiating between his course of travel and places merely mentioned in the general area of his "visit." A further obstacle to

---

[19] Pérez Embid, *Los descubrimientos*, 58.

[20] Fernández Armesto, *Before Columbus*, 152.

[21] George H. T. Kimble, Foreword to *Catalan World Map of the R. Biblioteca Estense at Modena* (London: Royal Geographical Society, 1934), 8.

understanding the itinerary is that many of the place-names have changed over the centuries, some cities mentioned no longer exist, and others are purely legendary. For the sake of simplicity, we offer here a synopsis of the narrator's course of travel. The outline will also serve to demonstrate the improbability of this journey, as the traveler constantly criss-crosses Europe, Asia, and Africa, returning to remote places, suddenly appearing in cities far from the last place mentioned without reporting his departure or arrival, and visiting fictitious locations.

The narrator begins his journey in Seville, sets out to Portugal, then north to Galicia. He travels east along the north coast of Spain, crosses the French border to visit Bayonne, then returns to Navarre. From here he traverses the Pyrenees and follows the western coast of France to the mouth of the Loire River. After traveling four days inland to Paris, he heads toward the north coast and sees Dieppe, Calais, then Bruges. Once he has toured several other cities in Belgium, the traveler proceeds to Cologne, passing through Germany and Austria to the Czech border. He returns to Cologne, traveling on to the Netherlands and Denmark, then to the northern coast of Germany. He follows the coast to Poland, apparently heads south to Krakow, then sets out for Lithuania before turning south into the area bordering Bohemia, Romania, and Ukraine.

Without mention of his departure from Ukraine, we suddenly find the narrator on the Swedish coast of the Baltic Sea, where he embarks for the island of Gotland, subsequently returning to Sweden. The journey continues to Norway, where the traveler boards an English ship for Denmark and then heads back to Norway. He now sails to Scotland, England, and Ireland, where he learns of a ship that is going to Spain. He boards it and proceeds first to the north, passing to the Orkney, Shetland, and Faröe Islands before reaching Iceland.

The boat then sails to Spain, landing at Pontevedra, and continues south to Algeciras and Gibraltar. Soon thereafter the narrator departs for Aragon and Barcelona. He next travels the coast to Ampurias, then Narbonne and along the southern coast of France, finally reaching Genoa. From here he heads inland to Lombardy, south to Tuscany, then on to Rome. At Rome he follows the coastline along the boot of Italy to Pescara, making his way to Sicily, rounding it from its northeast corner. The intrepid tourist now boards a galley and arrives at Naples, and subsequently repeats his trip around the Italian shore, this time reaching Venice.

At Venice the narrator follows the Adriatic seacoast to Albania. He suddenly speaks of cities in Hungary without mentioning having traveled there, and leaves this country once again heading for Albania, where he embarks

for Peloponnesus. From here he sails on to Rhodes, Crete, and along southern Turkey until he reaches Syria.

The traveler next progresses to North Africa on a voyage around the eastern Mediterranean to Cairo, then continues west along the northern coast of Africa. He arrives at Tunisia but directly leaves there for Sardinia and Corsica before returning to the African continent and moving on to Algeria. Once again he ventures off the straight course, this time visiting Majorca, then comes back to North Africa, disembarking in Ceuta or Melilla. By land he heads for Fez, then for the Atlantic coast of Morocco before going south and inland to climb the western part of the Atlas Mountains. Once more he finds himself on the Atlantic shore, traveling south in an oar-propelled boat to Cape Boujdour. Here he boards a Moorish ship that sets off for the Canary Islands, traveling also to the Selvage Islands, Madeira, and the Azores. He goes back to Boujdour, then crosses the Sahara on camels with another group of Moors. The party heads south for Senegal to the legendary Kingdom of Organa and on to the equally fictitious Kingdom of Tauser. From there the traveler heads north to Tlemcen (between Melilla and Oran) before leaving for the Nile, which he cruises with some Genoese merchants who are headed for Cairo and Damietta. Here the narrator embarks with some Christians and repeats his journey to Ceuta and the Atlas Mountains, boards a Moorish ship for the apocryphal River of Gold, and heads south of that to present-day Sierra Leone.

Once again on land, the indefatigable traveler crosses Africa and ends up in Aksum, an Ethiopian city, and Malsa, the imaginary city where the mythical Prester John was believed to reside. From this area he continues to Mogadishu, then north along the eastern side of the Red Sea, trekking into Iraq, then across Arabia to Mecca (which, apparently unknown to the author, at that time did not receive Christian visitors). He goes along the south coast of present-day Saudi Arabia to the Gulf of Aden before proceeding to the entrance of the Persian Gulf. From there he sails across the Arabian Sea to India, where he visits Delhi and other cities.

From India the narrator goes to Ceylon (Sri Lanka) and the Bay of Bengal, then east to Burma. Unexpectedly we find him in a merchant ship in the South China Sea heading toward Java, only to return to Burma. Then he journeys to Cathay, making a long trip to the legendary castle of Magog,[22] where he claims to have stayed "for a time." Leaving Magog he

---

[22] The story of Gog and Magog, followers of the Antichrist, appeared in the prophecy of Ezekiel. He predicted that they would rise up and take over the Earth on the Day of Judgement. They were believed to be found in northeastern Asia. Medieval lore has Alexander building a

moves on to a city called Norgancio, apparently located somewhere between the Caspian Sea and the Ural Mountains, and from there to Astrakhan (on the northwest corner of the Caspian) and on to the Persian Kingdom. Once in Persia the traveler visits Teheran, then goes south to Shiraz
before leaving Persia with some Christian merchants. They sail down a
spurious branch of the Euphrates River to Asia Minor (Turkey) and Tarabulus (Lebanon).

The narrator now boards another Christian ship which embarks for
Cyprus and Constantinople. They circumnavigate the Black Sea from west
to east, laying over at the Crimea and Trabizond (Turkey), an important
stopover on the trade route frequented by Genoese and Venetian merchants. Afterward he crosses Turkey with some other merchants, and they
traverse Georgia to Derbent (on the Caspian), then head south along the
eastern side of the sea. From there the traveler proceeds up the Volga River
to a lake named Tanais[23] into the Russian Kingdom of Sebu, near Moscow. He turns south to Ukraine before suddenly turning up on a branch of
the Volga in western Russia and equally as swiftly (without mentioning his
passage), he arrives in Sweden.

The incredible journey comes to an end as the unflagging traveler sails
down the Baltic coast of Sweden to Denmark, into Belgium, then abruptly
finds himself in Seville, from where he began his extraordinary travels.

Typically the geographers who have discredited the *Conoscimiento* based
upon its evident dependence on maps available at the time and the errors in
reading them which its author plainly makes, Leo Bagrow, Raymond Beazley, Georges Pasch, and J. K. Hyde,[24] all agree on these points. Kimble
singles himself out by saying that, although the book might seem at first to
be a false account, closer examination will demonstrate its veracity. In the
first place, he contends, the narrative is not plagiarized from earlier travel
books; therefore its originality attests to its truthfulness. This argument is not,
of course, logical. Even if the author did not copy his information from existing narrative examples this does not prove that it is a true story. Kimble also
finds in the book "the stamp of credibility" missing from known novelized

---

gate to contain them, a legend referred to in the *Conoscimiento*. On mappaemundi they are
depicted often as two giants. See A. R. Anderson's and Ian Michael's works on this subject in
the Bibliography.

[23] The Tanais appears to be the river Don, whose source is a lake, which could explain this
reference.

[24] Leo Bagrow, *History of Cartography* (Chicago: Precedent, 1985), 66; Raymond C. Beazley,
The Dawn of Modern Geography (London: H. Frowde, 1906), 3:416, n.1; Pasch, "Drapeaux du
Libro del Conoscimiento," 8; J. K. Hyde, "Real and Imaginary Journeys in the Later Middle Ages,"
Bulletin of the John Rylands University Library of Manchester 65:1 (1982): 144–45.

travel books such as the *Travels of Sir John Mandeville.* "Credible" to Kimble means that the author limited the number of times he mentions fantastic animals and humans and their unconventional behavior. He also considers references to the profit made by merchants or the author's visit to an African king to be "natural touches" of "a *bona fide* mode of expression which seems to belie the charge of fabrication." In addition, Kimble is impressed by the exactitude of the *Conoscimiento's* description of the coast of West Africa, and attributes it to the narrator's first-hand knowledge of the region.[25] But none of these lines of reasoning constitute plausible proof that such a voyage in fact did take place.

Some scholars believe that the author might have undertaken at least some of the journey, then invented the rest to complete his "tour" of the known world. Bonnet admits that it would have been impossible to cover so much ground in a reasonable amount of time: some estimates place the required time to complete this voyage at twenty years. He is taken, though, by the idea that the author was a Franciscan missionary and was probably present, therefore, in North Africa where he gleaned direct information about the area.[26] In his introduction to a facsimile of Jiménez de la Espada's edition of the *Libro del conoscimiento,* Francisco López Estrada comments that some of the facts put forth in the book might be true and might even be the product of personal experience, but others obviously originate in geographical lore and the works of others.[27] Martín de Riquer assumes that the author did not make the journey all at one time, but rather in segments over a twenty-year period.[28] While it is not inconceivable that the author in fact did make some of the voyage outlined in his book, as any merchant, herald, missionary, ambassador, or pilgrim might have done, it is difficult to accept that he personally took part in all of it. Even Clements Markham, who translated Jiménez de la Espada's edition into English, does not accept the literalness of the entire narrative. He does accept, however, the premise that the author was "a great traveller" who combined his own experiences with other geographical information he gathered.[29] Serrano y Sanz effectively sums up his reasons for not embracing the theory of author-

[25] Kimble, *Catalan World Map,* 111–13.

[26] Bonnet, "Las Canarias," 210–11.

[27] *Libro del conosçimiento de todos los reinos,* ed. Marcos Jiménez de la Espada (Madrid, 1877; reprint with a foreword by Francisco López Estrada, Barcelona: El Albir, 1980), no page.

[28] "La heráldica en el *LdC* y el problema de su datación," *Dicenda: Cuadernos de Filología Hispánica,* vol. 6 of *Estudios y textos dedicados a Francisco López Estrada* (Madrid: Universidad Complutense, 1987), 319.

[29] *Knowledge of the World,* ed. and trans. Clements Markham (London: Hakluyt Society, 1912), xi.

traveler: "De ser cierta su narración nos encontraríamos con el viajero más audaz y afortunado que registra la Historia, al lado del cual Marco Polo resultaría un vulgar turista" [If his narration were true we would find ourselves beholding the most audacious and fortunate traveler that History records, next to whom Marco Polo would result a common tourist].[30]

Some of those who have considered this issue have found errors in the book that belie the assumption that the author truly made the journey. Hyde, for example, points out several such inaccuracies. To reach Ireland from England, the traveler claims to have made a short crossing of only one mile, an inaccuracy. His knowledge of the Mediterranean seems second-hand, and he "does not follow any credible sailing route." Bosnia, according to the narrator, is the name of a mountain, and Crete is a city on Rhodes, whose position he mistakenly describes. These misrepresentations, Hyde conjectures, are probably due to the author's simple misreading of the information on a map he was consulting.[31] But they also strongly suggest that he never traveled to these particular places. Conti Rossini recognizes an error in the narrator's tale of his trip to Dongola (Nubia). Our traveler refers to Dongola as a Christian state, but it ceased to be one by the end of the thirteenth century; at the time of the *Conoscimiento*'s composition, the ruler of this state was Muslim, and had been so for some time. Conti Rossini therefore concludes that this fact affirms the rhetorical nature of the part of the book.[32] If the author were a Franciscan missionary, as so many scholars would have it, would he not be abundantly aware of this fact, given that the Franciscans first arrived in the north of Africa in 1220?

There are entirely fictitious elements of the story that, although apparently believed to be true by the author, are evidence to the modern reader of a falsified account. Among these many now conspicuous blunders are the narrator's sighting of Noah's Ark atop Mount Ararat, his stay at the legendary castle of Magog, a visit to mythical Malsa, home of the fictional Prester John, and trips to non-existent nations such as Organa.

Despite the geographical impossibilities and the inclusion of fantasy, the author of the *Conoscimiento* supplies some genuine touches of contemporary reality. His initial departure from and final return to Seville is well-chosen: besides being an important port at this time, Seville was also the starting point in the 1370s of several expeditions to the Canary Islands, sponsored

---

[30] Serrano y Sanz, *Autobiografía*, xli.
[31] Hyde, "Real and Imaginary Journeys," 144–45.
[32] Conti Rossini, "Il *Libro del Conoscimiento*," 665.

by Sevillian merchants interested in the slave trade.[33] The author was apparently also aware of the frenzied interest in the search for gold that was encouraged by the stories of the River of Gold. He probably used a common illustration on mappaemundi of the era that depicted Jacme Ferrer, who in 1346 set out to find the legendary river and abruptly disappeared. The author also wrote of African ants that dug up gold nuggets as they made their home underground, a legend that dates back to Herodotus.

Despite certain properties that have convinced some that the author recounted a personal experience, there are simply too many discrepancies and fantastic elements in the book to allow the informed reader to accept it as a totally true account. While it is possible that the anonymous author really did travel to some of these places at one or more points in his life, the ratio of real travel to invented journey seems to be quite small. The book can be therefore best described today as a geographical "novel," and not an authentic travel book.

POSSIBLE SOURCES

In the previous section we established with some certainty that the anonymous author of the *Libro del conoscimiento* could not have made the entire journey he describes in a reasonable amount of time. His geographical errors also support the argument that the narrative is not entirely a product of his own experience. Even if the author actually did participate in some of the travel he details, he would have required at least one other source to help him fabricate the remainder of his account. It is apparent enough that, for the necessary geographical data, one or more maps of the era would have served him well, since essentially all of the sites he claims to have visited (both real and imaginary) appear on a chart from the mid-fourteenth-century. But his narrative is not just a list of cities and countries and the routes that lead to them; in addition to a long catalogue of places, the author includes names of historical and legendary personages, references to historical events and early exploration, unusual animals and humans, legendary cities, and the coats of arms of more than one hundred states and rulers. While it might appear that he needed to have at his disposal a number of different works in order to research these various aspects, the author readily could have secured all of these items from but one source: a mappamundi.

---

[33] Some critics have supposed, therefore, that the author was from Seville, or at least Andalusian. See Russell, "La heráldica," 691.

Mappaemundi are more than simply maps of the world, as their name might imply; they contain an abundance of material and have a didactic purpose rather than an exclusively geographical one. Explorers, merchants, ambassadors and missionaries who required a reliable source of information for travel purposes did not use mappaemundi, but instead referred to maritime charts called portolans, which correctly illustrated coastlines and seas. Serious travelers had little use for the typical mappamundi, which included a combination of geographical places, historical facts and fiction, description of peoples both real and mythical, legends, unusual animals and plants, and often the coats of arms of the countries depicted.[34]

These works were meant almost exclusively for leisure reading and armchair traveling, not for use as an accurate reference for actual journeys. Two of the best known maps that date from the mid- to late fourteenth century are the Angelino Dalorto map (1339) and the Catalan Atlas (1375); they are also the most frequently mentioned by those who have studied the *Conoscimiento* and its possible sources. However, there were most likely numerous portolans and mappaemundi produced in the fourteenth and fifteenth centuries. Harley and Woodward say that we know of 180 such works dating from that era, charts which represent a "minute fraction" of the vast number that must have existed.[35] In this time of active land and sea travel accomplished by merchants, missionaries, ambassadors, pilgrims, and other such travelers, it is evident that each ship—and the total number of vessels and journeys over two centuries is incalculable—must have had on board at least one portolan chart. It is impossible to pinpoint the exact map of the very few remaining that the author of the *Conoscimiento* consulted when composing the work; the data he offers do not match precisely the details contained in any one of the extant maps. However, it is possible to determine that he used an atlas of the Catalan school, although not specifically the famous 1375 version.

In the late fourteenth century Abraham Cresques and his assistants were producing exceptional maps in their workshop on Majorca, and it was one of these that Pedro el Ceremonioso of Aragon commissioned as a gift for King Charles VI of France. Once housed in the Bibliothèque Royale, this exquisitely illuminated map is preserved today in the Bibliothèque Nationale in Paris. It is usually referred to simply as the Catalan Atlas of 1375. While it is the earliest known map that this school produced, one finds it

---

[34] J. B. Harley and David Woodward, *The History of Cartography* (Chicago: University of Chicago Press, 1987), 2:112.

[35] Harley and Woodward, *The History of Cartography*, 2:373.

difficult to accept that it is the first such map that they made. Kimble considers the Catalan atlas the work of an experienced cartographer capable of very accurate descriptions and in possession of excellent drafting techniques.[36] Its delineation of the Far East, for example, is the finest of the era and is not equalled until the middle of the fifteenth century. Cartographers generally agree that there must have existed early fourteenth-century prototypes of this map, although their whereabouts are unknown. The 1375 Atlas, probably based on a portolan chart, was executed splendidly because it was intended for the library of a king, and its preservation can be attributed to this fact. But it is reasonable to assume that the Majorcan school manufactured other, less grand works destined for more practical use and lesser collections, and that these examples simply have not survived the centuries.

There is a number of correspondences between the Catalan Atlas and the information contained in the *Conoscimiento* that suggests the author's dependence on a related map; it would be impractical to list them all here. Much of the data that the author offers to his readers can be found somewhere on the Catalan chart. A significant similarity is the relatively accurate placement of the Canary Islands and the Azores in the Atlantic, something not accomplished by many other documents of this era. Other coincidences between the Atlas and the *Conoscimiento* include the following: most of the cities and countries the author mentions, both real and imaginary, and the distances between them; many of the legends he writes about (for example, Prester John, Gog and Magog); references to earlier explorers (the doomed Vivaldi voyage and explorer Jacme Ferrer's ill-fated 1346 expedition to the River of Gold); drawings of different sea-going vessels and camels used for transportation; mention or sketches of monuments located in certain cities; drawings of rulers almost identical to those seen in some copies of the *Conoscimiento*; and colorful depictions of the coats of arms of these lands, some of them invented. (The shields are placed over the general location of the places they represent, since border delineations were not employed on such maps.) There is also a striking similarity in the language used by both the book and the atlas. In many of its inscriptions, the Catalan map begins the explanation with the word "sepiats" [know], while the author of the *Conoscimiento* often introduces explanatory material with the word "sabet," the Castilian equivalent.

But there are also differences between the Catalan Atlas of 1375 and the *Libro del Conoscimiento* that indicate that the author could not have relied specifically on this map. For example, the book's description of the area

---

[36] Kimble, *Catalan World Map*, 1.

south of the River of Gold on the west coast of Africa is not depicted on
the Catalan map; in fact, all existing maps of Catalan origin end in the south
at the latitude of this river.[37] In addition, the narrator's description of Asia
does not appear to originate from a reading of the Catalan charts. The Cresques atlases were based probably on information gleaned from Marco Polo's
writings; the description of these lands in the *Conoscimiento* does not resemble either the map or the Italian explorer's book. The anonymous author
presents his readers with two distinct travel routes that lead to Cathay; this
persuaded Hyde that he might have been using knowledge circulating
among merchants of the era, and that some of what he has to say also could
have been derived from the reports of missionaries who traveled the
East.[38] The narrator's account of the Tibetans is, according to Markham,
the earliest European description that exists.[39] But the author's ignorance
of the Eastern Mediterranean belies any personal experience there.

The other map commonly related to the *Libro del conoscimiento* is the
Angelino Dalorto work of 1339. Conti Rossini made an excellent comparison of the two more than eighty years ago, and his objective observations
and conclusions are still valid.[40] He notices agreement in the area of Nubia
and Ethiopia, whose ruler both the book and the map show as Abdeselib,
a name that does not appear on the Catalan atlas. In addition, the Dalorto
map legend at Nubia reads, in imperfect Latin: "Iste Rex saracenus habet
continuo guera cum christianos nubie et ethiopie qui sunt sub dominio prest
Iane christianus niger" [This Saracen king is at continuous war with the
Christians of Nubia and Ethiopia, who are under the rule of Prester John, a
black Christian]. The map legend refers also to the kingdom of Titimissen
(Tlemsen). The *Conoscimiento* offers this similar observation: "[L]legué a otro
rreinado que dizen Tremisin, et confina con el flumen Nilus et sienpre bive
en guerra con los cristianos de Nubia et de Etiopia" [I arrived in another
kingdom that they call Tremisin, and it borders on the river Nilus and it
always lives at war with the Christians of Nubia and of Ethiopia]. There are
also coincidences between the coats of arms depicted for this area. The
Dalorto map assigns to Christian Nubia (where Prester John was believed
to reside) a cross bearing three intersecting arms; the *Conoscimiento* attributes
this symbol to Prester John himself. Both the map and the narrative display
the same coat of arms in the cases of the kings of Dongola and Tlemsen.

---

[37] Kimble, *Catalan World Map*, 7.
[38] Hyde, "Real and Imaginary Journeys," 145–46.
[39] Markham, *Knowledge*, 49, n.3.
[40] Conti Rossini, "Il *Libro del Conoscimiento*," 656–79.

Each also locates Earthly Paradise south of Ethiopia, but the Dalorto map shows one river (evidently the Blue Nile) originating in Paradise, while the travel book describes four distinct rivers. It should be noted also, however, that the *Conoscimiento* does not make use of all the place-names found on this map. Sometimes the author corrects the names or adds others not listed by Dalorto.

Having compared and contrasted the 1339 Dalorto map with the *Conoscimiento*, Conti Rossini concludes that, despite their similarities, the author of the *Conoscimiento* did not consult the Dalorto map. This opinion is seconded by others who have studied the possible sources of the travel book, and concluded that the *Libro del conoscimiento* does not correspond exactly to any extant portolan or mappamundi because its author had at hand a work no longer available to us. Hyde, however, puts forth a theory which eliminates the necessity of such a missing link: "With all its faults the *Conoscimiento* marks a significant step in the drawing together of the world of merchants and missionaries and that of literature. . . . [T]he Castilian set out to portray the world as it was known in his time, basing his account almost entirely on up-to-date information and maps."[41] This contemporary data, as we have previously seen, would have consisted of accounts of missionaries and merchants, in addition to well-known legends. Could the author of the book have used as the basis for his narrative a map or maps, correcting and expanding the information according to other more accurate or current material he had obtained? This would explain the fact that his description does not completely match any known map; but it is, of course, a theory which conveniently explains this problem, although it is one that is difficult to prove with any certainty.

What can be surmised from the comparison between extant cartographical works was that the anonymous author of the *Libro del conoscimiento* had available to him a map similar to but later than the Angelino Dalorto work of 1339, a map that more closely resembles the Catalan Atlas of 1375. It was probably a work produced by the Catalan school. Whether he enhanced his writing with knowledge obtained from other sources, or whether any of the information was updated by later copyists, can only be left to conjecture.

---

[41] Hyde, "Real and Imaginary Journeys," 146.

THE DATE OF COMPOSITION

The anonymous author of the *Libro del conoscimiento* begins his work with a specific reference to his date of birth, 11 September 1305. In the course of his narrative he also refers to historical events, foreign rulers, and flags of other nations, all of which can can be dated easily. Over the years scholars have used these various clues to attempt to determine the book's date of composition. Despite the evidence available, it is not sufficient to fix a date: reference to a particular historical incident suggests only the earliest possible month and year of the text's composition, it cannot indicate the latest possible date. Examination of this information and other related facts that we are about to consider will help to demonstrate that the *Conoscimiento* was written probably in the last quarter of the fourteenth century, sometime after 1378 but before about 1402.

Scholars who have attempted to date the work often cite the following passage, near the beginning of the work, as significant evidence:

> Et de Ponte Vedra vine a una villa que es del rreyno de Castilla, que ya conté de suso, que dizen Tarifa, la qual pobló un alarabe muy poderoso que dixeron Tarif. Et sobre esta villa fue desbaratado et vençido Alboaçen, rrey de toda tierra del poniente de allen mar, et vençiólo et desbaratólo el muy noble rrey don Alfonso de Castilla, et rrobóle todos sus rreales et sus thesoros et todas sus mugeres, et matóle sus cavallerias.

> [And from Ponte Vedra I came to a town which is in the Kingdom of Castilla, of which I told above, that they call Tarifa, which a very powerful Arab, named Tarif, founded. And near this town Alboacen, King of all the western land beyond the sea, was defeated and conquered, and it was the very noble King Don Alfonso de Castilla who conquered and defeated him, and stole from him all his military camps and his treasures and all his women, and [Alboacen] was killed by his knights.]

This excerpt refers to the defeat of Abu-l-Hasan, King of Morocco, at the hands of Alfonso XI in the Battle of Salado in 1348. For this reason Bonnet, Pasch and Hyde are quick to conclude that the year 1348 is the work's *terminus post quem*.[42] Bonnet and Pasch, therefore settle on a date of compo-

---

[42] Bonnet, "Las Canarias," 207; Pasch, "Drapeaux du *Libro del Conoscimiento*," 9; Hyde, "Real and Imaginary Journeys," 145, n.65. Beazley, *The Dawn of Modern Geography*, 3:416, suggests c.1345; opting for c.1350 are Kimble, *Geography*, 109, and Joaquín Rubio Tovar, ed., *Libros españoles de viajes medievales (Selección)* (Madrid: Taurus, 1986), 63.

sition of about 1350, while Hyde extends the possibility to 1375, the date of the Catalan Atlas which he believes the author used as a reference for other facts included in the book.

Riquer finds another possible date of composition in the 1350s from a reference in *Conoscimiento*:

> Apres de Çerdeña es otra isla que dizen Corçega. Las señales dende son un pendon blanco con una cruz bermeja, por que la ganaron los ginoveses a los catalanes. Et por eso an oy dia guerra con ellos.

> [After Cerdeña there is another island they call Corcega. Its insignia is a white flag with a vermilion cross, because the Genoese took it from the Catalans. And for that reason there is war between them today.]

The first of the Genoese-Catalan battles took place in February, 1352, and a truce was signed in March of 1360. 1348 is not therefore, a reasonable date for the work; rather, sometime between the 1352 clash and the settlement eight years later. But there remains one bothersome issue: The critical remark "Et por eso an oy dia guerra con ellos" [And for that reason there is war between them today] appears in only one manuscript, *S*, which dates from the latter half of the fifteenth century. This singular occurrence of the remark could suggest that it might be a later interpolation made either by a fourteenth-century copyist who was responsible for one of the now lost exemplars of this era, or a fifteenth-century counterpart, who was perhaps seeking to add an historical flourish. Since the existence of this sentence in the original text remains questionable, its reference to an ongoing Catalan-Genoese conflict cannot be considered reliable. The allusion, therefore, should not be used to determine the probable date of the *Conoscimiento*.

These examples serve to demonstrate that allusions to datable incidents are not sufficient to determine the date of composition of the *Conoscimiento*. Such references are especially unreliable if the author adopted for his own use the numerous pieces of historical information included on the typical mappamundi. Because the author of this work evidently did copy this kind of material from a map or maps, Peter Russell has challenged justly the idea that the *Libro del conoscimiento* was created in 1348: the fact of Abu-l-Hasan's defeat probably was expropriated from a map which would have recorded this information some time after its occurrence, a map which would have been finished at least several years before the composition of the travel book.[43] It is feasible therefore that as many as ten years or more could

---

[43] Russell, "La heráldica," 691.

have passed since the battle, reference to it on a portolan chart or atlas, and its inclusion in the *Conoscimiento*. Russell conjectures that the text was written sometime between 1350 and 1370.

The author's evident reliance on information taken from cartographical works nevertheless provides some significant clues about the date of the book's composition. Angelino Dalorto's 1339 map which, as we have seen, can be linked to our text, shares several pieces of information with the *Conoscimiento*. While it would be difficult to prove conclusively that the anonymous author used the Dalorto map as a reference, it is possible to say that the travel book and the map at least had a common source, and that they both reflect geographical data—both new discoveries and old wisdom—that was available in about 1339. But that knowledge was not exclusive to these two works. Another map which contains information similar to that found in the *Conoscimiento* is the so-called Laurentian Atlas (or Medici Atlas of the Laurentian Library), begun in 1351. And many scholars who have noted similarities between the *Conoscimiento* and Abraham Cresques' Catalan Atlas—usually dated 1375—have assigned the travel book a date closer to that year. It is clear that there is no one map that can be identified as the definitive source of the book, but it is also true that the dates traditionally attached to these maps are questionable as well. Fernández Armesto points out that while the Laurentian Atlas begins with an almanac dated 1351, it is probably a collection of folios produced at different times by different hands; he believes that one folio might have been appended as late as 1385. In addition, the 1375 date typically given to the Catalan Atlas seems to be, according to Fernández Armesto, the year that the work on it commenced; the texts that accompany the map also contain the dates 1376 and 1377. For this reason, and because mapmaker Cresques is known to have sent the King of France a similar mappamundi in 1381, the date of the Catalan Atlas should probably be revised to the late 1370s or early 1380s.[44] So the lack of proof which might demonstrate the precise cartographical source of the *Libro del conoscimiento*, compounded with the uncertain dates of some of the possible map authorities, only serves to cloud further the issue of the book's date of composition.

The description of some of the coats of arms provides other clues about the *Conoscimiento's* date. The arms of England, for example, are described as: "un pendon a quarterones: en los dos quarterones ay flores de oro en canpo azul porque es el rrey de la casa de França; en los otros dos quartos ay en cada uno tres onças de oro luengas, et el canpo bermejo ..." [a quartered

---

[44] Fernández Armesto, *Before Columbus*, 159.

flag: in two quarters there are gold flowers on a field of blue because the king is of the House of Francia; in the other two quarters there are in each three long gold lynxes, and the field is vermilion]. Edward III of England claimed the French throne in 1340 and began to use this quartered coat of arms; in 1406 Henry IV ceased to display this flag. Another example, from MS. *R*, depicts the flag of Majorca with gold and red vertical bars; that is to say, the same as the Aragonese standard. Such correspondence can only be the case after October of 1349, when Pedro el Ceremonioso of Aragon defeated Jaime III of Majorca and seized his kingdom, incorporating it into his own. But perhaps the most significant coat of arms for the dating of the *Conoscimiento* is the shield of France, depicted with three gold fleurs-de-lis on a field of blue. Riquer uses this information to date more precisely the book after 1376, when the French began to use this modernized version of their flag, which was earlier entirely semy with fleurs-de-lis (i.e., covered with more than sixteen such symbols).[45]

In an article on the heraldic element of the *Libro del conoscimiento* and the problem of its date, also published in 1987, Riquer first agrees with Alan Deyermond that the book seems to have been written between 1350 and 1360,[46] based upon the reference to the Catalan-Genoese struggle of 1352–60. But Riquer soon thereafter mentions the book's inclusion of the new French arms which date from 1376. He realizes that this poses a contradiction, which he quickly justifies in a most enigmatic manner:

El autor debió de viajar durante muchos años, y aunque no alcanzara países lejanos que describe como si los hubiera visitado, es perfectamente aceptable que conociera los principales reinos de Europa y las islas del Mediterráneo occidental. Los viajes del anónimo franciscano debieron de efectuarse en diferentes momentos de su vida, y de cada uno de ellos conservaría notas o breves relaciones que iría incorporando a su libro, en el que el desorden es patente y los itinerarios muy poco convincentes. Pudo estar en Córcega entre 1352 y 1360, y así consigna que entonces había guerra entre catalanes y genoveses: y pudo visitar el reino de Francia después de 1376, cuando en el blasón del rey se había efectuado la reducción a tres flores de lis. ... [E]l anónimo franciscano, que invirtió tantos años de vida en viajes, era un septuagenario que recogía con ilusión, ingenuidad y malicia sus re-

---

[45] Riquer, "La heráldica en el *LdC*," 318.
[46] Alan D. Deyermond, *A History of Spanish Literature: The Middle Ages* (New York: Barnes and Noble, 1971), 276.

cuerdos, sus fantasías y el eco de sus lecturas sobre países exóticos y maravillosos.[47]

[The author must have traveled for many years, and although he might not have reached distant lands that he describes as if he had seen them, it is perfectly acceptable that he knew the kingdoms of Europe and the islands of the western Mediterranean. The trips of the anonymous Franciscan must have been made at different moments of his life, and from each one of them he must have conserved notes or short accounts that he would go along incorporating into his book, in which disorder is patent and the itineraries not very convincing. He could have been in Corsica between 1352 and 1360, and thus records that there was a war at that time between the Catalans and the Genoese: and he could have visited the kingdom of France after 1376, when the reduction to three fleurs-de-lis had been made on the coat of arms of the king. ... The anonymous Franciscan, who invested so many years of his life in travels, was a septuagenarian who gathered with joy, ingenuity and malice, his memories, his fantasies, and the echo of his readings about exotic and marvelous lands.]

Here, Riquer attempts to explain the obvious problem which arises from the incongruity between the author's stated year of birth in 1305 and the probable date of composition of his work after 1376, coupled with a seemingly "contemporary" reference to the Catalan conflict with the Genoese. As we have seen earlier in the section, mention of this conflict does not unquestionably represent information original to the work. There seem to be several possible explanations for the issue of the author's age. First, it is not impossible that the author of the *Conoscimiento* was more than seventy years of age when he wrote this book, but it was not a memoir of his actual travels. Why would he be reluctant to identify himself at the end of his life, when most likely he would have been proud of such accomplishments and knowledge? A second possibility is that the date of birth furnished for the narrator is simply another fiction created by an author already given to fictionalizing a medieval world tour; this notion supports the concept that the author and the narrator of the text are not meant to be one and the same person, as we shall discuss in the section about the authorship of the book. The other conceivable solution to the question of the author's age is that the description of the French coat of arms is a later interpolation. This is

[47] Riquer, "La heráldica en el *LdC*," 319.

especially feasible if the principal appeal of the *Conoscimiento* in the fifteenth century is, as we have previously mentioned, its depiction of the arms of Spain and other nations. It would be natural for a proficient preparer of the text or copyist to amend what the knowledgeable reader would recognize as an error in the flag of a familiar country.

It is worth noting that when Riquer and Russell published their articles on the use of heraldry and the dating of the *Conoscimiento* in 1987, they were unaware of each other's differing conclusions. In 1993, Riquer wrote his "La heráldica en el *Libro del conoscimiento* por tercera vez," which appropriately appeared in a volume of works in homage to Russell.[48] In this article Riquer states that Russell's arguments have convinced him that the author of this book was probably not a Franciscan friar, but maintains that this person indeed did travel to places for first-hand knowledge of heraldic devices in use at the time. (Russell contends that the author never undertook any of the travels at all.) Riquer concludes that the creator of this text began writing it in about 1352–60 and completed the project shortly after 1376, basing his work mostly on facts he took from various mappaemundi, but occasionally on information he gathered in his own journeys.

Another clue suggesting the work's earliest date of composition can found in a seemingly off-hand remark that the author makes about the city of Avignon. While he only mentions the place in passing, he identifies it as "una çibdat do mora el Papa de Roma" [a city where the Pope of Rome resides]. Clement VII moved his court there in 1378. Since all of the manuscripts we have contain this reference, it is probably in the original text and not a later insertion. It seems that, in spite of the various opinions concerning the text's earliest possible date, this brief allusion to the anti-pope's residence in Avignon provides the best evidence that the *Conoscimiento* could not have been written before the fall of 1378, when Clement became the first anti-pope and the Great Schism of the western Church began. Avignon ceased to be the papal residence in 1408.

So while there is virtually nothing in the text itself which identifies with exactitude the year or years of its composition, there is enough evidence to set its date of composition within a twenty-four-year span. If we consider the reference to the Pope's residence in Avignon as the *Conoscimiento*'s *terminus a quo*, then the book could not have been composed before late 1378. Russell judiciously maintains that the only real *terminus post quem* of

---

[48] Alan Deyermond and Jeremy Lawrance, eds., *Letters and Society in Fifteenth-Century Spain: Studies Presented to P. E. Russell on His Eightieth Birthday* (London: Dolphin, 1993), 149–51. Curiously, Russell's essay appeared in an homage volume to Riquer.

the work is around 1402, when the authors of *Le Canarien* used it as a reference for their own narrative of exploration. Unfortunately, the date of this book cannot be determined precisely either. It is nevertheless safe to assume that the *Conoscimiento* was composed in the last quarter of the fourteenth century.

AUTHORSHIP

When the authors of *Le Canarien* described the *Libro del conoscimiento de todos los reinos* they considered its creator a Spanish mendicant friar. This is apparently the first time that the author of the *Conoscimiento* is identified as a Franciscan, and most of those who subsequently wrote about the work followed this assertion without question. It is not clear, however, how the authors of *Le Canarien*, themselves members of religious orders, arrived at the conclusion that the anonymous author of the travel book was a Franciscan friar. None of the four extant manuscripts identifies him by profession, nor does the author make any comment within the work itself that would lead one to conclude that he belonged to a religious community. In fact, the narrator of the *Conoscimiento* only comments about his life at the beginning of the book, where he mentions that he was born in Castile during the reign of Fernando IV, on 11 September 1305, a year that he identifies in terms of the Christian and Hebrew ages, as well as the eras of Nabuchodonosor, Alexander the Great, and Caesar, in addition to time passed since the Great Flood. As Russell appropriately points out, it is strange that the author would define his date of birth in such specific terms but not identify himself in any other way; Russell suggests that by revealing his identity the author would have revealed also the fictional nature of the *Libro del conoscimiento*, since the author's contemporaries surely would have known that he never in reality made the trip he described.[49]

Most historians, geographers, and literary critics who have commented on the *Conoscimiento* have not made an issue of its authorship, reiterating without question that this person was a Franciscan. The scholar most convinced of this religious identity is the editor of the 1877 publication of the work, Jiménez de la Espada, whose fascination with and belief in the authenticity of the book led him to make some improbable affirmations about both the author and the text. In an attempt to identify positively the purported monk who composed the travelogue, Jiménez de la Espada engaged

---

[49] Russell, "La heráldica," 690.

the services of a Franciscan historian, who nevertheless did not succeed in determining a likely candidate for the book's authorship. Literary historian Morel-Fatio also objected to belief in the truthfulness of the book's assertions, and could not accept that if the author of this work was really a Franciscan, he would not be mentioned somewhere in the many existing biographies of Spanish members of this religious order.[50]

In some cases the assumption of a Franciscan identity has pre-determined other opinions about certain aspects of the *Conoscimiento*. Bonnet defends the truthfulness of the work in his article, maintaining that the fact that its author was a missionary in Africa accounts for how well he knew the parts of this continent cited in his narrative.[51] Miguel Angel Pérez Priego also subscribes to the theory of Franciscan authorship, but offers a quite reasonable justification for accepting the position that it is possible: "Aunque [el autor] no indica expresamente sus propósitos, su obra está inspirada por la idea clerical del saber: es un libro del 'conosçimiento de todos los reinos e tierras e señorios que son por el mundo' y también de 'las armas y los señores' que los gobiernan; es decir, un relato didáctico, una compilación geográfica con añadido de historia política y heráldica" [Although [the author] does not expressly indicate his purposes, his work is inspired by the clerical idea of knowledge: it is a book of 'knowledge of all the kingdoms and lands and lordships there are in the world' and also of the 'arms and lords' that govern them; that is, a didactic account, a geographic compilation with an addition of political and heraldic history].[52]

There are many reasons for not embracing the hypothesis that the author of the *Libro del conoscimiento* was a Franciscan missionary who traveled through almost every part of the world known in the mid-fourteenth century and subsequently wrote about his numerous stopovers. One good reason to challenge this assumption is simply the lack of textual evidence that upholds the theory. As we have seen, the author makes no disclosures concerning his particular vocation, either by straightforward statement or by implication, nor does he communicate to the reader the purpose of his travel. He mentions merchants but never counts himself among them; he refers to pagan persons he saw but does not express a desire to convert them; he recalls the exploits of early explorers but apparently is not seeking uncharted lands himself. Neither does he refer to making a pilgrimage. The

---

[50] Morel-Fatio, review of *Andanças e viajes*, 138.

[51] Bonnet, "Las Canarias," 211.

[52] Miguel Angel Pérez Priego, "Estudio literario de los libros de viajes medievales," *Epos* 1 (1984): 234.

withholding of such details of identity and purpose seems, as Russell has said, an intentional omission designed to conceal the author's identity.

We have examined already external evidence in two of the manuscripts which suggests that the author probably was not a member of a religious order, since the male figures depicted in the illuminations found in these codices are patently secular figures. Had he been a Franciscan, this information likely would have been known to the fifteenth-century copyists, who would surely have provided miniature portraits detailing his vocation, not a gentleman in court clothing.

Russell also doubts that the author was a Franciscan, basing his argument in part on the lack of religious references made throughout the work.[53] The fact is that the traveler makes very few allusions to things religious, and usually confines his comments to whether the peoples encountered were Christian or not. On the Island of Gropis (off the west coast of Africa), for example, he observes that it was a land abundant in all things, but the people were idolaters. But he says nothing further about this practice, which makes one wonder if a Franciscan missionary would make such an unsubstantial remark about this aberration. It does not seem likely that one whose vocation it was to convert non-believers would take such little interest in pagan activity, dismissing it with a superficial mention. Further doubt can be cast on the author's alleged profession by the fact that he visits neither churches (save Saint Sophia, in Constantinople, whose description he limits to its beauty and exact exterior dimensions) nor other holy landmarks: no stop is made in the Holy Land or any other place of religious significance. While enumerating places in France, the author only casually mentions that the Pope resides in Avignon. It is a lack of concern for religious matters that provokes doubt in the reader of a supposed "Franciscan" work.

And what interest might a Franciscan have had in the coats of arms of the cities and nations named in this book? The heraldic component, which signifies the worldly might and possessions of a ruler, would seem incongruous in a work written by one who should be more impressed with the might of God and the kingdom to come. That such a great portion of the book is allocated to heraldry which, in fact, gives structure to the narrative, is difficult to explain in a work presumably written by a missionary.

These observations make it hard to believe that a Franciscan could have written the *Libro del conoscimiento*. However, we are confronted still with the fact that in *Le Canarien*, written approximately twenty-five years after the

---

[53] Russell, "La heráldica," 690.

Conoscimiento was composed, the author of the *Conoscimiento* is referred to as a mendicant friar. The authors of this book on French exploration were working from a manuscript older than any we know today (the four extant copies date from about the mid-fifteenth century). Might an earlier copy, now lost, have mentioned his religious vocation? Did they arrive at this conclusion themselves because of their own knowledge of Franciscan missions in the north of Africa or their travels in conjunction with their missionary work? Existing accounts of such missionary travels, however, are rarely anonymous, as Franciscans were meticulous recorders of their works and voyages to missions in Asia and Africa.[54]

There is no doubt, however, that the author of the *Conoscimiento* was a person of considerable culture. He was familiar enough with a number of things historical and legendary to be able to integrate them into his text. As we will see later, the structure of his narrative seems to indicate that he had probably read or was otherwise acquainted with other medieval travel books, to whose general organization he appears to adhere. He had access to and could manage in a fundamental way a mappamundi of the era. He also had some basic knowledge of contemporary exploration and merchant commerce, even if only from the map or maps he consulted. But his evident interest in and comprehension of the heraldic convention is what most attracts our attention, details to be examined below.

What if the *Libro del conoscimiento* had been written by a herald? We have already proposed that the fifteenth-century audience was not interested in this book for its "travel" aspects (many of which were found to be erroneous by explorations that took place not long after the book was written), but for its illustration of more than 100 coats of arms of cities and nations. Is it not possible that a herald or an apprentice to this post (called *perservante* in Spain) might compile a roll of arms of the lands of the known world, using a travel itinerary as a pretext? Such a person certainly could have made at least part of the journey himself: the profession of herald (which finally became defined in the fourteenth century) required a knowledge of reading and writing, as well as a rudimentary ability in other languages, since travel was a necessary aspect of this work. According to Richard Wagner in his *Heralds and Heraldry in the Middle Ages*, "[M]any heralds led a wandering life from court to court and even from country to country, mingling always in what may be called chivalric circles; so that their oppor-

---

[54] Russell, "The Infante Dom Henrique," 264.

tunities for both collecting and spreading news of feats of arms and those who performed them would be ample."[55]

The existence of professional heralds in Castile in the mid-fourteenth century is difficult to demonstrate with any certainty. For example, there was no herald listed as a member of Pedro I el Cruel's household,[56] yet the chronicle of his reign clearly states that the king made use of heraldic devices on the flags and banners which accompanied him to the field of battle.[57] But even if there was no designated herald or king of arms, someone must have been responsible for this task. Heraldic symbols came into use in Spain at the end of the twelfth century when Alfonso VIII of Castile put the castle on his shield.[58] Edward, Prince of Wales (the so-called Black Prince) brought a herald with him to Spain when he came to support Pedro I in the struggles against his half-brother, Enrique de Trastámara. In fact, this herald was also entrusted with the task of messenger (a secondary and later common duty of the office) between the two camps, and was rewarded with expensive garments for his services.[59] Heralds from Spanish kingdoms also have been mentioned in other fourteenth-century works: there is reference in a French chronicle that in 1366 the heralds of Aragon and Navarre were in Brussels on the occasion of a tournament organized by the Duchess of Brabant.[60] Their identity is uncertain, however. The first herald to be baptized "Aragón" was Jean de Bar, in 1387; Martin Carbonel was named "Navarra" in 1369.[61] Both men may have practiced the office of heraldry prior to their official appointment. The first documentation of heralds in Castile has a late date (1429, in Juan II's chronicle) but the occupation might certainly have existed well before then, especially since it was

---

[55] Richard Wagner, *Heralds and Heraldry in the Middle Ages* (London: Oxford University Press, 1946), 28.

[56] Luis Vicente Díaz Martín, *Los Oficiales de Pedro I de Castilla* (Valladolid: Universidad de Valladolid, 1987).

[57] Pero López de Ayala, *Crónica del rey don Pedro*, eds. Constance L. Wilkins and Heanon M. Wilkins (Madison: Hispanic Seminary of Medieval Studies, 1985), 162.

[58] Martín de Riquer, *Heráldica castellana en tiempos de los Reyes Católicos* (Barcelona: Biblioteca Filológica, Quaderns Crema, 1986), 16.

[59] López de Ayala, *Crónica*, 163; also Chandos Herald, *Life of the Black Prince*, ed. Milfred K. Pope (Oxford: Clarendon Press, 1910), 155, 160; and Alfonso de Ceballos-Escalera y Gila, *Heraldos y reyes de armas en la corte de España* (Madrid: Colección El Perseverante Borgoña, 1993), 76–77.

[60] Wagner, *Heralds*, 34.

[61] Upon being named, heralds or kings of arms were usually baptized with the name of the kingdom or other some such designation, and henceforth were referred to with that name. Thus in Spain there were heralds called Castilla, Aragón, Navarra, Gerona, Trastámara, Cataluña, Valencia, etc. See Riquer, *Heráldica castellana*, 364–67.

common in the other two Spanish kingdoms and in Portugal at least sixty years before this time.

The anonymous author of the *Libro del conoscimiento* would have had at his disposal a limited but sufficient number of sources from which to copy heraldic shields. The typical portolan chart or mappamundi provided the coat of arms of a country or state in its general area on the map, but no extant map displays nearly as many such shields as our book does, which suggests, of course, that more than one source was employed in its manufacture. Other than geographical charts, there were few works that the author could have consulted. Rolls of arms existed in fourteenth-century England, Belgium, and Navarre, but these consisted mostly of the arms of rulers and nobles of each of those countries. The Parliament Roll of England, for example, was compiled in about 1312 and contains about 1100 banners of knights and noblemen. The herald of the Duke of Gelderland, named Gelre, produced between 1369 and 1400 an armorial of more than 1800 shields in which most of the countries of Europe were represented. The above mentioned herald Navarre (at the service of the kingdom's French ruler, Charles II) was responsible for the creation of an armorial of more than 1200 coats of arms, of which only fifteen belong to foreign sovereigns, with the remainder French.[62] Whether or not the author of the *Conoscimiento* had any of these works within reach is doubtful. Spanish rolls of arms do not begin to appear until the fifteenth century.

Russell notices that the use of heraldic language in the *Conoscimiento* is limited to only the most essential vocabulary;[63] in other words, the author employed common lay language when describing the colors, shapes, and illustrations on the coats of arms he had included. But this does not necessarily belie his possible identity as a herald, professional or otherwise. Other known masters of heraldry also have made use of everyday language in their descriptions of arms. A good example is the Castilian herald Garci Alonso de Torres, who composed his *Blasón de armas* [*Depiction of Arms*] sometime between 1476 and 1496. Despite his familiarity with established heraldic terminology for the colors of arms, he often wrote *verde* [green] instead of *sinopla* [vert], *amarillo* [yellow] rather than *oro* [or], *negro* [black] for *sable*, and *colorado* [red-colored] or *bermejo* [vermillion] for *gulas* [gules].[64] The author of the *Conoscimiento* also uses the common names for colors, at times interchanging them with the accepted terms. He applies a number of official

---

[62] Wagner, *Heralds*, 52–53.

[63] Russell, "La heráldica," 693.

[64] Riquer, *Heráldica castellana*, 72.

heraldic terms in his descriptions as well, which we shall consider later.

It is not impossible then, that the unknown author of the *Libro del conoscimiento* was a herald or at least a member of the court entrusted with the responsibility of this profession. He certainly possesses the required knowledge and culture that the position demands. And a person attached to the court would have access to the kinds of works he seems to have consulted in the compilation of the book: additional travel books, maps, historical treatises and other such texts.

The identity of the curious person who wrote the *Conoscimiento* probably will never be known, and evidently the author assured his own anonymity by his studied omission of remarks about his own person. His apparent desire to remain unnamed further confirms the fictional nature of his book. He is the author but not the narrator of the tale. He has created a pose, that of a traveler through the known world, as a means of offering his audience a description of places they would never go, and of people they would never see. This proposition is, of course, the principal purpose of medieval travel literature, factual or fictional. This particular voyage, it seems, amounts to a medieval joy-ride for the purpose of armchair tourism.

THE HERALDIC COMPONENT

The depiction of the coats of arms of rulers, states, and nations is a significant aspect of the *Libro del conoscimiento*, if not the most important feature of the work. After a brief account of his arrival in a place and any interesting characteristics of the region, its people, or curiosities, the author inevitably includes a blazon (written description) of the territory's heraldic arms, which usually also appears as a painted or sketched shield in the body of the text. As we have mentioned previously, the heraldic component of the *Conoscimiento* may account for its continued popularity into the fifteenth century, when the book's geographical information was known to have been largely misleading or entirely erroneous. It is in the 1400s that the Spanish reading public began to take a keen interest in the discipline of heraldry, as the growing number of works dealing with its norms and depicting Spanish arms attests. The *Conoscimiento* certainly can be considered one of these works for, as Riquer points out, the work is an authentic book of blazoned and illustrated arms, which gives it singular importance in the history of Spanish heraldry.[65]

---

[65] Riquer, "La heráldica en el *LdC*," 313.

The use of heraldic devices first appeared in Europe at the end of the eleventh century, and became firmly established by the middle of the next century.[66] Emblems were essentially a means of identifying and distinguishing persons; the need to use them for this purpose came about as a result of tournaments, where knights were heavily armored from head to foot and the public could not discover them easily. Therefore the participants put on their shields a symbol that could be associated with them; banners with the same emblems were flown when they jousted, and heralds were put in charge of documenting this aspect of the proceedings. When the practice became widespread, it became necessary to systematize and normalize the depiction of coats of arms. The norms included heraldic colors (*azure, gules, vert, purpure,* and *sable*) and metals (*argent* and *or*), geometric shapes called ordinaries (crosses, stripes or bands displayed at various angles, each with its own name), and other articles (called figures), which included a wide range of motifs such as animals or humans both real or fantastic, natural objects such as plants or flowers, or inanimate objects such as castles, cups, or keys. By the end of the twelfth century, most European heraldry conformed to these standards as well as to other instituted norms, such as avoiding the juxtaposition of metal and metal, or color and color.

Although heraldry was born in a milieu of combat, soon it was adopted by those who did not participate in tournaments. Within one hundred years the use of heraldic devices was taken up not only by kings and seignorial families, but by members of the bourgeoisie and even landed peasants. By the fourteenth century, cartographers began to use coats of arms on portolans and mappaemundi as a way of identifying kingdoms and states, since they did not ordinarily delineate the interior boundaries of these territories; they simply placed the flag associated with the region over its general area on the map.[67] But the design of these flags was by no means standard, and the selection of flags depicted on the maps also varied widely. At times the arms were invented by the mapmakers; sometimes the arms shown were incorrect or simply out of date because of the constant political turmoil in the Middle Ages. These inaccuracies make the flags on medieval maps an undependable source of historical data, as well as an unreliable method to date the maps on which they appear. As we have seen in the section on the *Conoscimiento's* sources, its author probably referred to one or more mappae-

---

[66] There are a number of good books on heraldry. Refer to Riquer, Wagner, and Woodcock in the Bibliography.

[67] See Harley and Woodward, *History of Cartography*, 1:399–401 on the use of flags on maps.

mundi and doubtless copied some of the coats of arms he described from these maps.

The four extant manuscripts of the *Libro del conoscimiento* each contain numerous coats of arms either completely painted or sketched. *N* offers the highest number, with 110 heraldic arms (plus eleven miniatures of people, things, or places supposedly encountered on the journey); *S* follows with 108 arms plus nine spaces intended for shields but left blank (and no other miniatures); *R* has 106 coats of arms, with blank spaces for sixteen more (as well as twelve other completed miniatures); *Z*, the most incomplete of the four codices, has ninety-eight flags of nations and rulers (plus eleven minia- tures).[68] It would be impractical and unnecessary to explain all of these coats of arms;[69] nevertheless, we shall refer to a few interesting examples.

In his study of these heraldic shields of *N*, *R*, and *S*, Pasch concluded that the artists who painted or drew the arms apparently worked indepen- dently from one another, providing miniatures created on the basis of the author's description of the shields in his text.[70] In this way Pasch accounts for the variation that occurs among the manuscripts. For his study he refers only to the flags provided in Markham's English translation; had he seen the original codices, Pasch would have noticed that, although there are occa- sionally differences in the depictions of the arms, *R* and *N* often agree with each other and differ from *S*. This reinforces our conclusion that *R* and *N* originated in the same or similar source, and that *S* had a distinctly different origin. Now that *Z* is available, it is possible to see that the arms that appear in it resemble those in *R* and *N*, which also suggests a similar source for all three codices. Take, for example, the arms of Navarre: in *S* the chains asso- ciated with the kingdom divide the shield into eight diagonally prescribed segments (gyronny); *R* and *N* depict the chains horizontally across the field, and above them are added three fleurs-de-lis not found in *S* (a possible

---

[68] Pasch, "Drapeaux du *Libro del Conoscimiento*," lists, describes, and provides sketches of 110 coats of arms, using the drawings in Markham's translation as his source. Markham, *Knowledge*, does not explain his criteria for selecting shields from the three manuscripts known to him, although he does identify the source of each coat of arms with an *S*, *R*, or *N*. Most of them he reproduces from *S*, but provides only eighty-nine of its 108 flags. He adds to this twenty-three from *N* and only seven from *R*, either to complete the set with flags missing from *S* or to show the variations that occur in the other two codices. Pasch, who obviously did not have access to any of the manuscripts, assumes that each has only the number of arms credited to it in Markham's work, well below the real number contained in each of them.

[69] See Pasch, "Drapeaux du *Libro del Conoscimiento*," and Riquer, "La heráldica en el *LdC*" and *Heráldica castellana* for more specific information.

[70] Pasch, "Drapeaux du *Libro del Conoscimiento*," 9.

allusion to the kings of France-Navarre).[71] Similarly, S shows the arms of Narbonne with a cross bottony in the center (each end of the cross ending in a clover-like figure), with four arrow-like shapes inside each quarter so formed; N, R, and Z all depict the field quartered by a plain cross, with a triangular shape in each quarter. Other comparative examples frequently give the same results, that is, that the shields appearing in S differ in an important way from those of the other three witnesses. There are, of course, errors such as mistaken attribution (in N, for example, the arms of Barcelona are shown for Toulouse), generally caused by an oversight on the part of the artist.

In addition to copying heraldic arms from another source or sources, the anonymous author of the Conoscimiento also invented devices for nations and rulers that did not really exist. But his doing so did not make him or his work unique in the fourteenth century, since imaginary heraldry was a commonplace in the Middle Ages, having begun about the same time as real heraldry was being standardized, in the mid-twelfth century.[72] Literary texts, tapestries, and paintings have all depicted the invented arms of non-existent persons and places, as well as the arms of people who lived before heraldry was created. Heraldic emblems have been created for such figures as Moses, Adam, Attila the Hun, Jupiter, Mars, King Arthur and his knights, Christ, the Devil, and Prester John (these last arms appear in the Conoscimiento), as well as for numerous fantastic kingdoms, countries, and institutions. Many of these fanciful arms later found their way into real armorials, such as Hierosme de Bara's 1579 work entitled Blason de armoires [Depiction of Arms].[73] The inventors of these shields generally conformed to the norms followed by heralds with respect to use of color, metals, and charges, but some (probably less familiar with heraldry than anxious to imitate it) committed errors in color or placement of figures. Besides the invention of arms for fictional persons or places, there existed the practice of creating one's own arms: a 1379 book on heraldic law confirms the legitimacy of designing one's own arms, as long as one did not expropriate those of another person or family not related.

When he invented arms for persons or places unknown to him, the author of the Conoscimiento usually followed accepted heraldic standards. Except for an error he made describing a Majorcan flag which probably never

---

[71] Unfortunately the miniature in Z has been intentionally darkened, making it impossible to see what might have been painted there.

[72] Michel Pastoureau, "L'heraldique imaginaire," Perpectives médiévales 10 (1984): 98–102.

[73] Riquer, Heráldica castellana, 33.

existed (juxtaposing the colors green and black[74]), the author seems to be well acquainted with the approved norms and applied them appropriately. As Russell has pointed out, the unidentified author seemed to think that the rulers of unfamiliar Asian and African countries used heraldic devices in the same way that Christian and Moslems rulers did.[75] The use of heraldry was probably so widespread that he must have assumed that all nations had arms, and set out to invent some for those with which he was unfamiliar. Knowing that heraldic charges were frequently symbols associated with a particular country, the author provided a flag with a pagan idol for an African nation he claimed was filled with idolaters; on the shield of another African realm of warm climate he placed palm trees. We must recall here that it was the credible description of these African arms that led the Béthencourt expedition to believe that the "mendicant friar" actually had reached these remote places and made them confident that they could duplicate his journey.

Another indication that the anonymous author was informed about heraldry is his frequent reference to the historical or other reasons for the pictorial aspect of arms. He tells the reader, for example, that Corsica's flag resembles that of Genoa "because the Genoese took it from the Catalans." This kind of information was not ordinarily found on portolans or mappaemundi, so even if he copied the physical attributes of the shield from such a source, he was aware that historical circumstances could determine its appearance and knew what those circumstances were. There are several such examples in *Conoscimiento*, regarding both real and imaginary realms. The author informs us that the flag of Naples displays fleurs-de-lis because its king belongs to the House of France, and with the same seriousness tells us that Nubia bears the arms of Prester John because he rules the area.

The unknown author of the *Conoscimiento* takes great care to make the blazoned arms of his work creditable. Where he describes coats of arms of real places, he is generally accurate and contemporary. (We must remember that the appearance of the French flag with only three fleurs-de-lis led Riquer to date the work after 1376, when these arms came into use.) Where he concocts the purported shields of realms and rulers unfamiliar to him, the author avails himself of standard heraldic norms and creates arms based on plausible premises. As we have said elsewhere, the journey attached to the text seems to be a pretext for the author's real intention, that is, to provide an armorial of all the places that appeared on contemporary cartographical works.

---

[74] Riquer, "La heráldica en el *LdC*," 315.
[75] Russell, "La heráldica," 694.

THE *LIBRO DEL CONOSCIMIENTO* AS TRAVEL LITERATURE

In the late eleventh century the First Crusade took fighting men, both knights and peasants, to the Holy Land. Those that returned did so with tales of their travels, stories of places they visited and people they met, foods they ate, and the hardships and dangers of the road. Some of the tales were embellished with yarns about miracles and fantastic creatures, humans and plants, fictitious things that were the essence of medieval legends. Medieval men and women were more willing to believe such fanciful stories because, unlike ourselves, they were not suspicious about things that they had not experienced first-hand. Some of these stories, which dated from antiquity, were conveyed as if they were fact. Therefore, medieval people believed in the existence of men without necks or with dog faces, birds that grew from buds on trees, ants who mined gold, and a wealth of other such lore. Because they did not distinguish between the "scientific" and the fictitious, the people of the Middle Ages were the ideal audience for books about travel to far-off places which they would never see; they longed for these exotic places to be filled with equally exotic things, unlike the familiar people and circumstances of their own lives. The authors of travel books were pleased to oblige their public, embroidering accounts of real (or sometimes fictitious) journeys with anecdotes about legendary cities or monsters that they supposedly encountered or heard about during their journeys. In this way they could satisfy the requirements of different reading publics, from the merely curious to those—such as prospective pilgrims, merchants, ambassadors, or explorers—who sought factual information about what to expect along the routes they planned to follow.

Beginning in the late thirteenth century, travel literature enjoyed a growing popularity. This coincided with authentic journeys of various kinds of people. In the mid-1200s, Franciscan missionaries concentrated their religious efforts in Mongol territory around the Volga River and in China. They are the first European travelers about which we have information, and the first to trek on land across Asia. John of Pian de Carpine, a Franciscan from Cologne, made the initial trip to the land of the Great Khan in 1245, returning home two years later. In 1251 or 1253, William of Rubruck, a friar from French Flanders, carried letters from King Louis to the Great Khan in Karakorum. Upon his return in 1254 or 1255 he wrote a detailed account of his journey. Dominican missionary groups also established themselves in other parts of Asia, India, Iran, and the central region of the continent. Later in the same century Marco Polo spent more than twenty years traveling throughout the Mongolian empire, China, and parts of Southeast Asia; the narrative of his adventures, entitled *Il Milione,* was a

work widely read not only during his lifetime, but for centuries thereafter, and it was translated into many languages.[76]

It is because of the curiosity of these travelers, both missionaries and merchants, that today we have an excellent idea of the medieval European perception of Asia. Not all those who made such voyages at that time were European. An important exception is the Islamic scholar, Ibn Battuta, who between 1325 and 1354 journeyed to virtually all the lands known to Moslem merchants in the fourteenth century. In Asia he journeyed all the way to Canton, and in Africa, to the Niger River. While his writings about this voyage are a valuable source of information to modern scholars, unfortunately his book was unknown to Europeans of the Middle Ages.[77]

During this period, these travelers had in common the desire to leave a written account of their experiences in distant lands, regardless of the intention of the finished work, which could range from serving as a travel guide, to promoting the work of the missions, or simply serving as a tool for disseminating knowledge. Most of those who wrote these books were not authors by profession, which the deficiency of their literary style often demonstrates. What reveals itself instead is an enthusiasm to relate their adventures against a backdrop of cities, mountains, seas, and other natural or manmade phenomena.

The narrator of the typical medieval travel book usually has a strong literary presence. He ordinarily identifies himself by name. The purpose of his journey (commerce, exploration, embassy, religious conversion, or pilgrimage) is made clear from the outset. Because he recounts personal experiences, the author customarily writes in the first person, a style that also draws the reader closer to the text, giving them a sense of participation. It was not only the itinerary of the trip that was of interest to the reader, but also the day-to-day experiences, observations, and conditions which the traveler underwent en route to his destination that held fascination. Most travel books contain comments on the various hardships that the journeyers had to endure. The narrators constantly complain of cold or heat and inadequate clothing to endure the climate; and transportation problems, including the fatigue that came from travel on foot or horseback. The travelers frequently refer to the accommodations they enjoyed or endured, as well as the quality of the food they ate at inns or monasteries. Both hunger and thirst are

---

[76] There are a number of informative books on medieval travel. See, for example, Labarge, Ladero, Newton, and Ohler in the Bibliography.

[77] Ibn Battuta, *Travels, A.D. 1325–54* (Cambridge: Cambridge University Press, 1958).

recurrent topics in these stories. The perils of the road, such as thieves or poor treatment by those they met along the way, is also a recurring theme in this literature, as is the inherent danger of the transportation itself, especially if by sea. There are tales of treacherous waters and near disasters, as well as illnesses that could befall travelers on long sea voyages. Some authors mention their traveling companions by name; or mention only those closest to them, and some mention no names at all. Once the traveling party arrived at a town or city, there could arise the problem of language and the consequent misunderstandings between the Europeans and the native people. The confusion and its results are typically explained in some detail.

A general characteristic of the medieval travel book is the personal account including ordeals endured and pleasant experiences enjoyed, described against an interesting geographical setting. In fact, the geographical data are relegated regularly to second place in significance, the most important component being the human element, the personal anecdote, the adventure. It is the almost total deficiency of these distinguishing attributes that sets the *Libro del conoscimiento* apart from other travel literature of this period. Although written as a first-person account, the work lacks the kind of personal remarks made in other books. The author makes no mention of traveling conditions, weather, accommodations, food, sickness or other problems or pleasures of the journey. Instead, he emphasizes the names of the places he claims to have visited and almost never fails to describe the coats of arms of the rulers of these distant lands. Despite these deficiencies, the narrator provides an identifiable structure and exhibits a certain style of his own, if a rather unadorned and often tedious one.

The purported itinerary forms the backbone of the *Conoscimiento*: the book offers a linear and chronological narrative of the places along the supposed route that the narrator followed. Most of the cities are enumerated in rapid succession, giving the reader the impression that they were merely passed by and not visited as the author would have us believe, or even copied from a map, as was probably the case. But he does follow an accepted and traditional composition in the narrative, conforming at least in a superficial way to a set of characteristics instituted in antiquity. Miguel Angel Pérez Priego provides an excellent summary of these established elements in his study of literary travel books.[78] The first of these aspects is, of course, the itinerary of the journey, which occupies the entire account from beginning to conclusion because the book ends when the voyage is over. The second characteristic is its chronological order which conforms most strictly in the

---

[78] Pérez Priego, "Estudio literario," 217–39.

more objective and truthful works and least rigorous in the more ficticious accounts.[79] The *Conoscimiento* adheres assiduously to the latter, as its narrator prefers to avoid definite reference to time spent in any pursuit. Some examples of his imprecise allusions are the following:

> "[E]t andudo aquella nao por alta mar tanto tienpo que llegamos a una isla que dizen Eterus." [And that ship traveled the high seas for so long a time that we arrived at an island they call Eterus.]

> "Et parti de Alcaara et fuy me para Damieta et fallé una nao de cristianos et entré en ella. Et andude un tienpo en esta nao fasta que descargaron en la çibdat de Çepta. . . . [E]t fuyme para Gazula, et moré ay un tienpo." [And I left Alcaara and went to Damieta and I found a ship of Christians and entered it. And I traveled a time in this ship until they unloaded in the city of Çepta. . . . And I went to Gazula, and lived there for a time.]

The narrator almost never gives explicit information about the number of days, weeks, or months he either traveled to or remained in a particular place, in part because he apparently had little idea of the time required to cover the ground about which he was writing. Already we have seen that probably it would have taken over twenty years to actually make the journey he describes, without taking into account the time he claims to have spent living in various cities, as he declares he did on eleven occasions.

Another established feature of travel books is the organization of the description of cities, the *de laudibus urbium*. The conventional structure includes information on the antiquity of the city in question, its geographical location, the fertility of its lands, the customs of its people, the buildings and monuments of note, and its celebrated men. In some such works the author breaks the rhythm of his narrative to expound at length on an unusually interesting aspect of a city. In the *Conoscimiento*, however, this kind of information generally is offered in a rather perfunctory manner, and there is never more than a paragraph's notice about any given place. The author uses repetitive and uninspired language to describe the sites according to the traditional requirements. Virtually all of his descriptions mention the regions' lands, and virtually all are depicted with the same adjectives: the land under consideration is always cold, temperate or hot, populated or unpopulated, large or small, abundant or barren. In one instance, the area is deemed dangerous, though for unstated reasons; in another, a city is delightful for

---

[79] Pérez Priego, "Estudio literario," 223–24.

equally unmentioned reasons. The choice of words is standardized and im-
personal, and probably originated in the legends of the map the author consulted, where such comments could be found. He sometimes furnishes
other information about the places of which he writes, but again the data
are kept to a minimum and can be consulted on the typical mappamundi.
He knows, for example, that the Pope was residing in Avignon at the time,
that the Magi were said to be buried in Cologne, that Rome was the head
of the Roman Empire, that Fez was the seat of the Benimerin, and so forth.
He largely ignores monuments, with the exception of the church of Saint
Sophia in Constantinople, and his description of it closely resembles its pictorial appearance on representative maps of the era.

   While many authors of medieval travel books dwell on the figure,
clothing, and customs of the people they come across, the narrator of the
Conoscimiento has little to say about the men and women of foreign places.
Like his remarks about the condition of the lands, his comments are usually
limited to a few words about their physical attributes, their intelligence, or
their religion. This last element is what he mentions most, and his typical
observations have to do with whether or not they are Christians: he calls
some schismatic Christians, others are not Catholic Christians, or are Greek
Christians; non-Christians are usually referred to as idolatrous, or "people
without religion who keep no commandments." The narrator, however,
never expands his comments or includes further details about their religious
practices. He makes a cursory reference to their appearance: some are described simply as beautiful, others simply as black. Unlike many other travel
writers of the era, he takes no interest whatsoever in the people's clothing
or lack thereof. He describes some of them only as cruel or vile, but he
offers no explanation of the behavior that merits these epithets. Most of the
people that the narrator encounters are simple-minded, but the Persians as
well as the inhabitants of parts of India are said to be wise, again without
explanation. The quality and quantity of the narrator's observations about
people he met on his journey do little to convince the reader that he speaks
from experience, compared to the abundance of particulars offered by his
literary counterparts.

   Travel literature of this period does not lack the fantastic element, especially in certain legends which had great impact on people, such as the existence of Prester John. These personages, together with fabulous humans,
animals, and plants, also appeared in medieval scientific encyclopedias such
as lapidaries or bestiaries and St. Isidore's *Etymologiae*. The stories of these
extraordinary creatures and phenomena, the *mirabilia*, came to the Middle
Ages from the works of Solinus, Pliny, Aristotle, and other ancient authors

who first alluded to them. The *Libro del conoscimiento* also has its share of such fantastical beings: there are the cynocephali (barking men who have dogs' heads and feet); the antipodeans (people who occupy the opposite end of the globe, known as the torrid zone, and are therefore black from sunburn); birds on the island of "Hibernia" that grow from well-watered trees, and are delicious either boiled or roasted; griffins on the island of Java; and on the River of Gold there were supposedly ants as big as cats that would unearth gold nuggets as they built their anthills.

The narrator of the *Conoscimiento* does know something of the more objectively scientific ideas of the period, for he refers at different moments to astronomy and climate. As we have seen in the section on the identity of the author, he begins the narrative with an explicit account of his date of birth, counting out the years in terms of the Hebrew, Christian, Islamic, and other calendars. He is aware that in the northern latitudes there are six months of daylight and six of night. He mentions the seven climates four times, a concept which came to medieval men through Macrobius, and appeared in the works of the Venerable Bede (eighth century) and Albertus Magnus and Roger Bacon (both of the thirteenth century). The narrator writes several times about astronomy, and informs the reader that it was discovered in Persia. But other than the reckoning of his birth date according to the ages of man, any of these scientific terms usually could be found on a mappamundi, so we cannot credit our author with either being knowledgeable enough about these matters to write of them, or consulting works more learned than a contemporary map.

Like other works of this genre, the *Conoscimiento* is written from the point of view of the narrator, but he seems only to imitate literary tradition in an attempt to lead his readers to believe in the truthfulness of the endeavor. To bring added authority to his writing, the author at times employs the first-person plural in order to imply that he had company during part of his journey. These companions are never cited more than once and then only by profession; they are generally merchants in whose ships he travels for a time. He often uses other modes of expression to lend an air of authenticity to what he claims to have seen or done. Sometimes he says "wise men told me this," or "they affirm that," "I heard marvelous things," "they showed me," or "they told me other secrets." But when telling of something quite fantastic (such as the existence of men without necks), the narrator generally adds the disclaimer "but I did not see them," apparently because he is not very convinced of what he is saying. Nevertheless, the author does affirm that he saw Noah's ark, which probably seemed more historically valid to him than reports of ill-formed humans and therefore

more believable to his intended readership. In contrast, William of Rubruck and Marco Polo continually stress that they have seen these things themselves, or were supplied the information by trustworthy witnesses.

His story-telling vocabulary is also limited and repetitive, based almost solely on the verb *contar*: "ya conté de suso"; "ya contaré"; "ya contamos"; "seria luengo de contar" [I already told of above; I will soon tell; we already told; It would be too long to tell]. Occasionally he uses the verb *fablar* [to speak] or *dezir* [to say]. The narrator frequently addresses his audience in the imperative form *sabet* [know]. Of particular interest is the terminology he utilizes to write of the act of traveling: never once does the verb *viajar* [to travel] appear in the text, nor the noun *viaje* [journey]. In fact, he uses no nouns at all to describe the journey; he reserves the word *jornada* [a day's-worth of traveling] for measuring the distance between two places or for the size of a region. The author instead makes use of a variety of verbal expressions relating to travel: *travesar, salir, llegar, partir, ir, pasar, ir por tierra, tomar camino* [to cross, to leave, to arrive, to depart, to go, to pass, to go by land, to take a road]. And he mentions only two ways of transportation: by sea, in various kinds of boats, ships, and galleys; and by land, he mentions only camels. The author does not remark whether he traveled on foot or horseback when trekking across land on anything other than a camel.

Because they are written by inexperienced authors, most medieval travel books hold little literary interest or have no notable literary value. Their style is straightforward and linear both geographically and chronologically; figurative language almost never appears in them. But the *Libro del conoscimiento* is a particularly prosaic narrative characterized by repetitive modes of expression, ponderous lists of place-names, commonplace epithets to describe people or sites, as well as a general scarcity of detail about the narrator's personal experiences or observations. In fact, precise description is reserved only for the coats of arms that appear both blazoned (verbally depicted) and painted or sketched at the end of each section concerning a place or ruler.

The special attention given the heraldic aspect of the *Conoscimiento* leads us to suspect that the geographical data in the book serve merely as a pretext for the blazoning and depiction of the coats of arms of more than one hundred states, cities, and rulers. The author nevertheless does not entirely neglect the geographical component of his work for, as we have seen in other sections, he generally provides up-to-date information on places such as the western coast of Africa. These two elements together were probably responsible for the book's apparent popularity in the 1400s; the combination of heraldry and political geography would have been more attractive to the

fifteenth-century reader or book collector than the pedestrian treatment that the journey receives.

It is not until the fifteenth century that Spain produces real travel books. Ruy González de Clavijo completed his *Embajada a Tamorlán* [*Embassy to Tamerlaine*] in about 1406. Written in the third person (which sets it apart from most other works of the genre), it is essentially the chronicle of an official embassy visit, an almost day-to-day record that Clavijo composed during his journey, and offers an abundance of details including exact dates and hours of the day, precise accounts of what he observed and heard, and an excellent physical description of the lands he saw. Pero Tafur's *Andanças e viajes* [*Journeys and Travels*] was written following his return from travels which lasted from 1436 to 1439, and is therefore a less explicit narrative than most. Nevertheless, Tafur offers accurate information of his voyages and the time he spent in this endeavor. Although intended to be a chronicle of the life of don Pero Niño, Count of Buelna, Gutierre Díez de Games's *El Victorial* essentially contains a travel narrative of the count's wanderings from 1403 to 1410. All of these works, whether told in the first or third person, are characterized by the strong personality of their narrators, and the exact purpose of the travels reported, be it a diplomatic mission or simple adventure. The *Conoscimiento* is very unlike these examples of travel literature.

ABOUT THE EDITION AND TRANSLATION

The present edition has been prepared using manuscript *S* as its base, since (as we have already seen in the section on the manuscript witnesses) it provides a complete text of the *Libro del conoscimiento* and contains the fewest number of errors of the four extant codices. Because all the available manuscripts date from the fifteenth century—and are therefore removed by some one hundred years from the work's date of composition—we have no "original" text upon which to base an edition. The edition offered here has been constructed with careful consideration to what would be the most correct and accurate text possible given the witnesses at hand.

I have made as few modifications of the text as possible, following current practice, and have made only alterations that would facilitate its reading. They are as follows:

1. All abbreviations have been resolved.
2. Words have been capitalized and punctuation has been added according to modern usage.
3. Orthographical changes have been made when the original makes

reading more difficult. This includes modernizing the spellings of u/v and i/j. When it occurs within a word or at the beginning of a word that need not be capitalized, R has been rendered rr.

The translation follows closely the original Spanish text; this has been done in order to maintain its characteristic narrative form. Therefore no attempt has been made to improve the text by changing such infelicities as its abundant and sometimes tedious use of the word "and," including its frequent appearance at the beginning of sentences. Place-names have been left as they appear in the Spanish text for several reasons: the reader will become aware of the often numerous variants found in the original; some cities and other places are identified mistakenly by the narrator (the correct toponyms are found in the notes to the edition and translation); and the imaginary places mentioned usually have no apparent translation in English. However, those names containing descriptive adjectives (e.g., Mar Mayor) have been translated (Great Sea).

The Spanish and English texts share the same set of footnotes.

The illustrations of the coats of arms mentioned in the text have also been prepared using S as the source. When they vary in the other manuscripts, variant arms are given as well. In some cases the illustration was missing in S, and one of the other manuscripts, usually N, was used to supply the arms.

The Roman numerals in square brackets in both the Spanish and English texts refer to the number of the illustration.

El Libro del conoscimiento
de todos los reinos

(The Book of Knowledge of All Kingdoms)

I. Castilla y Leon

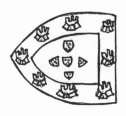

IIa. Portogal (S)

IIb. Portogal (N, R, Z)

III. Bayona

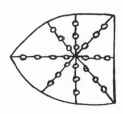

IVa. Navarra (S)

IVb. Navarra (N, R, Z)

Va. Tolosa (S)

Vb. Tolosa (R)

Vc. Tolosa (N, Z)

VI. Françia

VII. Flandes

VIII. Alemaña

IX. Frisa

X. Daçia

XI. Boemia

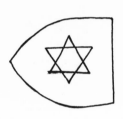

XII. Litefama, Catalant

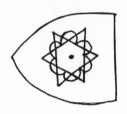

XIIIa. Polonia (S)

XIIIb. Polonia (N, Z)

XIIIc. Polonia (R)

XIVa. Leon (S)

XIVb. Leon (N, Z)

XVIc. Leon (R)

XV. Suevia

XVIa. Gotlandia (S)

XVIb. Gotlandia (N, R)

XVIc. Gotlandia (Z)

XVII. Gotia

XVIII. Noruega

XIX. Salanda

XX. Escoçia

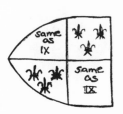

XXI. Inglaterra

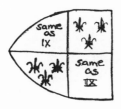

XXII. Irlanda

XXIII. Ibernia

XXIV. Granada

XXV. Aragon

XXVIa. Narbona (S)

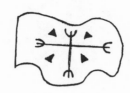

XXVIb. Narbona (N, R)   XXVIc. Narbona (Z)   XXVII. Genova

XXVIII. Lonbardia   XXIXa. Pisa (S)   XXIXb. Pisa (N, R, Z)

XXX. Florençia   XXXIa. Roma (S)   XXXIb. Roma (N, R, Z)

XXXIIa. Napol (S)   XXXIIb. Napol (N, Z)   XXXIIc. Napol (R)

XXXIII. Çeçilia

XXIV. Veneçia

XXXV. Esclavonia

XXXVIa. Boxnia (S)

XXXVIb. Boxnia (N, R, Z)

XXXVII. Narent

XXXVIII. Ungria

XXXIX. Morea

XL. Rodas

XLIa. Satalia

XLIb. Satalia (N, R, Z)

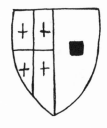

XLII. Turquia

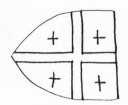

XLIII. Corincho

XLIVa. Cunio (S)

XLIVb. Cunio (N, R, Z)

XLVa. Savasco (S)

XLVb. Savasco (N, R, Z)

XLVI. Armenia Menor

XLVII. Chipre

XLVIIIa. Suria (S)

XLVIIIb. Suria (N)

XLVIIIc. Suria (R, Z)

XLIX. Damasco

L. Egipto

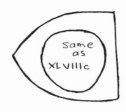

LI. Alexandria

LII. Luchon

LIII. Tolometa

LIV. Tripul

LV. Africa

LVI. Tunez

LVII. Cerdeña

LVIII. Corçega

LIX. Bona

LX. Costantina

LXI. Bugia

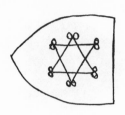

LXIIa. Brischan (S, Z)

LXIIb. Brischan (R)

LXIII. Mayorca

LXIV. Tremeçen

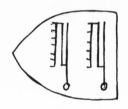

LXV. Çepta

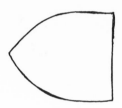

LXVI. Fez

LXVII. Marruecos

LXVIII. Çuçia

LXIX. Sugulmença

LXX. Tocoron

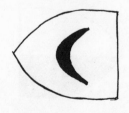

LXXI. Buda

LXXII. Guinoa

LXXIII. Organa

LXXIV. Tauser

LXXV. Tremisin

LXXVIa. Dongola (S, R)

LXXVIb. Dongola (N, Z)

LXXVII. Gropis

LXXVIII. Gotonie

LXXIX. Amenuan

LXXX. Graçiona

LXXXIa. Preste John (S)

LXXXIc. Preste John (N)

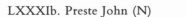

LXXXIb. Preste John (N)

LXXXId. Preste John (R, Z)   LXXXIIb. Magdasor (N, R, Z)

LXXXIIa. Magdasor (S)

LXXXIII. Bandacho   LXXXIV. Meca   LXXXV. Sicroca

LXXXVI. Lini   LXXXVII. Viguy   LXXXVIII. Oxanap

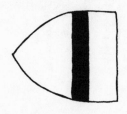

LXXXIX. Catayo   XC. Armalet   XCI. Gran Can

XCII. Sçim

XCIII. Bocarin, Cato

XCIV. Norgançia

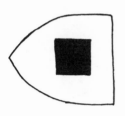

XCV. Persia

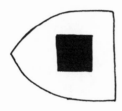

XCVI. Saldania

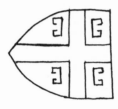

XCVIIa. Salonico (S)

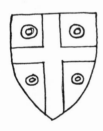

XCVIIb. Salonico (N, R)

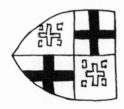

XCVIIIa. Constantinopla (S)

XCVIIIb. Constantinopla (N, R)

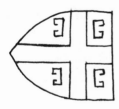

XCIXa. Lodomago (S)

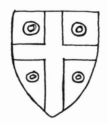

XCIXb. Lodomago (N, R)

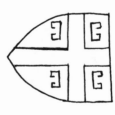

Ca. Meseber (S)

Cb. Meseber (N, R)

CI. Veçina

CII. Comania, Tana, Canardi

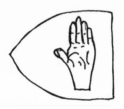

CIII. Sant Estopoli

CIV. Trapesonda

CVa. Semiso (S)

CVb. Semiso (N)

CVIa. Castelle (S)

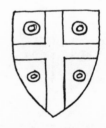

CVIb. Castelle (N)

CVIIa. Palolimen (S)

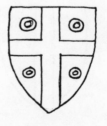

CVIIb. Palolimen (N)

CVIII. Feradelfia

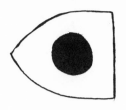

CIX. Atologo

CX. Derbent

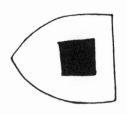

CXI. Caraol

CXII. Sara

CXIII. Sabur

CXIV. Roxia

CXV. Sicçia

CXVI. Xorman (N)

CXVII. Maxar

CXVIII. Silvana

CXIX. Yrcania (N)

EL LIBRO DEL CONOSÇIMIENTO DE TODOS LOS RREGNOS E TIERRAS ET SEÑORIOS QUE SON POR EL MUNDO

Este libro es del conosçimiento de todos los rregnos et tierras et señorios que son por el mundo, et de las señales et armas que han cada tierra et señorio por sy.

En el nonbre de Dios padre et fijo et spiritu santo que son tres personas indeviduas en una esençia: Yo fuy nasçido en el rreynado de Castilla, rreynante en uno el muy noble rrey don Fernando fijo del muy noble rrey don Sancho,[1] quando andava la era del mundo segund los abraicos en çinco mill et sesenta et çinco años, et la era del general diluvio en quatro mill et quatroçientos et siete, et la era de Nabucodonosor Rey de Caldea en dos mill et çinquenta et dos años, et la era del grande Alixandre de Maçedonia en mill et seysçientos et diez et siete años, e la era de Çesar Enperador de Roma en mill et tresientos et quarenta et tres años, et la era de Cristo en mill et trezientos et quatro años, et la era de los alarabes en sieteçientos et seys, en onze dias del mes de setienbre.[2] Et avia en el rreynado del dicho rreyno veynte et ocho çibdades et con otras muchas villas et castillos et logares. Las tres çibdades son arçobispados, que son Sevilla et Toledo et Conpostela, et las veynte et çinco çibdades son obispados, que son Algezira[3] et Cordova, Jahen, Murçia, Badajoz, Coria, Çibdat Rodrigo, Çamora,

---

[1] Sancho IV (1284–95) and Fernando IV (1295–1312).

[2] The various methods used to calculate the year of the author's birth create confusion about whether he was born in September of 1304 or 1305. The Jews consider that Christ was born in the year 3761 of Creation, therefore the year 5065 cited here seems to correspond to 1305; since the Hebrew New Year could fall between September 3 and October 6, however, September 11 of Hebrew year 5065 could have corresponded to 1304 A.D. According to the Alphonsine Tables, the Great Flood took place 3101 years and 319 days before the birth of Christ; the year 4407, therefore, would be the equivalent of 1305 A.D. The era of Alexander the Great began with his first conquests in 312 B.C.; 1617 years later also corresponds to 1305 A.D. Finally, the author apparently uses the year 598 (when Mohammed began to preach his doctrine) as the beginning point of the Islamic era; 706 years afterwards was 1304 A.D.

[3] Algeciras was conquered by Alfonso XI in 1344, a reference which helps determine that this book was composed after this date.

THE BOOK OF KNOWLEDGE OF ALL THE KINGDOMS, LANDS, AND LORDSHIPS IN THE WORLD

This is the book of knowledge of all the kingdoms and lands and lordships that there are in the world, and of the insignia and arms that each land and lordship has.

In the name of the Father and Son and Holy Spirit, who are three individual persons in one essence. I was born in the Kingdom of Castilla, during the reign of the very noble King Fernando, son of the very noble King Don Sancho, when the era of the world, according to the Hebrews, was 5065 years, and the era of the Great Flood 4407 years, and the era of Nebuchadnezzar King of Caldea 2502 years, and the era of Alexander the Great of Macedonia 1617 years, and the era of Caesar Emperor of Roma 1343 years, and the era of Christ 1304 years, and the era of the Arabs 706 years, on the eleventh day of the month of September.

And there were in the reign of said kingdom twenty-eight cities and many other towns and castles and villages. Three of these cities are archbishoprics, to wit, Sevilla and Toledo and Compostela; and twenty-five cities are bishoprics, namely Algezira and Cordova, Jahen, Murçia, Badajoz, Coria, Çiudad Rodrigo, Çamora, Salamanca, Plazençia, Avila, Segovia,

Salamanca, Plazençia, Avila, Segovia, Palençia, Cuenca, Osma, Astorga, Burgos, Leon, Oviedo, Orense, Tuy, Lugo, Mondoñedo, Calahorra, Çiguença. Et fallé en este rreinado prinçipalmente quatro montes altos: los montes de Bizcaya, que son rribera del Mar Oçidental[4] et que se tyenen con las sierras de las Asturias; al otro monte dizen la Sierra de Segovia, a do son muchas villas et logares; al otro monte dizen la Sierra Morena; al quarto monte dizen la Sierra de Segura, donde nasçen dos rrios muy grandes. Al uno dizen Guadalquevyr, que antiguamente dezian Betis, et pasa por Cordova et por Sevilla et entra en el Mar Oçidental en un logar que dizen Barrameda. Al otro rrio dizen Segura, et va por Murçia et entra en el mar Medio Terreno çerca de un lugar que dizen Guardamar. Et fallé en este rreinado seys rrios grandes: Guadalquivir, que ya conté; al otro rrio dizen Tajo, que corre por Toledo et por Santaren et entra en la Mar Oçidental çerca de una çibdat que dizen Lisboa en el rreynado de Portogal; al otro se dizen Duero, et corre por Soria et por Almaçan et por Santesevan de Gormaz et va por una çibdat que dizen Çamora et entra en el Mar de Poniente[5] çerca de la çibdat que dizen Portogallo; al otro rrio dizen Guadiana, et va por un lugar que dizen Calatrava et dende va a un lugar que dizen Merida et dende va por vna çibdat que dizen Badajoz et entra en la Mar de Poniente en un lugar que dizen Castro Marin; al otro rrio dizen Ebro, que va por Tudela et por Çaragoça (çibdades del rreinado de Aragon), et entra en el mar Medio Terreno çerca de una çibdat que dizen Tortosa. Et sabet que en este rreynado de Castilla et Leon tiene toda la marisma del poniente fasta Bayona la mayor, et parte con Navarra et Aragon et Granada. Las señales deste rrey deste rreyno es un pendon con dos castillos et dos leones fechos en quarterones, tales como estos que adelante se siguen. [I]

E party del rreynado de Castilla et fuy al rreinado de Portogal, et fallé en el quatro çibdades grandes: Lisbona et el Portogallo et Santaren et Bragaa. Et corren por ellas tres rrios grandes: Tajo et Guadiana et Duero, de que ya conté de suso. Et este rreynado parte con el Mar de Poniente et con el rreynado de Castilla et Leon. Et las señales del rrey deste rreyno son un pendon con castillos alderredor, et quynas en medio como aqui se siguen. [II]

E parti de Portogal et fueme por la marisma del Mar Oçidental a la provinçia de Gallizia, al puerto de Bayona de Miño,[6] et desi a Ponte Vedra, et dende fuy a Sant Ander et a Castro de Urdiales et a Bilbao et a Sant Sabastian, que es toda esta marisma del señor Rey de Castilla. Et dende fuy a

---

[4] The Atlantic, called the Western Ocean since ancient times.
[5] Another name for the Atlantic Ocean is the Poniente, so named for its position.
[6] A city in Galicia near the mouth of the River Miño.

Palençia, Cuenca, Osma, Astorga, Burgos, Leon, Oviedo, Orense, Tuy, Lugo, Mondoñedo, Calahorra, Çiguença. And in this kingdom there are four principal ranges of high mountains: the mountains of Bizcaya, which are on the coast of the Western Sea and border on the Asturian sierra; they call the other mountains the Sierra of Segovia, where there are many towns and villages; they call the other mountains the Sierra Morena; they call the fourth mountain range the Sierra de Segura, where two great rivers originate. One they call the Guadalquevyr, which they formerly called Betis, and it passes through Cordova and Sevilla and enters the Western Sea at a place called Barrameda. The other river they call Segura, and it goes through Murçia and enters the Medio Terreno Sea near a village called Guardamar. And there are in this kingdom six great rivers: Guadalquivir, of which I have already told; the other river they call the Tajo, which runs by Toledo and Santaren and enters the Western Sea near a city they call Lisboa in the kingdom of Portogal; they call the other the Duero, and it runs through Soria and through Almaçan and Santestevan de Gormaz, and goes through a city called Çamora, then enters the Western Sea near a city they call Portogallo; the other river they call Guadiana, and it flows near a place called Calatrava and then goes to a town named Merida, then to a city called Badajoz, and enters the Western Sea in a village called Castro Marin; they call the other river the Ebro, which flows through Tudela and Çaragoça (cities in the Kingdom of Aragon), and enters the Medio Terreno Sea near a city they call Tortosa. And know that this Kingdom of Castilla and Leon has swampy land in the west near Bayona Major, and it borders on Navarra and Aragon and Granada. The insignia of the king of this kingdom is a flag with two castles and two lions, quartered like these that now follow. [I]

And I left the Kingdom of Castilla and went to the Kingdom of Portogal, where I found four great cities: Lisbona and Portogallo and Santaren and Bragaa. And three great rivers run through them: Tajo and Guadiana and Duero, which I have already told of above. And this kingdom borders on the Western Sea and the Kingdom of Castilla and Leon. And the insignia of the king of this kingdom is a flag with castles around it and escutcheons in the center, in this manner. [II]

I left Portogal and went along the swampy coast of the Western Sea to the province of Gallizia, to the port of Bayona de Miño, then to Ponte Vedra, from where I went to Sant Ander and to Castro de Urdiales and to Bilbao and to Sant Sabastian, coastal lands which all belong to the King of Castilla. And from there I went to Bayona la Mayor, which is in Gascueña,

Bayona la Mayor, que es en Gascueña, que está asentada entre el Mar de Poniente et los Montes Pirineos. El señor desta Bayona a por señales un pendon blanco con una cruz bermeja atal. [III]

Parti de Bayona et entre por Navarra, un rreynado muy viçioso, en que ay tres çibdades grandes, conviene a saber: Panplona et Tudela et Estela. Et corren por él tres rrios grandes, que son Ebro et el flumen Sinca et el flumen Sigre. Et el rrey della a por señales éstas que se siguen.[7] [IV]

E parti de Navarra et atravesé los montes Perineos que allegan fasta el condado de Anpurias, et destos montes nasçen quatro rrios grandes. Al primero dizen Sinca, al segundo Sigre, al terçero Giron,[8] al quarto Ebro. Et a la parte esquyerda destos montes es el condado de Burdeo et Limogines, Caorz et Armeñaque et Piteos,[9] et la noble çibdat de Tolosa, do son los estudios de las artes liberales. Et el señor desta Tolosa a por señales un pendon bermejo con una cruz de oro pintada atal.[10] [V]

E parti de Tolosa et torné a la marisma al condado de Burdeo, et dende fuy a la Rochela, una rrica çibdat de Françia, et dende fuy a la punta de Sanmae, que es en la provinçia de Bretaña, et dende fuy al golfo de Samalo, et dende a la provinçia de Lormandia,[11] que es todo esto en el rreinado de Françia, do son muchas çibdades et villas et logares. Et parti de Lormandia por la marisma et fuy al golfo de Loira, en el qual entra un grand rrio que dizen Saina,[12] que nasçe de los montes que dizen Pirineos, et traviesa todo el rreinado de Françia et entra por medio de la grand çibdat de Paris, et entra por el mar del golfo de Loira. Et deste golfo fasta Paris son quatro jornadas. Et sabed que el rreynado de Françia parte con el Mar Medio Terreno en una çibdat que dizen Narbona, et parte con los Alpes Alsaçie, et con toda la marisma de Flandes et toda la Gascueña fasta los montes

---

[7] S illustrates the familiar arms of Navarre, with its four chains that cross at the center. Markham explains its origins: "The King of Navarre and his knights broke the chain which defended the approach to the Almohade Sultan's tent, at the battle of Las Navas de Tolosa in 1212. From that time the Kings of Navarre bore the chain on their coat of arms, and on their flag" (*Knowledge of the World*, 4).

Both *N* and *R* depict three horizontal chains, above which are found three fleurs-de-lis.

[8] Jiménez de la Espada proposes that this is the Ter River, called Giron here because it passes through Gerona (205).

[9] According to Jiménez de la Espada, this might refer to the county of Poitiers or Pitou (193).

[10] S and R each provide the banner described here. In N, despite the fact that the same description is given, there appear instead the arms of Barcelona, an apparent error made by the illuminator.

[11] The first is probably the Pointe St.-Mathieu (near Brest), which appears on the Catalan map as Samae. The others are the Gulf of St.-Malo and Normandy.

[12] The Seine.

which is located between the Western Sea and the Pirineos Mountains. The lord of this Bayona has as his insignia a white flag with a vermilion cross, in this manner. [III]

I left Bayona and entered Navarra, a kingdom of great abundance in which there are three great cities, to wit, Pamplona and Tudela and Estela. And through it run three great rivers, the Ebro and the Sinca and the Sigre. And the king of it has as his insignia the one that follows. [IV]

And I left Navarra and crossed the Pirineos Mountains that extend to the County of Anpurias, and from these mountains four great rivers originate. The first they call Sinca, the second Sigre, the third Giron, and the fourth Ebro. And on the left side of these mountains is the County of Burdeo and Limogines, Caorz and Armeñaque and Piteos, and the noble city of Tolosa, where the Liberal Arts are studied. And the lord of this Tolosa has as his insignia a vermilion flag with a cross of gold painted in this manner. [V]

And I left Tolosa and returned to the coast to the County of Burdeo, and from there to Rochela, a rich city in Françia, and from there I went to the Punta de Sanmae, which is in the province of Bretaña, and from there I went to the Golf of Samalo, and from there to the province of Lormandia, all of this in the Kingdom of Françia, which has many cities and towns and villages. And I left Lormandia for the coast and went to the Gulf of Loira, in which there enters a great river that they call Saina, which originates in the mountains called the Pirineos and crosses the whole Kingdom of Françia, and passes through the center of the city of Paris, and enters the sea at the Gulf of Loira. From this gulf to Paris there is a four-day journey. Know that the Kingdom of Françia borders on the Medio Terreno Sea at a city called Narbona, and borders on the Alpes Alsaçie and the whole coast

Pireneos. El Rey de Françia a por señales un pendon azul con tres flores de lises de oro atales. [VI]

E parti de Paris et fuy a Roan et a Chalon, et dende torné a la marisma a una çibdat que dizen Diepa del rreyno de Françia. Et parti dende et fue a la punta de Calés, una rrica çibdat que es en la provinçia de la Picardia.[13] Et sabed que desde Calés fasta la isla de Inglatera es una pequeña traviesa de ocho millas. Et party de Calés et fuy al condado de Flandes a una noble çibdat que dizen Brujas. Et el señor dende a por señales un pendon de oro con un leon prieto atal. [VII]

Desde ende fuy me por la marisma a una çibdat que dizen Solanda et dende a otra que dizen Maxa, et otra Leobet, que son çibdades de Alemaña. Et dende pasé a Dodret,[14] una grand çibdat et rrica, et pasa por ella un gran rrio que dizen Rinus que nasçe de los Alpes Alemaña, el qual rrio pasa por Coloña, una grand çibdat de Alemaña. Et en esta Coloña diz que yazen soterrados los tres Reyes Magos que adoraron a Jesu Cristo en Beleen, pero que quando fuy en el inperio de Catayo en una çibdat que dizen Solin, me mostraron tres monimentos muy onrrados et dixeron me que eran de los tres Reyes Magos que adoradon a Jesu Cristo, et que de ally fueron na-turales.[15] Et en esta Alemaña son unos montes muy altos que llaman Alpes Alemanie, et nasçen dende tres rrios. Al uno dizen Ruedano, que va por una çibdat que dizen Leon,[16] et ayuntase a el otro rrio muy grande que nasçe de los Alpes Alsaçie. Et van por Lurdevit et por Aviñon, una çibdat do mora el Papa de Roma, et entra en el Mar Medio Terreno apres de una çibdat que dizen Arle. Et estas çibdades son del rreyno de la Proençia.[17] Al otro rrio dizen Rinus, et va por la çibdat de Coloña de que ya conté de suso, et entra en la Mar de Alemaña. Al otro rrio dizen Danubio, et traviesa

---

[13] After Paris, Rouen, Chalons, Dieppe, and Calais.

[14] The first is the province of Zeeland (Netherlands). Jiménez de la Espada (226) and Markham (64) identify the second as Maastricht. Jiménez de la Espada (220) suggests that Leobet might be either Leuven or Limbourg (both in Belgium), while Markham (64) believes it is Lièges, but it is not clear which city the narrator had in mind. The last place mentioned is Dordrecht; the supposed itinerary does not help determine what Leobet might be, since the narrator would have traveled from Zeeland southeast to Maastricht, then northwest to Dordrecht after the intermediary stop in Leobet.

[15] Besides this reference to Cologne, there are various legends about the burial place of the Magi. Marco Polo reported that their tomb could be found in Persia, while the Catalan Atlas illustrates it in the eastern part of Turkestan. Another story is that Saint Helena had them removed from India and brought to Milan. See Markham (6, n.1) and Jiménez de la Espada (123).

[16] The Rhone River, which passes through Lyon.

[17] Perhaps this is Luc-en-Diois, southwest of Lyon on the Drome River. The kingdom mentioned is Provence.

of Flandes and Gascueña, up to the Pireneos. The King of Françia has as his insignia a blue flag with three gold fleurs-de-lis, in this way. [VI]

I departed Paris and went to Roan and to Chalon, and from there I turned toward the coast to a city they call Diepa, in the Kingdom of Françia. And I left there and went to the point of Calés, a rich city in the province of Picardia. Know that from Calés to the isle of Inglatera there is a short crossing of eight miles. And I departed Calés and went to the County of Flandes to a noble city they call Brujas. And the lord of it has as his insignia a flag of gold with a black lion. [VII]

From there I went along the coast to a city they call Solanda and from there to another they call Maxa and another named Leobet, which are all cities in Alemaña. And from there I traveled on to Dodret, a great and rich city, through which flows a great river they call Rinus that originates in the Alpes Alemaña and passes through Coloña, a great city in Alemaña. And in the Coloña they say the Three Magi who adored Jesus Christ in Beleen lie buried, but when I went to the Empire of Catayo to a city they call Solin, they showed me three much honored monuments and told me they were for the Three Magi who adored Jesus Christ, who were born there. And in this Alemaña there are some very high mountains that they call the Alpes Alemanie, from which three rivers originate. They call one Ruedano, which runs through a city called Leon and converges with another great river that originates in the Alpes Alsaçie. And they flow through Lurdevit and Aviñon, a city where the Pope of Roma resides, and enter the Medio Terreno Sea after a city they call Arle. And these cities are in the Kingdom of Proençia. The other river they call Rinus, and it runs through the city of Coloña of which I told above, and enters the Sea of Alemaña. They call the other river Danubio, and it crosses all of Alemaña and enters through the

toda la Alemaña et entra por medio del rreino de Ungria,[18] et faze y diez yslas muy grandes que adelante contaré. Et fazen en la provinçia de Barbaria un grand lago de agua dulçe que dizen Lacus Danoye, et va por una çibdat que dizen Varispona et entra por la provinçia de la Germania, por una çibdat que dizen Tusna.[19] Et despues entra en la provinçia de Panonia et va por Patania et por Ebruc et por Viana et por Arrisnar.[20] Et despues entra por el rreyno de Ungria et traviésalo todo, et entra en el Mar Mayor çerca de una çibdat que dizen Veçina,[21] et faze apres della una ysla muy grande. Et el Enperador de Alemaña a por señales un pendon amarillo con una aguila prieta coronada atal. [VIII]

Party de Coloña et fuy a una çibdat que dizen Colanda en el rreyno de Frisa. Et pasa por ella un grand rrio que dizen Albia,[22] que nasçe de las sierras de Boemia. Et aqui faze el Mar de Alemaña[23] un grand golfo que dizen el Golfo de Frisa, en el qual golfo son quatro islas. A la una dizen Ruyna, a la otra dizen Erria, a la otra Finonia, a la otra dizen Ganglante.[24] Et el Rey de Frisa a por señales un pendon de oro con tres leones prietos luengos atales. [IX]

Partime del rreyno de Frisa et entré luego en el rreyno de Daçia de Danes, el qual es todo çercado del Mar de Alemaña, et del otro cabo lo çerca el Golfo de Frisa de manera que todo este rreyno non a mas de una entrada sola. En el qual rreyno son doze çibdades grandes. A la mayor dizen Burbena, et en esta coronan los rreyes de Daçia. A la otra dizen Burgalensis, a la otra que dizen Bina, otra que dizen Abenbrut, otra que dizen Tandeus,

---

[18] "Ungría" is a name applied to an area which comprises modern-day Hungary, plus parts of Yugoslavia, Romania, and Bulgaria.

[19] According to Markham (6), this is Lake Donaueschingen, just north of the French border near the Rhine River; Jiménez de la Espada (217) nevertheless considers it imaginary. Varispona is Ratisbon (Regensburg), on the Danube. Markham (6) believes that Tusna is the present-day Donaustauf, also on the Danube, although Jiménez de la Espada (263) would have it be Cham, a little farther north on the Regen River.

[20] Jiménez de la Espada (237) identifies Panonia as an old province bordered on the north by the Danube. Patania is Passau, while Ebruc might be Enns (Austria, also on the Danube), followed by Vienna and Bratislava, on the Austrian-Czech border.

[21] Both Markham (6) and Jiménez de la Espada (123) mention Vidin, in Bulgaria, although it is far from the Black Sea (here called the Mar Mayor, or Great Sea). But Jiménez de la Espada goes on to explain that on the Catalan Atlas and other related maps Vidin was located wrongly near this body of water.

[22] Jiménez de la Espada (124) believes that the narrator made an error in calling "Colanda" a city, and that he actually was referring to "Çelanda" or "Holanda," and that this confusion also can be seen on some ambiguous labeling of places on the Catalan Atlas. The Albia might be the Ohre River.

[23] The Baltic.

[24] See Jiménez de la Espada n.viii for more. Fyn and Lolland are Danish islands. According to Wright (*Geographical Lore*, 327) Frisia Minor was adjacent to Denmark.

middle of the Kingdom of Ungria, and forms ten islands about which I will tell below. And in the province of Barbaria they form a large sweet-water lake that they call Lacus Danoye, and it runs through a city they call Varispona and enters the province of Germania near a city called Tusna. And afterwards it enters the province of Panonia and runs through Patania and Ebruc and Viana and Arrisnar. And later it enters the Kingdom of Ungria and crosses all of it and enters the Great Sea near a city they call Veçina, and it forms a very large island near it. And the Emperor of Alemaña has as his insignia a yellow flag with a crowned black eagle. [VIII]

I departed Coloña and went to a city they call Colanda in the Kingdom of Frisa. A great river they call Albia, which originates in the Sierra de Boemia, runs through it. Here the Sea of Alemaña forms a large gulf that they call the Gulf of Frisa, in which there are four islands. One they call Ruyna, the other Erria, another Finonia and the other they call Ganglante. The King of Frisa has as his insignia a gold flag with three long, black lions, like these. [IX]

I left the Kingdom of Frisa and then entered the Kingdom of Daçia de Danes, which is entirely surrounded by the Sea of Alemaña, and on the other end is the Gulf of Frisa, so that this kingdom has no more than one entrance. In this kingdom there are twelve great cities. The largest they call Burbena, and in it they crown the kings of Daçia. The other they call Burgalensis, and they call the other Bina, another they call Abenbrut, another they call Tandeus, another they call Artuz, another Orens, another Ardonxep,

otra que dizen Artuz, otra Orens, otra Ardonxep, otra Damesmare, otra Corp, otra Dandora, otra Dasia, otra Bonia.[25] Et desta punta Daçia fasta Noruega son sesenta millas de traviesa. Et el rrey esta Daçia a por señales un pendon de oro con tres leones prietos atales. [X]

E parti del rreino de Daçia et tornéme para Alemaña a una çibdat que dizen Lubet, que es en el ducado de Xaxonia, et dende a Rostot et a Bondizmague, que son çibdades de Alemaña la alta, et dende a una çibdat que dizen Grisualdiz, que es rribera de un grand lago de agua que dizen Alechon.[26] Et pasélo et fuy a una çibdat que dizen Corverit, et dende a la çibdat de Escorpe, et dende a otra que dizen Dançicha. Et por esta Dançicha pasa un grand rrio que dizen Turonie, que sale de las Sierras de Boemia et metese en el Mar de Alemaña.[27] Et en el rreyno de Boemia son siete çibdades grandes, conviene a saber: Grisua et Posna et Sirca et Noxia et Furent.[28] A la mayor çibdat dizen Praga, do coronan los rreyes de Boemia. Et esta Praga es toda çercada de una alta sierra que dizen los Montes de Boemia. Et en medio es una grand nava et en medio está la çibdat asentada, çercada enderredor de un rrio grande que dizen Albia. Et nasçe otrosi otro rrio mas grande que dizen Vandalor,[29] çerca de una grand tierra que dizen Avandalia por nonbre del rrio. Et las gentes desta tierra Avandalia conquyrieron antiguamente el Andaluzia de España et pusieronle su nonbre, conviene a saber, Andaluzia. Et el Rey de Boemia a por señales un pendon blanco con un leon bermejo coronado desta manera. [XI]

E parti de Boemia et fuy a una provinçia que dizen Sant Mirio, et otra que dizen Curconia et Culman,[30] que son grandes provinçias que son entre Alemaña et el Mar Mayor. Et como quiera que sean pobladas de cristianos, pero son sismaticos. Et allegué a Litefama et a Catalant,[31] dos grandes

---

[25] The capital of the Danish kingdom was Viborg. The other places mentioned are: Bornholm, Ribe, Åbenrå, Randers, Århus, Odense, Haderslev, Gotorp, and Tønder. Danesmare seems to be a misinterpretation of Danes Mare, and might refer to one of the bodies of water surrounding this area. Jiménez de la Espada (185 and 197) suggests that the narrator mistook the name of the kingdom Dasia (Dacia) for a city within it, and that Bonia is simply a misreading of Dania, the other part of this toponym.

[26] Lübeck, Rostock, Straslund, and Greifswald, although this last town is not on the shores of any lake. The closest lake to it is Kummerower See, just southwest of Greifswald.

[27] Kolobrzeg, Stolpe Bank, and Gdansk are all on the north coast of Poland. The River Wista also passes through the city of Torun, and seems to receive a related name (Jiménez de la Espada 263).

[28] The narrator seems to refer to cities in present-day Germany, Poland, and the Czech Republic as the Kingdom of Bohemia.

[29] The Rivers Labe (Elbe) and Vltava pass through Prague.

[30] Could the narrator be referring to Sandomierz, Kraków, and Łwow in Poland?

[31] Markham (64) suggests that these are Livonia and Courland, regions in the former Soviet Union, and not cities as they are identified here.

another Danesmare, another Corp, another Dandora, another Dasia, another
Bonia. And from this point from Daçia to Noruega there is a crossing of
sixty miles. And the king of this Daçia has as his insignia a flag of gold with
three black lions, like these. [X]

I departed the Kingdom of Daçia and turned toward Alemaña to a city
they call Lubet, which is in the Duchy of Xaxonia, and from there to Rostot and to Bondizmague, cities in Upper Alemaña, and from there to a city
they call Grisualdiz, on the shores of a great lake they call Alechon. I passed
it and went to a city they call Corverit, and from there to the city of
Escorpe, and from there to another that they call Dançicha. And through
this Dançicha runs a great river called Turonie, which comes out of the
Sierra de Boemia and runs to the Sea of Alemaña. In the Kingdom of
Boemia there are seven great cities, to wit, Grisua, and Posna, and Sirca,
and Noxia, and Furent. The largest city they call Praga, where they crown
the kings of Boemia. And this Praga is totally surrounded by a high mountain range that they call the Mountains of Boemia. And in the middle is a
great plateau, and in the middle of this the city is located, surrounded by a
great river that they call the Albia. And yet another, larger river originates
here, which they call Vandalor, near a great land that they call Avandalia
after the river. And the people of this land Avandalia in ancient times
conquered Andaluzia in Spain and gave it its name, that is, Andaluzia. The
King of Boemia has as his insignia a white flag with a vermilion crowned
lion, in this manner. [XI]

I left Boemia and went to a province they call Sant Mirio, and to
another called Curconia and Culman, which are great provinces between
Alemaña and the Great Sea. And although they are populated with Christians, they are schismatics. I arrived in Litefama and Catalant, two great

çibdades que son entre el Mar Mayor et el Mar de Alemaña. Et es tierra muy poblada. Et el rrey dende a por señales un pendon blanco con esta señal prieta.[32] [XII]

Dende parti de Litefama et entré en el rreynado de Polonia, do son çinco çibdades grandes, la mayor dellas Santa Maria, do se coronan los rreyes, otra que dizen Rinalia, otra Uçibant, otra que dizen Nugradia, otra Birona. Et sabet que entré en estas dos çibdades Nugradia et Virona, et corre el grand rrio que nasçe del grand lago que dizen Tanaiz, de que adelante contaré. Et a este rrio dizen Nu[33] et entra en el Mar de Alemaña, a do se acaba el golfo porque el Mar de Alemaña es golfo que entra del Mar Oçidental fasta la provinçia de Palonia et pasa entre Alemaña et las sierras de Noruega et acaba en la provinçia de Palonia. Otrosi por esta Palonia corre otro rrio muy grande que dizen Echan, et nasçe de las nieves que se fazen en las sierras de la trasmontana, et faze un grand lago apres de Virona. Et el rrey desta Polonia a por señales un pendon verde con esta señal bermeja atal.[34] [XIII]

Party del rreynado de Polonia et fuyme al rreyno de Leon (los alemanes dizenle Lunbret), en que son çinco çibdades grandes. La primera dizen Leon, otra China, otra Basadino, otra Trues, otra Çever. Et sabet que este rreino de Leon parte con la provinçia de Romania et con el rreyno de Suana.[35] Et el rrey desta Leon a por señales un pendon verde con una cruz bermeja segund que aqui se sigue.[36] [XIV]

Despues desto tornéme por la otra marisma desta Mar de Alemaña a la parte de la trasmontana que dizen la Tierra de Europa,[37] de que adelante contaré, et entra por una grand provinçia que dizen Suevia. Et fallé una grand çibdat que dizen Roderin, muy rrica et muy poblada como quier que la tierra es muy fria. Et avia en ella nueve çibdades grandes, convien a saber Tarsa, otra Andine, otra Chicobergis, otra Landis, otra Ystat, otra Formeans. Et en este rreynado son dos lagos muy grandes. Al uno dizen Laco Escarse,

---

[32] The emblem depicted in all three manuscripts is a six-pointed star, like the Star of David. Pasch ("Drapeaux du *Libro del conoscimiento*," 18) does not think it has anything to do with a Jewish community there, and says that it is a "mysterious" usage of the star.

[33] Jiménez de la Espada (217) identifies this lake as the supposed origin of the Rivers Volga, Don, and Dvina. The River Nu is the Nogat, that flows into the Baltic.

[34] *S* depicts a hexagram decorated with a scalloped border. *N* and *R* show a cross mounted on an upturned crescent not only for Poland, but also for the next kingdom mentioned, Leon (Lwow).

[35] This seems to be an area where Poland, the Czech Republic, Romania, and the former Soviet republics meet. Markham (9) believes that Leon is the province Galicia in the southeast corner of Poland.

[36] In *S*, the banner bears no cross.

[37] Finland, Sweden, and Norway.

cities that lie between the Great Sea and Sea of Alemaña. It is a densely populated land. Its king has as his insignia a white flag with this black emblem. [XII]

From there I departed Litefama and entered the Kingdom of Polonia, where there are five great cities, the largest of which is Santa Maria, where they crown their kings, another that they call Rinalia, another Uçibant, another that they call Nugradia, another Birona. And know that I entered these two cities Nugradia and Virona, and through them runs a great river that originates in the great lake they call Tanaiz, of which I will tell later. They call this river Nu, and it enters the Great Sea where the gulf ends, because the Sea of Alemaña is a gulf that enters the Western Sea near the province of Palonia, and passes between Alemaña and the sierras of Noruega, and ends in the province of Palonia. In addition, another very large river, which they call Echan, runs through this Palonia, and it origi-nates in the snows that are made in the sierras of the north, and forms a large lake after Virona. The king of this Polonia has as his insignia a green flag with this vermilion emblem, like this. [XIII]

I departed the Kingdom of Polonia and went to the Kingdom of Leon (which the Germans call Lunbret), in which there are five great cities. They call the first Leon, another China, another Basadino, another Trues, and the other Çever. And know that this Kingdom of Leon borders on the prov-ince of Romania and the Kingdom of Suana. And the King of Leon has as his insignia a green flag with a vermilion cross, as is seen here. [XIV]

After this I turned toward the other shore of the Sea of Alemaña, to the northern part they call the Land of Europe, which I will mention later on, and entered a great province they call Suevia. And I found there a great city they call Roderin, which is very rich and populated, although it is a very cold land. And there were in it nine great cities, which are Tarsa, another is Andine, another Chicobergis, another Landis, another Ystat, another For-means. And in this kingdom there are two large lakes. One they call Laco

al otro Laco Estocol.[38] Et el rrey desta Suevia a por señales un pendon amarillo con dos leones bermejos, uno contra otro, desta manera que se sigue. [XV]

Parti de la çibdat de Roderin, entré en una nao, et pasé a una isla que dizen Gotlandia, et fázese en cabo del Golfo de Alemaña. En la qual isla es una grand çibdat que dizen Bisuy, en que son noventa perrochias, et la isla era toda poblada. Apres della es otra isla mas pequeña que dizen Oxilia.[39] Et el rrey destas islas a por señales un pendon con vandas amarillas et cardenas atravesadas desta manera que se sigue.[40] [XVI]

Party de Gotlandia et tornéme para Gotia, una provinçia que es entre Suevia et Noruega, et fallé y tres çibdades grandes. La primera dizen Estocol, a la otra Calman, a la otra Surdepinche.[41] Et apres desta çibdat Estocol faze el Mar de Alemaña un grand golfo rribera del qual son muchas çibdades. Et el mar deste golfo es toda quajada et elada de los muy grandes frios de la trasmontana. Et las gentes desta Gotia conquirieron a España et fueron señores della muy grand tienpo. Et las señales deste rreynado son un pendon amarillo con dos leones bermejos, uno contra otro, tales como se siguen aquy. [XVII]

Party de Gotia et sobi a la altas sierras de Noruega, que es en un rreinado muy fuerte en que son quatro çibdades grandes. A la mayor dizen Regis, do coronan los rreyes. A la otra dizen Nidroxia, a la otra Tronde, a la otra Trimberet. En las montañas desta Noruega crian muchas aves girifaltes, açores, falcones. Otrosi crian muchas animalias fuertes, javalis blancos, osos blancos. Et dizen que un infante fijo del Rey de Noruega conquyrio el condado de Flandes en el tienpo del rrey Artur de Bretaña.[42] Et sabed que de Noruega adelante contra la trasmontana es tierra desabitada en que faze el año todo un dia et una noche, seys meses dura el dia et otros seys meses la noche, et que ay unas gentes que an las cabeças fixas en los pechos,

---

[38] All are apparently cities on the Swedish coast, while the lakes mentioned are probably fjords near Stockholm.

[39] The city in Gotland is Wisby. The other island is probably Osel, which now belongs to Russia.

[40] The bends shown in N and R are diagonal, and Pasch (17) affirms that this corresponds to this flag as drawn on many portolan charts. S displays horizontal stripes.

[41] Gotia seems to refer to the southern area of Sweden, with the cities Stockholm, Kalmar, and Söderköping.

[42] There seems to be no historical basis for this anecdote, which probably originates in the story of the Knight of the Swan (who was not Norwegian): he rescued the daughter of Thierry III of Cleves from her oppressors, then married her. Later they founded a dynasty in Flanders.

Escarse, the other Laco Estocol. And the king of this Suevia has as his insignia a yellow flag with two vermilion lions, one facing the other, in the following manner. [XV]

I left the city of Roderin, embarked a ship, and went on to an island they call Gotlandia, which is at the end of the Gulf of Alemaña. On this island is a great city they call Bisuy, in which there are ninety parishes, and the island was totally populated. After it is another smaller island they call Oxilia. And the king of these islands has for his insignia a flag with yellow and cardinal red crossed bands, in the following manner. [XVI]

I departed Gotlandia and went to Gotia, a province that is between Suevia and Noruega, and there I found three great cities. They call the first Estocol, the other Calman, and the other Surdepinche. And beyond the city of Estocol the Sea of Alemaña forms a great gulf on the shores of which there are many cities. And the water of this gulf is completely immobilized and frozen because of the great cold of the north. And the people of this Gotia conquered Spain and were lords of it for a long time. And the insignia of this kingdom is a yellow flag with two vermilion lions, one facing the other, such as follows here. [XVII]

I departed Gotia and ascended the high sierras of Noruega, which is in a very important kingdom in which there are four great cities. The largest they call Regis, where they crown their kings. They call the other Nidroxia, the other Tronde, and the other Trimberet. In the mountains of this Noruega they raise many gerfalcons, hawks and falcons. They also raise many wild animals, white boars, white bears. And they say that a son of the king of Noruega conquered the County of Flandes in the time of King Arthur of Bretaña. Know that from Noruega onward toward the north the land is uninhabited, and the year is all one day and one night, the day lasting six months and the night the other six months, and there are some people whose heads are attached to their shoulders, who do not have necks

que non an cuellos ninguno, pero yo non las vy.[43] El rrey desta Noruega
a por señales un pendon de oro con un leon prieto segund aquy se sigue.
[XVIII]

Parti de Noruega en una nao de ingleses et tomamos camino contra el
poniente, et venimos a una isla que dizen Insola Cola, et dende venimos a
otra isla que dizen Lister, et dende venimos a otra que dizen Insola Bondola, et dende venimos a otra isla muy grande que dizen Ynsula Salanda, et
fázese a la entrada del Golfo de Frisa que ya conté de suso. Et esta Isla
Salanda era muy poblada et avia en el quatro çibdades muy grandes. A la
una dizen Salandi, a la otra Risent, a la otra Esçendin, a la otra Alenda.[44]
Et el rrey desta isla a por señales un pendon de oro con un leon prieto,
como el de Noruega. [XIX]

Parti de la Isla de Salanda en la dicha nave et andovimos grand camino,
et llegamos a otra isla que dizen Insula Tille, et dende llegamos a la Isla de
Escoçia. Et fallé en ella quatro çibdades grandes. A la una dizen Donfres,
Eneruit, otra Donde, otra Veruit.[45] El rrey desta Escoçia a por señales un
pendon bermejo con tres leones de oro luengos, como aquy se sigue. [XX]

Parti por tierra d'Escoçia et fuyme para el rreino de Inglaterra. Et sabed
que es tierra muy poblada. Et fallé en ella onze çibdades grandes. La mayor
de ellas, do coronan los rreyes, llaman Londres, otra Gunsa, do son los estudios generales, otra dizen Antona, et Bristol et Artamua et Premua et Miraforda. Et en esta isla de Inglaterra ay una grand provinçia que dizen Galas
en que ay una grand çibdat que dizen Dirgales.[46] Et con esta Galas parte
otra tierra que dizen Morgales, que es del señorio de Inglaterra. Et el rrey
destas tierras a por señales un pendon a quarterones: en los dos quarterones
ay flores de oro en canpo azul porque es el rrey de la casa de Françia; en los

---

[43] Men without necks are common in medieval lore, but appeared much earlier in Pliny and
Solinus.

[44] Although the author says that he travelled west, such a route would not have taken him
to the places he mentions. The first island is Öland (Sweden), followed by the Swedish peninsula
Listerlandet, then Bornholm and Sjælland, both Danish islands. Copenhagen, Ringsted, and Stor
Hedding are found on Sjælland. The author apparently mistook the name of the Danish island
Lolland, just south of Sjælland, for that of a city. Jiménez de la Espada (126) notes that the same
error can be seen on the Catalan Atlas, which also contains the same remarks about the animal
life of Norway.

[45] Might Insula Tille be Telemark, a region in the south of Norway, or Thyland, a province
in northwest Denmark? The four Scottish cities referred to are Dumfries, Edinburgh, Dundee,
and Berwick. During the era in which this book was probably written, the King of Scotland was
David Bruce; Robert Bruce had secured Scotland's independence in 1314.

[46] After London, possibly Windsor (although there were no studies to be had there), then
Southampton, Bristol, Dartmouth, Plymouth, and Milford. Jiménez de la Espada (208) suggests
that Dirgales might be "Virgalles" in Wales, although it is not clear to what town he is referring.

at all, but I did not see them. The King of this Noruega has as his insignia a gold flag with a black lion, as follows. [XVIII]

I left Noruega in a ship of Englishmen and we took a course to the west and came to an island they call Insola Cola, from which we arrived at another island they call Lister, from which we came to another they call Insola Bondola, from which we came to another very large island they call Ynsula Salanda, and it is found at the entrance to the Gulf of Frisa which I already mentioned above. And this Isla Salanda was very populated and there were four great cities in it. One they call Salandi, the other Risent, the other Esçendin, the other Alenda. And the king of this island has as his insignia a gold flag with a black lion, like the King of Noruega. [XIX]

I departed the island of Salanda in the boat I mentioned and we traveled for a long time, and arrived at another island that they call Insula Tille, from which we came to the island of Escoçia. And I found there four large cities. They call the first Donfres, [the second] Eneruit, another Donde, another Veruit. The king of this Escoçia has as his insignia a vermilion flag with three long gold lions, as follows here. [XX]

I left Escoçia by land and went to the Kingdom of Inglaterra. And know that it is a very populated land. And I found in it eleven great cities. The largest of them, where they crown their kings, they call Londres, another Gunsa, where there are liberal studies, another Antona, and Bristol and Artamua and Premua and Miraforda. And in this island of Inglaterra there is a great province they call Galas in which there is a great city they call Dirgales. And this Galas borders on another land they call Morgales, which belongs to the lordship of Inglaterra. And the king of these lands has as his insignia a quarterly flag: in two quarters there are gold flowers on a field of blue because the king is of the House of Françia; in the other two quarters

otros dos quartos ay en cada uno tres onças de oro luengas, et el canpo bermejo como estas que siguen.[47] [XXI]

Sali de la isla de Inglaterra en un barco et entré en la isla de Irlanda, que es pequeña traviesa de una milla.[48] Et dizenle antigua mente Ibernia. Et sabed que es isla muy poblada et tierra muy tenplada, et fallé en ella seys çibdades grandes. A la mayor do coronan los rreyes dizen Estanforda, otra Ymeric, et Gataforda, et otra Rois, et Donbelin, Adrosda. Et en esta isla es un grand lago de agua que dizen el Lago Afortunado[49] porque rribera del fueron fechos muchos encantamentos antigua mente. Et el rrey desta insula a por señales tales commo el Rey de Inglaterra.[50] [XXII]

Conteçio que yo estando en Irlanda salio dende una nao para España et fuy con ellos, et andudo aquella nao por alta mar tanto tienpo que llegamos a una isla que dizen Eterus, et dende a otra que dizen Artania, et a otra que dizen Çitilant, et a otra que dizen Ibernia.[51] Et son estas islas a la parte do se pone el sol en el mes de junio, et todas estas islas eran pobladas et abondadas et tierra muy tenplada. Et en esta isla de Ibernia avia arboles que la fruta que llevavan eran aves muy gordas quando los arboles son muy bien labrados et rregados. Et estas aves eran muy sobrosas de comer, quyer cozidas quier asadas.[52] Et en esta isla son los omes de muy grand vida, que algunos dellos biven dozientos años los que y son nasçidos et criados, de manera que non pueden morir demientra que estan en la ysla. Et quando son muy flacos de vegedat sacanlos de la isla et mueren luego. Et en esta isla non ay culebras nin bivoras nin sapos nin moscas nin arañas nin otra cosa

---

[47] The background of the banner in S has been colored, but otherwise left blank. "Onças" (ounces) are heraldic leopards.

[48] According to Hyde (144), this very short crossing from England to Ireland was the result of the narrator's misreading of a map, and not based on fact.

[49] The places mentioned are: Strangford, Limerick, Waterford, Rosslare, Dublin, and Drogheda. Other maps of the era also refer to "el Lago Afortunado" (Markham 12, Jiménez de la Espada 217). It might be the Erne, in present-day Northern Ireland. In his *Topographia Hiberniae*, completed in 1188, Giraldus Cambrensis writes of a large lake near Ulster, the Lough Neagh, whose origin he attributes to a flood meant to punish the crimes of the people of this region (Wright 208).

[50] The outline of the flag is drawn in S, but left blank. Both N and R repeat the English flag.

[51] The first are probably the Faröe Islands, followed by the Orkneys, the Shetland Islands, and Iceland, which is mistakenly called Ibernia. Dublin is mentioned below, but Markham (13) believes that the comment about it is a copyist's intercalation suggested by the erroneous mention of this Irish city.

[52] Jiménez de la Espada (128–29) reports that reference to animal-bearing plants originated in Arabic travel accounts. In the twelfth century Giraldus Cambrensis (see also nn.49 and 53) describes trees in Ireland that bear ducks; later, pseudo-traveler John Mandeville mentions edible birds that grow on trees in England.

there are in each three long gold leopards, and the field is vermilion, like the one that follows. [XXI]

I departed the island of Inglaterra in a boat and entered the island of Irlanda, which is a short crossing of one mile. And they formerly called it Ibernia. Know that the island is very populated and the land is very temperate, and I found in it six large cities. The largest, where they crown their kings, they call Estanforda, another Ymeric, and Gataforda, and the other Rois, and Donbelin, Adrosda. And on this island there is a great lake that they call the Fortunate Lake, because on its shore many spells were cast in ancient times. And the king of this island has as his insignia the same as the King of Inglaterra. [XXII]

It happened that while I was in Irlanda a ship was leaving there for España, and I went with them, and that ship sailed on the high seas for so long that we arrived at an island they call Eterus, and then to another they call Artania, and another they call Citilant, and another they call Ibernia. And these islands are on the western horizon in the month of June, and all these islands were populated and abundant and of very temperate land. And on this island of Ibernia there were trees whose fruit were very fat birds when the trees are well tended and watered. And these birds were delicious to eat, whether boiled or roasted. And on this island the men are very old, since some of them live two hundred years, that is, those who are born and raised there, so that they cannot die as long as they are on the island. And when they are weak with age they take them off the island and then they die. And on this island there are no snakes nor vipers nor toads nor flies nor

veninosa.[53] Et en esta Ibernia es una çibdat arçobispal que dizen Dubilin. Et son gentes muy fermosas, como quier que son muy sinples. Et es tierra do non ay pan, como quiera que an muy grand abondo de carnes et de leche. Et sabet que esta isla es fuera de las siete climas. Et el rrey desta isla a por señales un pendon de oro con un leon prieto, commo el Rey de Noruega. [XXIII]

Despues desto parti de la isla de Ibernia en una nao et andude tanto por el Mar de Poniente fasta que aporté a la cabeça de la fin de la tierra oçidental, Ponte Vedra en la provinçia de Gallizia. Et de Ponte Vedra vine a una villa que es del rreyno de Castilla, que ya conté de suso, que dizen Tarifa, la qual pobló un alarabe muy poderoso que dixeron Tarif. Et sobre esta villa fue desbaratado et vençido Alboaçen, rrey de toda tierra del poniente de allen mar, et vençiólo et desbaratólo el muy noble rrey don Alfonso de Castilla, et rrobóle todos sus rreales et sus thesoros et todas sus mugeres, et matóle sus cavallerias.[54] Et parti de Tarifa et fuy a la çibdat de Aljezira, et dende a la Peña de Gibraltar, que son los logares del rreyno de Castilla, et dende pasé a Malaga, una çibdat muy viçiosa et abondada del rreynado de Granada, en el qual rreynado son tres çibdades grandes. La mayor dellas do coronan los rreyes es Granada, et las otras dos son Malaga et Almaria. Et este rreynado parte con el Mar Medio Terreno et con el rreyno de Castilla. Et en este rreyno es un monte muy alto que llaman las Sierras de Granada, et traviesa todo el rreyno fasta la villa de Lorca, que es del rreyno de Castilla. Et las señales deste rrey son un pendon bermejo con letras de oro aravigas como las traya Mahomad su profeta, et son estas que se siguen.[55] [XXIV]

Parti del rreinado de Granada et fuy al rreyno de Aragon, un rreynado muy viçiosso et abondado. Et fallé en el çinco çibdades grandes: la mayor, do coronan los rreyes, es Çaragoça; otra dizen Valençia et a la otra Tarragona et a la otra Tortosa et a la otra Barçelona. Et corre por este rreino el rrio de Ebro et el flumen Sinca. Este rreynado parte con Navarra et con Castilla et con Françia et con los Montes Pireneos. Et el rrey dende a por señales nueve bastones amarillos et bermejos atales. [XXV]

---

[53] In his *Topographia Hiberniae*, Giraldus Cambrensis writes that no poisonous creatures could survive in Ireland because of some deficiency in the land's soil, and thus dismisses as fiction the story of St. Patrick's ridding the country of snakes (Wright 212).

[54] The narrator is referring to the Battle of Salado, where Alfonso XI of Castile defeated King Abu-l-Hasan of Morocco in 1348. The Moroccan king's wife Fatima was first taken prisoner, then killed by her captors; historical accounts also mention the enormous amount of booty taken by the Christians in this battle.

[55] The "Arabic letters" that follow are simple fantasy.

spiders nor anything else that is poisonous. And on this Ibernia there is an archiepiscopal city they call Dubilin. And they are very beautiful people, although they are very simple. And it is a land where there is no bread, although there is a great abundance of meats and of milk. Know that this island lies outside the Seven Climates. And the king of this island has as his insignia a gold flag with a black lion, like the King of Noruega. [XXIII]

After this I departed the island of Ibernia in a ship and traveled a distance on the Western Sea until I reached port at the head of the end of the western land, Ponte Vedra in the province of Gallizia. And from Ponte Vedra I came to a town which is in the Kingdom of Castilla, of which I told above, that they call Tarifa, which a very powerful Arab, named Tarif, founded. And near this town Alboaçen, King of all the western land beyond the sea, was defeated and conquered, and it was the very noble King Don Alfonso de Castilla who conquered and defeated him, and stole from him all his military camps and his treasures and all his women, and [Alboaçen] was killed by his knights. And I left Tarifa and went to the city of Aljezira, and from there to the Peña de Gibraltar, which are towns in the Kingdom of Castilla, and from there I went to Malaga, a very luxurious and abundant city in the Kingdom of Granada, in which kingdom there are three great cities. The largest of them, where they crown their kings, they call Granada, and the others are Malaga and Almaria. And this kingdom borders on the Medio Terreno Sea and the Kingdom of Castilla. And in this kingdom there is a very high mountain they call they Sierra de Granada, and it crosses the entire kingdom all the way to the town of Lorca, which belongs to the Kingdom of Castilla. And the insignia of this king is a vermilion flag with gold Arabic letters, such as that of Mohammed, his prophet, and this is it that follows. [XXIV]

I departed the Kingdom of Granada and went to the Kingdom of Aragon, a very luxurious and abundant kingdom. And I found in it five large cities: the largest, where they crown their kings, is Çaragoça; the other they call Valençia, and the other Tarragona and the other Tortosa and the other Barçelona. And through this kindom the rivers Ebro and Sinca flow. This kingdom borders on Navarra and Castilla and França and the Pireneos Mountains. And its king has as his insignia nine yellow and vermilion pales in this manner. [XXV]

Party de Barçelona et fuyme por la marisma al condado de Anpuria, et dende a la çibdat de Narbona, que es rribera del Mar Medio Terreno. El señor della a por señales un pendon blanco con una cruz bermeja como la de Tolosa, et en cada quarto una tal señal, porque esta çibdat fue de don Remondo, Conde de Tholosa. Et es esta que se sigue.[56] [XXVI]

Parti de Narbona et fuy a Malagona, et dende a Monpesler,[57] et dende pasé aguas muertas et travesé el rrio de Ruedano, et fuy me para Arle, una noble çibdat et rrica que es en la Proençia. Et apres desta rribera del Ruedano es Aviñon, una rrica çibdat donde mora la corte de Roma et el Papa et los cardenales. Otrosy es Letduena, una çibdat del Rey de França. Despues pasé a Marsella que es cabeça de la Proençia, et fuy me por la marisma a Frenit, et dende a Nista, et pasé por Monago, et dende a Arbenga et a Saona.[58] Et subi en los montes de Genova, do es una rrica çibdat que dizen Genova, rribera del Mar Medio Terreno. El señor della a por señales un pendon blanco con una cruz bermeja. Ençima está escripto "Justiçia" desta manera.[59] [XXVII]

Parti de Genova et entré en Lonbardia do son muchas çibdades rricas, conviene a saber Medio Lanensis, et Clamona, et Boloña, morada de los philosofos, et Padua, et Panonia, et Pavia, et Burga, et Ravena, et Plazençia.[60] Las señales deste rreynado son estas que se siguen, un pendon vermejo atal.[61] [XXVIII]

Parti de Lonbardia et entré por Pisa, una tierra muy viçiossa et tenplada. El señor della a por señales un pendon todo colorado. [XXIX]

Sali de Pisa et entré por Toscana en la qual es una rrica çibdat que dizen Florençia. El señor della a por señales un pendon blanco con una cruz bermeja atal. [XXX]

---

[56] In S, a cross with scalloped edges centered on the flag; in each space formed by the arms of the cross there is a triangular object. Pasch (12) believes that the narrator confused this with the cross on the arms of Toulouse.

In N and R, a straight cross completely divides the flag into four areas; in each division appears the same triangular object.

[57] Between Narbonne and Montpellier there is no town with a name resembling Malagona.

[58] Letduena is Lyon. The others are Marseilles, Fraînet, Nice, Monaco, and the Italian towns Albenga and Savona.

[59] Pasch (14) says that the addition of this word is an innovation not found elsewhere.

[60] In Lombardy are found Milan, Cremona, Bologna, Padua, Parma, Pavia, Bergamo, Ravenna, and Piacenza. Wright (320) remarks that in the Middle Ages this was the best-known region of Italy to those beyond the Alps. The narrator singles out Bologna because of its university, which achieved great fame in the twelfth century for the study of law.

[61] The illustrators of N and R mistakenly have interchanged the arms of Pisa and Piacenza. The correct banner of the latter shows a white square on a red background. The flag of Pisa is plain red. In S, Piacenza's arms are left blank, and Pisa's are illustrated correctly.

I left Barçelona and went along the shore to the county of Anpuria, and from there to the city of Narbona which is on the shore of the Medio Terreno Sea. The lord of this city has as his insignia a white flag with a vermilion cross like that of Tholosa, and in each quarter an emblem like this one, because this city belonged to Don Remondo, Count of Tolosa. And it is this one, as follows. [XXVI]

I departed Narbona and went to Malagona and from there to Monpesler, and from there I crossed stagnant waters and the Ruedano River and went to Arle, a noble and rich city which is in Proençia. And beyond the shores of the Ruedano is Aviñon, a rich city where the Court of Roma and the Pope and the Cardinals live. Letduena is also there, a city belonging to the King of Françia. Afterwards I went on to Marsella, which is the capital of Proençia, and I went along the shore to Frenit, and then to Nista, and I passed through Monago, and from there to Arbenga and Saona. And I climbed the Mountain of Genova, where there is a rich city they call Genova on the shores of the Medio Terreno Sea. The lord of it has as his insignia a white flag with a vermilion cross. On it is written "Justicia" in this manner. [XXVII]

I left Genova and entered Lonbardia, where there are many rich cities, which are Medio Lanensis, and Clamona, and Boloña, home of the philosophers, and Padua, and Panonia, and Pavia, and Burga, and Ravena and Plazençia. The insignia of this kingdom is that which follows, a vermilion flag in this manner. [XXVIII]

I departed Lonbardia and entered Pisa, a very luxurious and temperate land. Its lord has as his insignia an entirely red-colored flag. [XXIX]

I left Pisa and entered Toscana in which there is a rich city they call Florençia. Its lord has as his insignia a white flag with a vermilion cross in this manner. [XXX]

Parti de Toscana et fuy me a la noble çibdat de Roma, que es cabeça del inperio de los rromanos. Et corre por ella un rrio que dizen Tibre, que nasçe de los Alpes de Albernia et va por la Mar de Ancona[62] et por el patrimonio, et entra en el Mar Medio Terreno en el puerto de Roma. Et destos montes de Albernia nasçe otro rrio muy grande que dizen Arno, que va por Toscana et va por Florençia et entra en el Mar Mediterraneo en la çibdat de Pisa. Et apres desta Roma son estas çibdades: Veya, et Santa Sedra, et Ostia, et Taraçona, et Gayeta, et Montedragon.[63] Et sabed que Roma et Pisa et Toscana et tierra del prinçipado son entre'l mar Medio Terreno et el golfo de Veneçia. Et las señales de Roma son un pendon bermejo con una vanda de oro con unas letras que dizen Senatus Populusque Romanus, et esta cruz blanca ante de las letras, desta manera que se sigue.[64] [XXXI]

Parti de Roma et fuy me a Romana et por la tierra del prinçipado, et entré en el rreinado de Napol, una tierra muy viçiosa, et abondada, et tenplada, en la qual son las provinçias de Pulla et de Calabria, en que son muchas çibdades et rricas. Las mayores son Surenti, Salerno, Policastro, Scalea, Rezo, Girazo, Cotrun, Tarento, Entranto, Brandizo, Monapoli, Bar, Barleto, Monfrodoye, Pescara, Schilazo.[65] El Rey de Napol a por señales un pendon cardeno con flores de oro por que'l rrey es de la casa de Françia. Et ençima es una lista bermeja que dizen el rrestello atal.[66] [XXXII]

Party de Napol et pasé a la ysla de Çeçilia, por mar una pequeña traviesa, una tierra muy viçiosa et abondada, en que son ocho çibdades grandes. Es a saber Meçina, Catania, Sirracusana, Girenti, Trapana, Palermo, Cafallu, Pari.[67] Et el rrey desta Çeçilia a por señales un pendon a quarterones, los dos

---

[62] The narrator seems to refer to the Apennine Mountains and the Adriatic Sea, called Ancona because of the city of the same name on its coast.

[63] Cività Vecchia, Santa Severa, Ostia, Terracina, Gaeta, and Mondragone, all on the western coast of Italy, near Rome.

[64] In S, the initials shown are S P Q B.

[65] On the coasts of what the author identifies as the regions of Apulia and Calabria are found the cities of Sorrento, Salerno, Policastro, Scalea, Reggio, Squillace, Cotrone, Taranto, Otranto, Brindisi, Monopoli, Bari, Barletta, Manfredonia, and Pescara. He has, in effect, rounded the boot from Naples to Pescara. Squillace nevertheless is misplaced at the end of this list; in reality it is near the southwestern coast of Italy.

[66] From 1268 to 1442 the Kingdom of Naples was under Angevin rule; in 1282, however, Sicily was lost to the Aragonese.
The arms of Naples are drawn differently in each of the manuscripts. In S, there are three fleurs-de-lis above a band with one scalloped border. N shows the same band with three fleurs-de-lis above and six below. R is similar to N, but there are only four fleurs-de-lis below the decorative band.

[67] In Sicily, he purports to visit Messina, Catania, Siracusa, Agrigento, Trapani, Palermo, Cefalù, and Patti, rounding the island from its northeast extremity. It was as a result of the Sicilian Vespers (1282) that the island came into the hands of the crown of Aragon.

I departed Toscana and went to the noble city of Roma, which is the capital of the Roman Empire. And a river they call Tibre runs through it and begins in the Alpes de Albernia and goes through the Sea of Ancona and the patrimony, and enters the Medio Terreno Sea at the port of Roma. And from these mountains of Albernia comes another very large river they call the Arno, which flows through Toscana and Florençia and enters the Medio Terreno Sea in the city of Pisa. And beyond Roma are these cities: Veya, and Santa Sedra, and Ostia, and Taraçona, and Gayeta, and Montedragon. Know that Roma and Pisa and Toscana and the land of the principality are between the Medio Terreno Sea and the Gulf of Veneçia. At the insignia of Roma is a vermilion flag with a band of gold with letters that say Senatus Populusque Romanus, and a white cross before the letters, in the following manner. [XXXI]

I departed Roma and went to Romana and through the land of the principality, and I entered the Kingdom of Napol, a very luxurious and abundant and temperate land, in which the provinces of Pulla and Calabria are, in which there are many and rich cities. The largest are Surenti, Salerno, Policastro, Scalea, Rezo, Girazo, Cotrun, Tarento, Entranto, Brandizo, Monapoli, Bar, Barleto, Monfrodoye, Pescara, Schilazo. The King of Napol has as his insignia a cardinal red flag with gold flowers because he is of the House of França. And on the upper part is a vermilion stripe which they call the lambel, in this manner. [XXXII]

I departed Napol and passed on to the island of Çeçilia, by sea a short crossing, and it is a very luxurious and abundant land in which there are eight large cities. To wit, Meçina, Catania, Sirracusana, Girenti, Trapana, Palermo, Cafallu, Pari. And the king of this Çeçilia has as his insignia a quarterly flag,

quartos son blancos con dos aguilas prietas, et los otros dos quartos bastones bermejos et amarillos, por que el rrey es de la casa de Aragon. [XXXIII]

Aqui en Çeçilia entré en una galea et tornéme a la marisma de Napol, a Rezo, desi a Girazo,[68] et entré a la çibdat de Entranto, que es en la punta del golfo de Veneçia. Et entré en el golfo et fuy a Brandiza, et dende a Monapoli, et tomé la parte esquierda del golfo contra Napol et fuy a Barleto, desy a Pescara, et a Antona, et a Revena, et dende a la çibdat de Veneçia, que está cabo del golfo dentro en la mar. Et confinan sus terminos con la Lonbardia, et con la Mar de Ancona, et con tierra del patrimonio, et con la parte de llevante con la Esclavonia.[69] El señor desta Veneçia a por señales un pendon blanco con un leon bermejo con alas, commo el evangelista Sant Marcos. [XXXIV]

Despues desto parti de Veneçia en la dicha galea et tomé la marisma contra la Esclavonia, et pasé por una çibdat que dizen Aquylea, et otra que dizen Triesa, et dende fuy a Parenzo, et llegué a una çibdat que dizen Sena que es en la Esclavonia, et otra que dizen Jara.[70] Et el rrey desta Esclavonia a por señales un pendon ameitades, en la meitad bermeja que está çerca la vara está una estrella blanca, et la otra meitad del cabo es amarilla atal. [XXXV]

En el rreynado de la Esclavonia es una sierra muy alta que dizen los Montes de Boxnia, donde naçen quatro rrios muy grandes. Al primero dizen flumen Sar, al otro flumen Raba, al otro flumen Ur, al quarto dizen flumen Rabeza.[71] Et todos estos quatro rrios entran por el rreyno de Ungria et ayuntanse al grand rrio Danubio que nasçe de las Alpes de Alemaña. Et sabet que esta sierra Boxnia parte la Germania, et la Pavonia, et la Ungria, et la sierra está en medio, et son montes muy poblados de gentes, et tierra muy abondada de todas las cosas, pero non son cristianos catholicos. Et el señor destos montes a por señales tales commo el Rey de la Esclavonia.[72] [XXXVI]

---

[68] Between Reggio and Otranto there is no city with a name resembling this, although both Jiménez de la Espada and Markham identify it as Girace.

[69] Sebenica, in former Yugoslavia.

[70] The traveler passes through the Italian towns of Aquileia and Trieste, then continues the journey on the eastern side of the Adriatic. Both Jiménez de la Espada and Markham keep the name Parenzo, but it is not clear what place this might be, unless it refers to Premantura, a town south of Trieste on the same coast. Sena is also difficult to identify, but may be present-day Senj. Jara is evidently Zara or Zadar, further south.

[71] In the mountains of Bosnia originate the Rivers Sava, Raab, and Drava. Both Jiménez de la Espada and Markham identify Rabeza as a tributary of the Raab. Notice, however, that the author believes that Bosnia is simply the name of a mountain.

[72] In S, the arms of Bosnia are shown exactly as the preceding banner of Sebenica. In N and R, however, a circle divided by a cross is added to the plain half of the flag.

two of whose quarters are white with two black eagles, and [in] the other
two quarters vermilion and yellow pales, because the king is of the House
of Aragon. [XXXIII]

Here in Çeçilia I embarked a galley and headed for the shores of Napol,
to Rezo, [and] from there to Girazo, and I entered the city of Entranto,
which is on the tip of the gulf of Veneçia. And I entered the gulf and went
to Brandiza, and from there to Monapoli, and I went along the left side of
the gulf by Napol and went to Barleto, [and] from there to Pescara and to
Antona and to Ravena, and from there to the city of Veneçia, which is at
the end of the gulf in the sea. And it borders with Lonbardia and with the
Sea of Ancona, and with the land of the patrimony, and on the eastern side
with Esclavonia. The lord of this Veneçia has as his insignia a white flag
with a vermilion winged lion, like the Evangelist Saint Mark. [XXXIV]

After this I departed Veneçia in the aforementioned galley and traveled
the shore by Esclavonia, and I passed by a city they call Aquylea and another they call Triesa, and from there I went to Parenzo, and arrived at a
city they call Sena which is in Esclavonia, and another they call Jara. And
the king of this Esclavonia has as his insignia a flag divided in two vertical
stripes: in the vermilion stripe near the staff is a white star, and the other
stripe is yellow, like this. [XXXV]

In the Kingdom of Esclavonia there is a very high sierra they call the
Mountains of Boxnia, where four great rivers originate. The first they call
the River Sar, the other the River Raba, the other River Ur, the fourth
the River Rabeza. And all of these four rivers enter the Kingdom of Ungria
and converge with the great River Danubio that originates in the Alpes de
Alemaña. Note that this Sierra of Boxnia borders on Alemaña and Pavonia
and Ungria, and the sierra is in the center, and these mountains are quite
populated with people, and the land abundant with all things, but they are
not Catholic Christians. And the lord of these mountains has as his insignia
the same as the King of Esclavonia. [XXXVI]

E parti de Boxnia et torné a la marisma a la çibdat de Sara, et dende a
Sinbichon, et a Narent.[73] Et el rrey desta tierra a por señales un pendon a
quarterones, los dos quartos cardenos, et los dos blancos atales.[74] [XXXVII]

Con esta Narent confina una çibdat que dizen Dulçerno et con los
Montes de Açervya, una tierra muy viçiosa et abondada. Con este rreynado
de Açervya confina el rreyno de Bulgaria et el rreyno de Daraze, que son en
la provinçia de la Esclavonia. Et destos montes nasçen dos rrios muy
grandes. Al uno dizen Dranoya, al otro dizen flumen Pirus, los quales entran
por el rreyno de Ungria et se ayuntan al grand rrio Danubio.[75] Et fazen en
Ungria diez islas, a la primera dizen Ungria la Mayor, onde tomó este nonbre el rreyno de Ungria, a la segunda dizen Jaurin, a la terçera Unda, a la
quarta Firmia, a la quinta Signa, a la sesta Maçesno, a la septima Drinago, a
la octava Posga, a la novena Ungria la Menor, a la dezena Servia.[76] Et
todos estos rrios que fazen estas islas entran en la Mar Mayor çerca de una
çibdat que dizen Veçina, de que adelante contaré. Et sabet que en esta
Ungria son muchas çibdades et rricas, es a saber Ungria, Çevana, Casot,
Biver, Castro Ferrun, Jaurin, Servia, Strugonun, Bagamos, Beat, Drinago,
Saladino, Myrria, et otras muchas. Este rreinado de Ungria parte con
Greçia, et con Alemaña, et con la Esclavonia, et con Palonia, et con Bulgaria. Et las señales deste rreynado es un pendon ameitades, la una meitat
con flores de França por que es el rrey de la casa de França, et la otra
meitad vandas bermejas et blancas desta manera. [XXXVIII]

Party del rreino de Ungria et torné a la marisma a una çibdat que dizen
Durazo, et sobi en una nao et fue a la Isla de la Morea. Et son en ella siete
çibdades grandes, es a saber Trareoza, Patris, Coranto, et Neapoli, et Marbaxa,

---

[73] From Zara, the narrator travels south along the Adriatic coast to Gabela. Of the latter,
Jiménez de la Espada (232) remarks that its former name was Narona or Narbona, for its
proximity to the River Neretva.

[74] In R, the artist has drawn diagonal lines through both white quarters. Markham (plate 8,
facing p. 17) indicates that the arms of Narent are different in each of the manuscripts: for S and
R he shows flags with a large center cross (more like a dagger in S) surrounded by four smaller
crosses. In fact, the only difference among the three manuscripts is the addition in R of the
diagonal lines mentioned above. Pasch (19), who apparently had no first-hand experience with
any of the codices, copies all three banners in the manner of Markham.

[75] Near the former Narona was the city of Dulcigno (Jiménez de la Espada 229). Durazzo
(Durrës) is a city on the eastern coast of Albania. The first of the rivers is the Drava, but Jiménez
de la Espada (240) maintains that the Pirus is a fictional body of water.

[76] Jiménez de la Espada (265) refers to these as "penínsulas fluviales."

And I departed Boxnia and went down the shore to the city of Sara, and from there to Sinbichon and to Narent. And the king of this land has as his insignia a quartered flag, two [of its] quarters cardinal red, and two white, like these. [XXXVII]

This Narent borders on a city they call Dulçerno and the Mountains of Açervya, a rich and abundant land. This kingdom of Açervya borders on the Kingdom of Bulgaria and the Kingdom of Daraze, which are in the province of Esclavonia. And in these mountains two very large rivers originate. One they call Dranoya, the other they call the river Pirus, which enter the Kingdom of Ungria and converge with the great River Danubio. And in Ungria they form ten islands: the first they call Ungria Major, which took this name from the Kingdom Ungria, the second they call Jaurin, the third Unda, the fourth Firmia, the fifth Signa, the sixth Maçesno, the seventh Drinago, the eighth Posga, the ninth Ungria Minor, the tenth Servia. And all the rivers that form these islands enter the Great Sea near a city they call Veçina, about which I will tell further on. Know that in this Ungria there are many rich cities, to wit, Ungria, Çevana, Casot, Biver, Castro Ferrun, Jaurin, Servia, Strugonun, Bagamos, Beat, Drinago, Saladino, Myrria, and many others. This Kingdom of Ungria borders on Greçia and Alemaña and Esclavonia and Palonia and Bulgaria. And the insigne of this kingdom is a flag per pale, one pale with the flowers of Françia because the king is of the House of Françia, and the other pale [with] vermilion and white bands in this manner. [XXXVIII]

I departed the Kingdom of Ungria and went along the shore to a city they call Durazo, and I embarked a ship and went to the island of Morea. And there are on it seven large cities, to wit, Trareoza, Patris, Coranto, and

et Colon, et Mutam.[77] El prínçipe desta ysla a por señales estas que se siguen, un pendon blanco con esta señal amarilla perfilada de vermejo.[78] [XXXIX]

Parti de la isla de la Morea et fuy a la isla de Rodas do es una rrica çibdat que dizen Creta.[79] Esta isla es de la Orden de Sant Iohn, e tales son sus señales, commo estas que aqui se siguen, un pendon vermejo con una cruz blanca atal commo esta.[80] [XL]

Salli de la isla de Rodas et fuy a la isla de Candia, et dende a otra isla que dizen Negro Ponte, que ganaron los veneçianos. Et dexé a la mano siniestra la entrada de la Mar Mayor[81] et de Costantinopla, de que adelante contaré, et fuy a una çibdat que dizen Satalia,[82] que era de cristianos griegos. Et esta Satalia a por señales un pendon con ondas blancas et cardenas, et çerca de la vara un signo atal.[83] [XLI]

La çibdat de Satalia et Sinbichon, de que ya conté de suso, et las otras que diré fasta Armenia la Menor,[84] son todas en la provinçia de la Turquya, la qual antigua mente dezian Asia la Menor, do son muchas provinçias departidas et muchos señorios que son graves de contar porque esta Turquya llega fasta el Mar Mayor. Et sabet que es tierra muy rrica de todos bienes abondada. Et las señales de Turquia son estas que se siguen, un pendon a meytades, la meytad amarilla con esta señal vermeja, et la otra meytad blanca con çinco cruzes vermejas atales commo estas.[85] [XLII]

Fuy me por la marisma desta Turquia a una çibdat que dizen Candebor, et dende a otra que dizen Antroçeta, et a Corincho. Et en esta Turquya son

---

[77] Some of the cities on Morea (Peloponnesus) seem to be Troezen, Pátrai, Corinth, Neapolis, and Monemvasia; Colon and Mutam are more difficult to identify.

[78] The emblem in question is a circle that contains arcing spokes, as depicted in N and R. The flag is left blank in S. Markham (plate 8, facing p. 17) mistakes the following coat of arms in N, which belongs to Rhodes, for that of Morea.

[79] Notice that the narrator believes that Crete is a city on Rhodes.

[80] The Knights of St. John (Hospitallers) were a religious military order originally dedicated to caring for the sick. Later they became a purely military order whose purpose was defending pilgrims to the Holy Land. The Knights conquered Rhodes in 1307 and formed an independent feudal state there. The banner mentioned here was their coat of arms. Only its outline can be seen in S.

[81] Candia is Crete, and the body of water the narrator heads toward is the Black Sea.

[82] Satalia (Adalia) was on the southern coast of Asia Minor.

[83] S illustrates a flag completely covered with waves, on which is superimposed a six-point star. Both N and R divide the banner, with the star above and waves below.

[84] Armenia Minor is the ancient Cilicia.

[85] Only the outline of the flag is shown in S; Markham (plate 9, facing p. 19) nevertheless provides an illustration he labels as being from this manuscript. N and R depict vertically divided flags: on the left, a cross (a dagger in R) surrounded by four smaller crosses; on the right, a red square on a yellow field.

Neapoli, and Marbaxa and Colon and Mutam. The prince of this island has as his insignia the one that follows, a white flag with this yellow emblem outlined in vermilion. [XXXIX]

I departed the island of Morea and went to the island of Rodas, where there is a rich city they call Creta. This island is of the Order of Saint John, and this is its insignia, like the one that follows, a vermilion flag with a white cross like this one. [XL]

I left the island of Rodas and went to the island of Candia, and from there to another island they call Negro Ponte, that the Venecians conquered. And I left on my left side the entrance to the Great Sea and to Constantinopla, about which I will tell further on, and I went to a city they call Satalia, which belonged to Greek Christians. And this Satalia has as its insignia a flag with gold and cardinal red bars wavy, and near the staff an emblem like this one. [XLI]

The city of Satalia and Sinbichon, about which I already told above, and the other cities about which I will tell up to Armenia Minor, are all in the province of Turquya, which they formerly called Asia Minor, where there are many scattered provinces and many lordships that are difficult to enumerate, because this Turquya extends to the Great Sea. Note that it is a land rich and abundant in all things. And the insignia of Turquia is the one that follows, a flag per pale, one pale yellow with this vermilion emblem, and the other half white with five vermilion crosses like these. [XLII]

I went along the shore of this Turquia to a city they call Candebor, and from there to another they call Antroçeta and to Corincho. And in this

muchas provinçias departidas: Escapadoçia, Feliçia, Boesçia, Vitilia, Gala, Çililidia, Frigia do es Troya, Panfilia, Isauria.[86] El rrey desta tierra a por señales un pendon prieto con çinco cruzes blancas atales. [XLIII]

Salli de Corincho et fuy a una çibdat que dizen Feradelfia o Feradelfin,[87] la qual confina con los terminos de Troya, la que destruyó el rrey Menalao de Greçia. Et antigua mente esta Troya era cabeça de toda Asia la Menor, que agora dizen Turquia. Et sus señales son un pendon ameytades, la una meitad blanca con una cruz bermeja tal, et la otra meitat amarilla con una quadra bermeja atal.[88]

En esta Turquia ay otra provinçia que dizen Cunio en que ay una rrica çibdat que dizen Cunyo, con muchas tierras.[89] Et el rrey dende a por señales un pendon con ondas blancas et bermejas tales. [XLIV]

Otrosi en esta Turquia es otra provinçia que dizen Savasco. Et antigua mente dezian a esta Turquia Savasco, et tomó este nonbre de una çibdat que dizen Savasco, que antigua mente era cabeça de las otras çibdades. Et a esta çibdat de Savasco dezian antigua mente Samaria.[90] Aun agora es Savasco cabeça del rreynado, et a por señales un pendon blanco con çinco cruzes bermejas atales. [XLV]

En esta Turquia son dos çibdades a la parte de Armenia la Menor, que dizen a la una Chotay, et a la otra Silia.[91] Parti dende et entré en Armenia la Menor, la qual es toda çercada de montes muy altos que dizen los Montes de Armenia, et dentro de los montes es tierra llana en que son trezientas et sesenta villas, et castillos, et logares, et es rribera del Mar Medio Terreno en el logar do acaba. Et sabed que antigua mente dezian a esta Armenia la Isla de Colcos, por que en esta Armenia entra un golfo del mar en que está una isla pequeña, et dizenle Porto Bonel.[92] Et aquy fue el tenplo donde estava el carnero dorado encantado, el qual desencantó Jason el griego. Et dentro

---

[86] Both Jiménez de la Espada and Markham believe that Candebor is present-day Alanya, on Turkey's south coast, followed by Antioch and another city difficult to identify. The provinces referred to are Cappadocia, Cilicia, Boeotia (a geographic error, according to Jiménez de la Espada 184), Bithynia, Galatia, a repeat of Cilicia, Phrygia, Pamphilia, and Isauria.

[87] Philadelphia, in Phrygia (Turkey).

[88] Markham (plate 10, facing p. 20) interchanges this and the following banner (Iconium). The square (*cuadra*) does not seem to be a heraldic device.

[89] Iconium (Konya).

[90] Savasco was the ancient name for Turkey. Jiménez de la Espada (248–49) believes that the narrator erred in calling this city Samaria, confusing it with a place in modern Jordan (now Sebastiyah).

[91] If Chotay refers to Kütahya (as Jiménez de la Espada and Markham would have it), it is out of place in the area described by the author. The other city may be Cilicia.

[92] Jiménez de la Espada and Markham affirm that there is such an island as Port Bonel in the small gulf near the ancient city of Alexandretta, now called Iskenderun (Turkey).

Turquya there are many scattered provinces: Escapadoçia, Feliçia, Boesçia, Vitilia, Gala, Çililidia, Frigia, where Troya is, Pamfilia, Isauria. The king of this land has as his insignia a black flag with five white crosses like these. [XLIII]

I left Corincho and went to a city they call Feradelfia or Feradelfin, which borders on the limits of Troya, which King Menalaus of Greece destroyed. And in ancient times this Troya was the capital of all Asia Minor, which they now call Turquia. And its insignia is a flag per pale, one pale white with a vermilion cross, the other pale yellow with a vermilion square like this.

In this Turquia there is another province they call Cunio in which there is a rich city they call Cunyo, which has many lands. And its king has as his insignia a flag with white and vermilion bars wavy in this manner. [XLIV]

Also in this Turquia there is another province they call Savasco. And in ancient times they called Turquia Savasco, and it took this name from a city they call Savasco, that was formerly the capital of the other cities. And they formerly called this city of Savasco Samaria. Savasco is still the head of the kingdom, and has as his insignia a white flag with five vermilion crosses, in this manner. [XLV]

In this Turquia there are two cities on the side of Armenia Minor, [and] they call one Chotay and the other Silia. I departed there and entered Armenia Minor, which is entirely surrounded by very high mountains that they call the Mountains of Armenia, and within the mountains is a flat land in which there are three hundred sixty towns and castles and villages, and it is on the coast of the Medio Terreno Sea in the place where it ends. Know that they formerly called this Armenia the Isla de Colcos, because into this Armenia there enters a gulf of the sea in which there is a small island, and they call it Port Bonel. And here there was a temple where the enchanted golden ram was found, whose spell was undone by Jason the

en Armenia son quatro çibdades grandes, es a saber Laiso, Curquo, et Tarso, et Siçia, et Danabu.[93] El rrey dende a por señales un pendon blanco con un leon vermejo en canpo blanco atal commo este.[94] [XLVI]

Apres desta Armenia es la isla Chipre, et en esta Chipre son quatro çibdades grandes. La primera dizen Famagosta, a la otra Nycoxia, a la otra Lamiso, a la otra Bafa.[95] Et el Rey de Chipre a por señales un pendon ameytades, la una meytad cardena con flores de oro porque el rrey es de la casa de Françia, et la otra meytad çinco cruzes bermejas atales.[96] [XLVII]

Sale desta Chipre una punta que dizen la punta de Santander et dende fasta Alixandreta, una çibdat de la Suria son treynta et seys millas, et parti de Chipre et fuy Alixandreta et dende a Antiocha, una noble çibdat et rrica, la qual ganaron los françeses quando conquistaron la Suria. A esta Antiocha dezian antigua mente Repeleta. Et dende fuy a Solin et a Tortosa, et dende a Tripul de la Suria, et dende fuy a Solin, la que ganaron don Remondo, Conde de Tolosa, padre de don Alfonso Enperador de España.[97] Et dende fuy a Eburut et dende a la çibdat de Acre, que era de los frailes de San Juan, et dende fuy a Çesaria et a Escalona. Et a esta Escalona dezian antigua mente Palestina. Et fuy al puerto de Jafa donde toman el camino los pelegrinos para Iherusalem.[98] Et sabet que en la Suria son estas çibdades que dichas son, con otras muchas villas et logares et castillos. En la Suria son çinco montes altos. Al primero dizen el Monte de Libano, donde salen dos rrios que dizen al uno Jor, al otro Dan, et ayuntanse amos et dizenles Jordan. Esta tierra por do corre el rrio Jordan dezian antigua mente Tiberia,

---

[93] The first four were cities in southern Turkey, and the last is exclusive to S.

[94] S mistakenly gives the arms of Cyprus (which is the next land described) in this place. Markham (plate 10, facing p. 20) includes only this erroneous banner, ignoring the lion rampant of N and R, and Pasch (21) follows suit.

[95] Famagosta, Nicosia, Limassol, and Paphos. From 1376 to 1464, Famagusta was the dominion of the Genoese.

[96] The outline is drawn but left blank in S. Markham, nevertheless, depicts the flag as in N and R (vertically), then labels it S. As we mentioned in n.94, S erroneously attributed the Cypriote arms to "Armenia la Menor," which Markham shows on the same plate, next to the flag of Cyprus, but as a horizontal banner; the similarity which would have revealed his mistake does not seem to have occurred to him.

[97] The country in question is Syria. Antioch was the site of a patriarchal seat of the early church and of a long struggle during the First Crusade, when it was captured in 1098. After Antioch, the narrator's dubious itinerary takes him south to Seleucia (Samandagi), then north to Tarsus (both in Turkey), before heading south again to Tripoli (now Tarabulus, Lebanon). The Franks established themselves in this area after the First Crusade. The Don Remondo referred to here was the father of Alfonso, Conde de Tolosa, not of Alfonso VII of Castile, as the author would have it.

[98] Continuing south along the Mediterranean coast, the traveler arrives in Beirut, Acre (now Akko), Caesarea, and Ashqelon, which were commercial centers at the times of the Crusades.

Greek. And within Armenia there are four large cities, to wit, Laiso, Curquo, and Tarso, and Siçia, and Danabu. Its king has as his insignia a white flag with a vermilion lion in a field of white, like this one. [XLVI]

After this Armenia is the island Chipre, and on this Chipre there are four large cities. The first they call Famagosta, the other Nycoxia, the other Lamiso, the other Bafa. And the King of Chipre has as his insignia a flag per pales, one pale cardinal red with gold flowers because the king is of the House of França, and the other pale [has] five vermilion crosses like these. [XLVII]

Jutting from this Chipre is a point that they call the Point of Santander, and from there to Alixandreta, a city in Suria, there are thirty-six miles; and I departed Chipre and went to Alixandreta and from there to Antiocha, a noble and rich city, which the French took when they conquered Suria. They formerly called this Antiocha Repeleta. And from there I went to Solin and to Tortosa, and from there to Tripul de la Suria, and from there to Solin, which was conquered by Don Remundo, Count of Tolosa, father of Don Alfonso Emperor of España. And from there I went to Eburut and from there to the city of Acre, which belonged to the friars of Saint John, and from there I went to Çesaria and to Escalona. And they formerly called this Escalona Palestina. And I went to the port of Jafa where the pilgrims set off for Iherusalem. And know that these aforementioned cities are in Suria, with many other towns and villages and castles. In Suria there are five high mountains. They call the first the Mount of Libano, where two rivers originate, which they call Jor and the other Dan, and they both converge and they call them Jordan. This land through which the River Jordan flows was

despues le dixeron Siria. Et corren por medio de la Suria et fazen dos lagos muy grandes, al uno dizen el Mar Muerto et al otro el Mar de Galilea. Et afirman que en estos dos lagos fueron las dos çibdades que dezian Sodoma et Gomorra. Et en estos dos lagos se sume el rrio que non pareçe mas. Al otro monte dizen Monte Ermon, al otro Monte Galat, al otro Monte Abraren, al otro Seyr.[99] Et sabet que en esta Suria es la çibdat de Iherusalem que fue santificada por el santo tenplo que fizo en ella Salamon, el qual fue consagrado por la sangre de Nuestro Señor Jesu Cristo. Et esta tierra de Iherusalem antigua mente fue dicha Cananea porque fue de Can, fijo de Noe, et despues ovo nonbre Judea, de Juda fijo de Jaco. Et sabed que esta provinçia ganaron los françeses quando la conquysta de ultra mar. Las señales desta provinçia son un pendon todo blanco con cruzes bermejas en canpo blanco, desta manera.[100] [XLVIII]

Con la Suria parte la tierra de Jafet, et con esta Jafet parte terminos la çibdat de Damasco, que es çibdat muy rrica et abondada de todos los bienes. Et corre por esta Damasco el flumen Eufrates, et antiguamente le dezian Lairag.[101] Et el rrey dende a por señales un pendon amarillo con una luna blanca desta manera.[102] [XLIX]

Otrosi con la Suria confina Egipto. Antigua mente le dezian Egipto Exia. Et dende vine por la marisma a un puerto que's en la Suria que dizen el Puerto de la Risa, et dende vine al Puerto Descrion, et dende al Puerto de Tenexe que es ya en Egipto. Et tomé camino contra el poniente et vine a Damianta, una noble çibdat, et çerca la toda el flumen Nilus.[103] Et sabet que aquy fue cativo el Rey de Françia et desbaratado quando pasó a la conquista de Ultra Mar.[104] Et rribera de este flumen Nilus está asentada la

---

[99] The area now near the Syrian-Lebanese border. Presently Mount Hermon is called Jabal ash-Shaykh.

[100] N and R correctly depict the flag described here. S, however, shows a banner divided into four parts by a cross; each of the resulting fields also contains a cross. According to Pasch (22), the true coat of arms of Jerusalem is like the one illustrated in S. Nevertheless, he copies the banner provided by Markham (plate 11, facing p. 22) which shows the arms as they appear in N or R, but which he has labeled S; Pasch, therefore erroneously believes that the artist of S has drawn a fanciful flag, although it is only correct in S.

[101] Damascus was a well-irrigated market and holy city which reached its greatest moment in the thirteenth century. Lairag, according to Jiménez de la Espada (217), was called Al-Hirac (Iraq).

[102] All three manuscripts show the same shape flag, triangular with rounded edges. Markham provides a rectangular banner with a scalloped edge, which is the coat of arms of Luchon as it appears in S below.

[103] The traveler is in the area of El Arish, from which he continues to Damietta.

[104] Louis IX held Damietta in 1248–49, and was taken prisoner near there in April of 1250 (Markham 22, Wright 300, Jiménez de la Espada 132).

formerly called Tiberia, and afterward they called it Siria. And they run through the middle of Suria and form two great lakes; they call one the Dead Sea and the other the Sea of Galilea. And they confirm that in these two lakes were the two cities they called Sodoma and Gomorra. And in these two lakes the river submerges and disappears. The other mountain they call Mount Ermon, the other Mount Galat, the other Mount Abraren, the other Seyr. And know that in this Suria is the city of Iherusalem that was sanctified by the sacred temple that Solomon built in it, [the temple] sanctified by the blood of Our Lord Jesus Christ. And this land of Iherusalem was in ancient times called Cananea because it belonged to Cam, son of Noah, and afterward it was named Judea, for Judah, son of Jacob. And know that the French took this province during the Great Overseas Expedition. The insignia of this province is an entirely white flag with vermilion crosses in a field of white, in this manner. [XLVIII]

Suria borders on the land of Jafet, and Jafet borders on the city of Damasco, which is a city rich and abundant in all things. And through this Damasco the River Eufrates flows, and they formerly called it Lairag. And its king has as his insignia a yellow flag with a white moon in this manner. [XLIX]

Suria also borders Egipto. In ancient times they called Egipto Exia. And from there I came along the coast to a port that is in Suria, that they call the Port of La Risa, and from there I came to Port Descrion, and from there to Port Tenexe, which is in Egipto. And I set off toward the west and came to Damianta, a noble city, and the River Nilus completely surrounds it. And note that the King of França was taken captive and defeated when he went on the Great Overseas Expedition. And on the shores of this River

grand çibdat de Alcaira, do coronan los rreyes de Egipto, et aquy fue coronado Melicnasçar, el señor de los turcos magnos, que llaman el Soldan de Egipto. Et en esta Alcaara sobre dicha son quatro pueblos. Al primero dizen Alcaara, al otro Babilonia por que la poblaron los que escaparon de la destruyçion de Babilonia, el otro dizen Roda, el quarto dizen Lajuza.[105] Et las señales deste rreinado son un pendon blanco et en medio una luna de azul atal. [L]

Party de Alcaira et fuyme por la marisma a la çibdat de Alixandria, que es noble çibdat et rrica. Et desta Alixandria fasta la isla de Roxeto[106] son diez leguas, todo poblado de aldeas. El rrey della a por señales un pendon amarillo et en medio una rrueda prieta, et en la rrueda un leon pardo atal. [LI]

Parti de Alixandria et vineme por la marisma ayuso al puerto de Ribas Alvas, et dende a Partalbert, et fuy a una çibdat que dizen Luchon.[107] Et el rrey della a por señales una señal amarilla con una luna blanca atal. [LII]

Parti de Luchon et fuy al Puerto de Tarabut, et dende vine a Mon de Barcas, et a Bona Andrea, que es en medio de la Berberia, et dende a Tolometa, que es rribera del mar.[108] El rrey dende a por señales unos tovajones amarillos en çima de una lança fechos en esta manera.[109] [LIII]

De Tolometa fuy a Brenichon et a Zunara. Et en esta Zunara faze la mar un grand golfo que llaman el Golfo de Sçin. Et con los terminos desta Zunara confinan los Montes Claros que los antiguos dizen Carena, de que adelante diremos quando fablaremos de la tierra firme. Et party del Golfo de Sçin et fuy a Puerto Magro et dende fuy a Tripul de la Berberia. Et dizenle Tripul por que confina con los montes de Tripolitana. Et esta Tripul es una rrica çibdat.[110] El rrey della a por señales un pendon blanco con una palma verde et dos llaves bermejas atales. [LIV]

Parti de Tripul a Rahasa et dende a Capiz, et a Faquiz, et desi a Africa, una rrica çibdat. Et sabet que a treinta et seis millas desta Africa es la grand

---

[105] Malek Nasser was crowned in Cairo after he defeated the Mongols in Damascus in 1303. He died in 1341, a fact not mentioned here, which might indicate that it was a relatively recent event. The towns (or sections of Cairo) are: Cairo, Babilonia of Egypt, Roddah, and El Giza.

[106] Rachid, formerly Rosetta.

[107] He continues along the coast of North Africa.

[108] This is the north coast of Libya, heading west toward the Barbary Coast.

[109] *Tovajones* do not seem to be a usual heraldic device. In the drawing that follows they resemble long, fringed sashes.

[110] The traveler now finds himself in the area of Benghazi and the Gulf of Sirte (Libya). The Montes Claros are the Atlas Mountains, in present-day Morocco and Algeria. Puerto Magro might refer to Leptis Magna, an ancient town just east of Tripoli, where the narrator is headed next.

Nilus is seated the great city of Alcaira, where they crown the kings of Egipto, and here Malek Nasser was crowned, who was the lord of the great Turks, and whom they call the Sultan of Egipto. And in this aforementioned Alcaara there are four towns. They call the first Alcaara, the other Babilonia because those who escaped the destruction of Babilonia founded it, the other Roda, [and] they call the fourth Lajuza. And the insignia of this kingdom is a white flag with a blue moon in the center, like this. [L]

I departed Alcaira and went along the coast to the city of Alixandria, which is a noble and rich city. And between this Alixandria and the island Roxeto there are ten leagues, all populated with villages. Its king has as his insignia a yellow flag with a black wheel in the center, and in the wheel a brown lion, like this. [LI]

I departed Alixandria and came southward along the coast to the Port of Ribas Alvas, and from there to Partalbert, and I went to a city they call Luchon. And its king has as his insignia a yellow flag with a white moon, in this way. [LII]

I departed Luchon and went to the Port of Tarabut, and from there I came to Mon de Barcas, and to Bon Andrea, which is in the middle of Berberia, and from there to Tolometa, which is on the seacoast. Its king has as his insignia yellow sashes atop a lance, done in this manner. [LIII]

From Tolometa I went to Brenichon and to Zunara. And in this Zunara the sea forms a great gulf that they call the Gulf of Sçin. And Zunara borders on the White Mountains that the ancients called Carena, of which we will speak further on when we speak of *terra firma*. And I departed the Gulf of Sçin and went to Port Magro and from there to Tripul de Berberia. And they call it Tripul because it borders the Tripolitana Mountains. And this Tripul is a rich city. Its king has as his insignia a white flag with a green palm tree and two vermilion keys, like these. [LIV]

I departed Tripul for Rahasa, and from there to Capiz, and to Faquiz, and from there to Africa, a rich city. And know that thirty-six miles from this Africa is the great tower they call Ligen, and from this tower Ligen to

torre que dizen Ligen, et desta torre Ligen fasta Alcarahuan do se tornó
moro Mahomat son quarenta millas. Et sabet que en esta Alcarahuan fue
desbaratado Alboaçen, rrey de toda Africa fasta el poniente, et fueron rro-
bados todos sus rreales.[111] Et el Rey de Africa a por señales un pendon
blanco con una luna cardena atal. [LV]

Dende vine me para Çuçia[112] et dende para Tunez, que es una grand
çibdat, et rrica, et muy abondada, et es cabeça de toda la Berberia. El rrey
dende a por señales un pendon blanco con una luna prieta tal. [LVI]

Apres desta Tunez es la Isla de Çerdeña, que es una grand tierra en que
son dos montes muy altos. Al uno dizen Mons Barvaria, et al otro dizen
Mons Arbolea.[113] El Rey de Çerdeña a por señales bastones del Rey de
Aragon, commo éstos. [LVII]

Apres de Çerdeña es otra isla que dizen Corçega. Las señales dende son
un pendon blanco con una cruz bermeja, por que la ganaron los ginoveses
a los catalanes.[114] Et por eso an oy dia guerra con ellos. [LVIII]

Dende torné a Bona donde fue obispo Sant Agostin.[115] Es una rrica
çibdat. El rrey della a por señales un pendon blanco con una luna prieta
atal. [LIX]

Parti de Bona et fuy a la çibdat de Costantina,[116] la qual es toda çercada de un rrio enderredor. El Rey de Costantina a por señales un pendon
ameitades blanco et amarillo atal. [LX]

Sali de Costantina et vine a una çibdat que dizen Astora, et dende Alcom, et Gigar, et llegué a Bugia. Et pasa por ella un rrio que dizen Guadal-
quiujr,[117] et es çibdat muy fuerte et antigua. Et el rrey desta Bugia a por
señales un pendon bermejo con una ballesta amarilla atal. [LXI]

Parti de Bugia et vine a Titeliz, et dende a Arguer, et desi a Brischan,

---

[111] Jiménez de la Espada (132) remarks on the historical error that places Mohammed in this
area, which he did not visit. After Tripoli the narrator continues to the coast of Tunisia. Ligem,
according to Jiménez de la Espada (261) was a fortress. Abu-l-Hasan was defeated by Ahmed, an
Almohad, in Qairouan in 1348. This is one of the latest events mentioned in this book.

[112] Sousse, on the Tunisian coast south of Tunis.

[113] It is unclear to which mountains the narrator refers.

[114] The author is referring to the 1347 Genoese takeover of Corsica, one of the latest
historical occurrences mentioned in the text.

[115] After Sardinia and Corsica, the traveler returns to the north coast of Africa, to what is
now Annaba (Algeria); it was called Hippo in ancient times.

[116] Markham (25) remarks that in 311 A.D. Constantine restored this town after a civil war
with Maxentius.

[117] These are towns between Constantine and Bejaïa, all in the north of modern Algeria.

Alcarahuan, where Mohammed became a Moor, there are forty miles. And know that in the Alcarahuan Abu-l-Hasan was defeated, [who was] king of all Africa toward the west, and all his military camps were taken. And the King of Africa has as his insignia a white flag with a cardinal red moon, like this. [LV]

From there I came to Çuçia and from there to Tunez, which is a great city, and rich and very abundant, and it is the capital of all Berberia. Its king has as his insignia a white flag with a black moon, like this. [LVI]

Beyond this Tunez is the island of Çerdeña, which is a great land that has two high mountains. They call one Mons Bavaria, and they call the other Mons Arbolea. The King of Çerdeña has as his insignia the pales of the King of Aragon, like these. [LVII]

After Çerdeña there is another island they call Corçega. Its insignia is a white flag with a vermilion cross, because the Genoese took it from the Catalans. And for that reason there is war between them today. [LVIII]

From there I went to Bona where Saint Augustine was bishop. It is a rich city. Its king has as his insignia a white flag with a black moon, like this. [LIX]

I departed Bona and went to the city of Costantina, which is totally surrounded by a river. The King of Costantina has as his insignia a flag per pales white and yellow, like this. [LX]

I left Costantina and came to a city they call Astora, and from there Alcom and Gigar, and I arrived at Bugia. And through it runs a river they call Guadalquivyr, and it is a strong and ancient city. And the king of this Bugia has as his insignia a vermilion flag with a yellow crossbow, like this. [LXI]

I departed Bugia and came to Titeliz and from there to Arguer, and

una çibdat rribera del mar.[118] El rrey della a por señales un pendon blanco con un signo tal commo aquy está.[119] [LXII]

Sally desta Brischan et pasé a la isla de Mayorca en la qual es una noble çibdat, et rrica, et abondada. El rrey della a por señales bastones verdes prietos.[120] [LXIII]

De Mayorca tornéme a la rribera et fuy a Tensse et Algezer, et desi a Maganga, et a Oran, et a Sersel, que son del rreynado de Tremeçen, el qual es entre el Mar Medio Terreno et los Montes de Carena, que dizen los Montes Claros. Et sabet que sobresta Tremeçen mataron a Beacob, rrey del poniente.[121] El Rey de Tremeçen ha por señales un pendon blanco con una luna azul. [LXIV]

Parti de Tremeçen et torné a Une (et a esta Une dezian Numedia), dende al rrio de Miluya, desi a Alcudia et a Moçena, et dende a Bediz, et llegué a la fuerte çibdat de Çepta. Et sabet que Çepta es en derecho de Algezira et de Gibraltar, logares del rreino de España. Et pasa entre esta Çepta et Gibraltar el golfo del mar que llaman el Mediterraneo. Et porque va el mar en aquel lugar mucho estrecho, llaman los Estrechos de Marruecos et el Angostura del Lazocaque.[122] El rrey desta çibdat a por señales un pendon bermejo con dos llaves blancas atales. [LXV]

Salli de Çepta et fuy ver la noble çibdat de Fez do moran sienpre los Reyes de Benamarin. Et corre por ella un rrio que llaman Fexe, et nasçe de los Montes Claros, et entra en la Mar del Poniente apres de una çibdat que dizen Çale.[123] Et en esta Fez coronan los rreyes. Aquy fazen su morada. El rrey dende a por señales un pendon todo blanco. [LXVI]

---

[118] The first two are Dellys and Alger, but it is not clear what coastal town Brischan might be. South of Constantine there is a city named Biskra, but it is not on the shore, as the author would have it.

[119] The emblem shown is a six-point star. In S, the points are ornamented with curls; in R, they are not, and a heart pierced by an arrow appears at its center. Because of a *lacuna* in N, the flag does not appear.

[120] In 1375 Pedro IV of Aragon annexed Mallorca, thus changing the colors of the flag from green and black (sinople and sable) pales to red and yellow (gules and or). This might suggest that the book was written before that date. Although the flag is only an outline in S, Markham (plate 13, facing p. 25) nevertheless illustrates it as described, then labels it S.

[121] The narrator returns to Algeria after visiting Mallorca, arriving in Mostaganem, Oran, and Tlemcen. According to Markham (25), Abu Yakub Yusuf Almansor, a Benimerin king, was assassinated by a slave here in 1307 after a conflict with Abu Said, King of Tlemcen. Pasch (23) reports that the kingdom of Tlemcen was founded in 1285 and lasted until 1554.

[122] The traveler continues west on the north coast of Africa, stopping in Melilla and Ceuta. Jiménez de la Espada (178) identifies the last body of water as the "Mar de Zakak," the present-day Straits of Gibraltar.

[123] From Ceuta he travels south to Fez, then west to Salé, on the Atlantic coast of Morocco just north of Casablanca.

from there to Brischan, a city on the seacoast. Its king has as his insignia a white flag with an emblem like the one that is here. [LXII]

I left this Brischan and went on to the island of Mayorca, in which there is a noble and rich and abundant city. Its king has as his insignia green and black pales. [LXIII]

From Mayorca I traveled along the coast and went to Tunez and Algezir, and from there to Maganga, and to Oran, and to Sersel, which are in the Kingdom of Tremeçen, which is between the Medio Terreno Sea and the White Mountains. And note that near Tremeçen they killed Abu Yakub, king of the west. The King of Tremeçen has as his insignia a white flag with a blue moon. [LXIV]

I departed Tremeçen and went to Une (they used to call this Une Numedia), and from there to the river of Miluya, from there to Alcudia and to Moçena and from there to Bediz, and I arrived at the fortified city of Çepta. And note that Çepta faces Algezira and Gibraltar, towns in the kingdom of España. And between this Çepta and Gibraltar passes a gulf of the sea that they call the Mediterraneo. And because the sea enters that narrow place, they are called the Straits of Marruecos and the Strait of Lazocaque. The king of this city has as his insignia a vermilion flag with two white keys, like these. [LXV]

I left Çepta and went to see the noble city of Fez, where the Kings of Benemerin always reside. And through it runs a river they call Fexe, and it originates in the White Mountains and enters the Western Sea beyond a city they call Çale. And in this Fez they crown their kings. They make their home here. Its king has an entirely white flag as his insignia. [LXVI]

Parti de Fez, a la qual antigua mente dezian Cotamanfez, et fuy a
Miquynez et a Ribate, et torné a Tanjar rribera del mar et dende a Arzila,
et fuyme por la marisma a la Raxy, et dende a Çale, una çibdat rribera del
Mar Oçidental. Et en esta çibdat sotierran los rreyes. Et dende fuy a Nife,
et a Azamor, et a Çafi. Et en esta Çafi entra en la mar un rrio que dizen
Gux et nasçe de los Montes Claros.[124] Et sabet que en esta provinçia es
la muy noble çibdat de Marruecos que solian llamar Cartago la Grande, la
qual conquirio un consul de Roma que dixeron Çipion el Africano, en el
tienpo del señorio de los rromanos. Despues la señorearon los godos que
fueron señores de España.[125] Et el Rey de Marruecos a por señales un
pendon bermejo con un axedrez prieto et blanco atal. [LXVII]

Despues desto parti de Marruecos et fuy a Admet, una çibdat muy
antigua et muy viçiosa, en la qual son soterrados Benabit Rey de Sevilla et
su muger la Romaiqua. Et dende fuy a Çafi et a Modogor, puertos del Mar
Oçidental. Et subi en las sierras de Çuçia la alta, que es una tierra muy
viçiosa et abondada de todos los bienes. Et sabet que son unos montes muy
altos et tierra muy peligrosa, que non an mas de dos sobidas peligrosas muy
mucho. En estos montes escapó el rrey Myramamolin quando lo desbara-
taron los marines, et oy dia esta Çuçia es del linaje del Miramamolyn.[126]
El rrey dende a por señales un pendon blanco con un leon prieto. Et sabet
que en esta sierra Çucia comiençan los Montes Claros que los cristianos
dizen Acalanes et los antiguos dizen Carena, et son en luengo dos mill et
seisçientas et setenta et çinco millas, que son ochoçientas et noventa et una
leguas et dos terçios de legua. [LXVIII]

Parti de la Çuçia et entré por la Gazula, una provinçia muy viçiosa et
muy grande çercada de sierras muy altas, et abondada de aguas et muy frias.
Et sabet que es a la parte do se pone el sol en el mes de dezienbre, et por
eso la Gazula es fria en el estio et caliente en el ynvierno. Et los pobladores

---

[124] Meknes is east of Salé and Rabat, on the coast south of it. The narrator turns north again
to Tanger, then south to Asilah and down the Moroccan coast to Safi.

[125] The narrator confuses Morocco with Tunis. The Goths mentioned here are the Vandals,
who crossed the Straits of Gibraltar in A.D. 429 and conquered Mauritania.

[126] Benabit or Al-Mutamed-ala-Illah, King of Seville from 1069 to 1091, was dethroned by
the Almoravids and exiled to the castle of Aghmat, where he died and was buried in 1095. His
favorite wife was named Romeykiyyah, whose capriciousness was immortalized in Exemplum
XLI of Don Juan Manuel's *Conde Lucanor*: Because Romeykiyyah yearned to see snow, her
husband had almond trees planted throughout Cordoba so that their white blossoms would
mollify her desire.

Leaving Aghmat, the narrator passes through the port cities of Safi and Essaouira (formerly
Mogodor), then climbs the western part of the Atlas Mountains.

At the end of the thirteenth century, the Miramamolin Almortada lost a battle against the
Beni Merini in Meknes, then fled to the Atlas Mountains. See Jiménez de la Espada (139–41).

I departed Fez, which they formerly called Cotamanfez, and went to Miquynez and to Ribate, and on to Tanjar on the seacoast, and from there to Arzila, and I went along the coast to Raxy, and from there to Çale, a city on the coast of the Western Sea. And in this city they bury their kings. And from there I went to Nife and to Azamor and to Çafi. And in this Çafi a river called Gux enters the sea, and originates in the White Mountains. And know that in this province is the very noble city of Marruecos that they used to call Cartago la Grande, which a Consul of Roma that they called Scipio Africanus conquered, in the time of the rule of the Romans. Afterwards the Goths, who were lords of España, governed it. And the King of Marruecos has as his insignia a vermilion flag with white and black checky, like this. [LXVII]

After this I departed Marruecos and went to Admet, a very ancient and rich city in which Benabit the King of Sevilla and his wife Romaiqua are buried. And from there I went to Çafi and Mogodor, ports on the Western Sea. And I climbed the high sierras of the White Mountains, which is a very rich and abundant land in all things. And know that the mountains are very high and the land is very dangerous, as there are no more than two very dangerous paths up them. In these mountains the King Miramamolin escaped when the Benimerins defeated him, and today this Çuçia is of the Miramamolin lineage. Its king has as his insignia a white flag with a black lion. And know that in this sierra the White Mountains begin, which the Christians call Acalanes and the ancients call Carena, which are 2675 miles long, which are 891 leagues and two-thirds of a league. [LXVIII]

I departed Çuçia and entered Gazula, a very rich and large province surrounded by very high sierras, and abundant in very cold waters. And know that it is on the side where the sun sets in the month of December, and for this reason Gazula is cold in the summer and hot in the winter. And its

della nunca quysieron rrey pero que han un juez, et son gentes muy esentas. Et party de la Gazula et torné a la marisma a un puerto que dizen Zamatana, et dende fuy al cabo de Na en el Mar Oçidental.[127] Et es tierra yerma pero que ay gentes malas crueles que biven en los canpos. Et fuy por la rribera adelante sienpre en un panfilo[128] fasta que llegué al cabo de Sant Bin. Et dende fallé toda la marisma desabitada que non ay çibdat, nin villa, nin logar. Et andove por la marisma muy grand camino et atravesé todas las playas arenosas que non son abitadas de omes, et llegué a la tierra de los negros a un cabo que dizen de Buyder, que es del Rey de Guynea, çerca de la mar. Et ally fallé moros et judios. Et sabet que desde'l cabo de Buyder fasta el Rio del Oro son ochoçientas et sesenta millas, toda tierra desabitada. Et deste logar se tornó el panfilo, et yo finqué ally un tienpo et fuy ver las Islas Perdidas que llama Tolomeo las Islas de la Caridat. Et sabed que desde el cabo de Buider fasta primera isla son çiento et diez millas.[129]

Sobi en un leño con unos moros et llegamos a la primera isla, que dizen Gresa, et apres della es la isla de Lançarote, et dizen le asi porque las gentes desta isla mataron a un ginoves que dezian Lançarote. Dende fuy a otra isla que dizen Vezimarin et a otra que dizen Rachan, et dende a otra que dizen Alegrança, et otra que dizen Vegimar, et otra que dizen Forte Ventura, et otra que dizen Canaria. Et fuy a otra que dizen Tenerefiz, et a otra que dizen la Isla del Infierno, et fuy a otra que dizen Gomera, et a otra que dizen

---

[127] Djezula is to the southwest of the Atlas Mountains. Traveling on the coast in a northerly direction, one reaches the port of Samota, then Cape Non.

[128] This was a kind of boat equipped with oars used in the Mediterranean from the thirteenth to fifteenth centuries (Jiménez de la Espada 141). Hyde (145) believes that it was possible to cruise down the African coast in such a boat, but not sail over to the Canary Islands in a Moorish ship, as the narrator soon claims.

[129] Traveling south from Morocco along the western African coast, the narrator reaches Cape Boujdour. The kingdom of Guinea (Guinoa), according to Jiménez de la Espada (209), was "una gran región del Africa indefinida y cada vez más extensa, a contar de la altura del cabo Bojador hacia el S. y alcanzando hasta el Niger o Djoliba; muy otra de la que los portugueses denominaron después de aquella manera, y la misma que los españoles conocíamos, frecuentábamos, y quizá poseíamos a principios del siglo XV" (". . . a great region of and undefined and ever more extended Africa, from the point of Cape Boujdour toward the south and extending to the Niger or Djoliba; very different from what the Portuguese called by that name, and the same that the Spanish knew, and frequented and maybe even possessed at the beginning of the fifteenth century").

The River of Gold was the "El Dorado" of the Middle Ages, an illusory place that incited men to explore Africa. See Taylor's article for information on the expeditionary frenzy caused by the belief that gold could be found easily along the shores of this imaginary waterway.

Arab geographers had named the Canaries the Lost Islands, also called in Spanish "las Islas de la Caridat" (Al-Kalidat), which means Fortunate Islands, the name that the Romans had given them previously.

The Canaries were re-discovered in 1312 by the Genoese explorer Lancelloto Malocello, for whom the island of Lanzarote was named.

inhabitants never wanted a king but they have a judge, and they are very free people. And I departed Gazula and followed the coast to a port they call Zamatana, and from there I went to Cape Na in the Western Sea. And it is barren land but there are some cruel and bad people that live in the countryside. And I went onward along the shore, always in a *panfilo,* until I arrived at the Cape of Sant Bin. And from there I found the whole coast uninhabited, for there is no city nor town nor village. And I traveled along the coast a very long way and crossed all the sandy beaches that are not inhabited by men, and I arrived at a land of black people, at a Cape they call Buyder, which belongs to the King of Guynea, near the sea. And there I found Moors and Jews. And know that from Cape Buyder to the River of Gold there are 860 miles, all uninhabited land. And from this place the *panfilo* turned, and I stayed there a time and went to see the Lost Islands that Ptolemy calls the Fortunate Islands. And know that from Cape Buyder to the first island there are 110 miles.

I embarked in a sailing vessel with some Moors and we arrived at the first island, which they call Gresa, and beyond it is the island of Lançarote, and they call it that because the people of this island killed a Genoese man named Lançarote. From there I went to another island they call Vezimarin, and another they call Rachan, and from there to another that they call Alegrança, and another they call Vegimar, and another they call Forte Ventura, and another they call Canaria. And I went to another that they call Tenerefiz, and another they call Isla de Infierno, and another they call Gomera,

la Isla del Ferro, et a otra que dizen Aragavia, et a otra que dizen Salvaje, et
a otra que dizen la Isla Desierta, et a otra que dizen Lecmane, et a otra el
Puerto Santo, et a otra la Isla del Lobo, et a otra la Isla de las Cabras, et a
otra la Isla del Brasil, et a otra la Colunbaria, et a otra la Isla de la Ventura,
et a otra la Isla de Sant Jorge, et a otra la Ysla de los Conejos, et a otra la
Isla de los Cuervos Marines.[130] Et en tal manera que son veynte et çinco
yslas. Et de todas estas yslas non eran pobladas de gentes mas de las tres que
son Canaria et Lançarote et Forte Ventura. Et las gentes que ende moran
son atales commo estas que se siguen.

Tornéme al cabo de Buyder donde sally, et fuyme por la Zaara con unos
moros que llevavan oro al Rey de Guinoa en camellos. Et fallamos unos
montes muy grandes et muy altos en medio de la Zahara, et dizenles Zichialhamera. Et despues andovimos muy grand camino por la Zaara fasta que
llegamos a otro monte que dizen Isfurent, et deste Isfurent me parti de los
dichos moros et fallé otros que venian al Algarbe. Et vine me con ellos por
la Zahara fasta que llegué a Mascarota, que es una villa del Rey de Benamarin que está al pie de la sierra de la Çuçia. Et alli moré un tienpo, et
despues fuy a Sulgumença, una rrica çibdat que es en la Zaara, et çercala un
rrio que viene de los Montes Claros.[131] Et el rrey della a por señales un
pendon blanco con una rraiz de palma verde desta manera. [LXIX]

E parti de Sulgumença et fuy al rrio de Dara que dura seys jornadas,
todo poblado allende et aquende. Et es tierra muy poblada et muy abondada
de todos los bienes, maguer está en la Zaara. Et parti del rrio de Dara con
unos moros que yvan a la Guynoa et fuy con ellos por la Zahara fasta que
llegamos a Tocoron, que es una çibdat que está en unos montes. Et es tierra

---

[130] The narrator groups together all these Atlantic islands. He first travels east to west
through the Canary Islands: Graciosa, Lanzarote, one he calls Vezimarin (Vesci marini on the
Dulcert map, now Isla de Lobos), Rachan (El Roque), Alegranza, (followed by a repeat of the
Isla de Lobos), Fuerteventura, Gran Canaria, Tenerife and Infierno (which is also Tenerife),
Gomera, Hierro, and finally Palma.

Bonnet (216–19) points out some important facts about the appearance of the names of the
Canary Islands in this book. This is the first document that enumerates them all, and does so
with great accuracy. It is also the first time that Tenerife is referred to as such: on Italian and
Mallorcan maps of the era it is called "Insula del Inferno" (notice that this is the duplicate name
that the author of the *Conoscimiento* gives to this island. See also Cortesão, *Cartografia portuguesa*,
304.) The first map to include all the islands was the 1339 Dalorto map.

After the Canaries the traveler moves north to the Savage, the Desert, and the Madeira
Islands, referred to here with the name Lecmane, a variant of the Italian *legname* (wood). Nearby
is Puerto Santo. Traveling northeast, the narrator arrives at the Azores (see Bonnet, "Las
Canarias," 218–19).

[131] The narrator seems to be in the Atlas Mountains of Morocco once again, traveling south
into Algeria. Segelmessa (or Sigilmesa) was the capital of the kingdom of the same name which
was destroyed (Jiménez de la Espada 255).

and another they call Isla de Ferro, and another they call Aragavia, and another they call Salvaje, and another they call Isla Desierta, and another they call Lecmane, and another Puerto Santo, and another Isla del Lobo, and another Isla de las Cabras, and another Isla del Brasil, and another Colunbaria, and another Isla de la Ventura, and another Isla de Sant Jorge, and another Isla de los Conejos, and another Isla de los Cuervos Marines. And in this manner there are twenty-five islands. And of all these islands no more than three were populated by people, which are Canaria and Lançarote and Forte Ventura. And the people who live there are like those that follow.

I turned back to Cape Buyder from where I left, and went to Zaara with some Moors that were taking gold on camels to the King of Guinoa. And we found some very large and high mountains in the middle of the Zahara, and they call them Zichialhamera. And later we traveled a long way through the Zaara until we arrived at another mountain they call Isfurent, and from this Isfurent I took leave of the aforementioned Moors and encountered others that were coming to the Algarbe. And I came with them through the Zahara until I reached Mascarota, which is a town belonging to the King of the Benimerins that is at the foot of the Sierra of Çuçia. And I stayed there for a time, and afterward went to Sulgulmença, a rich city that is in the Zaara, and a river that comes from the White Mountains surrounds it. And its king has as his insignia a white flag with the root of a green palm, in this manner. [LXIX]

And I departed Sugulmença and went to the River Dara which is a six-day journey, all populated here and there. And it is a very inhabited land and very abundant in all things, although it is in the Zaara. And I departed the River Dara with some Moors that were going to Guynoa and went with them through the Zahara until we reached Tocoron, a city which is in some mountains. And it is an abundant land although it is hot, and the

abondada como quiera que es caliente, et las gentes son negras.[132] Et el rrey desta Tocoron a por señales un pendon blanco et en medio un monte prieto, commo el Rey de Guynoa. [LXX]

E dende fuy a Tibalbert, que es una çibdat que está en unas sierras muy altas. Et dende fuy a otro monte que dizen Sydon, en que ay dos çibdades. A la una dizen Sidan, a la otra Dan, que son del Rey de Guinoa. Et de alli pasé a Buda,[133] otra çibdat muy abondada que está asentada en çima de un monte. Et sabed que esta çibdat pobló un rrey de Tremeçen porque era malo et fazia malas obras, et despechava a los pueblos. Quisieron lo matar, et fuyó con sus thesoros a este logar, et fizo esta çibdat de Buda.[134] Et sus señales son un pendon blanco con una luna bermeja tal como esta. [LXXI]

Despues parti de Buda et fuy por la Zahara a otro monte que dezian Ganaht, en que ay un rrica çibdat et abondada de todos los bienes, et dizen le Ganaht.[135] Et es cabeça del rreyno de Guinoa. Et el rrey desta Guinoa ha por señales un pendon de oro et en medyo un monte prieto. [LXXII]

Parti de Ganaht et fuy a Crima, otra çibdat que es en la Zahara, et dende a Mesça, una rrica çibdat. Et corre por ella un rrio que nasçe de los Montes Claros. Et sabed que en este rrio fenesçe el rrio de Guynoa, que es muy ancho et muy luengo, en que ay muchas tierras yermas et pobladas, de manera que a en luengo sesenta et çinco jornadas et en ancho quarenta. Et Guinoa quyere tanto dezir como siete montes, por que en Guynoa son siete montes muy poblados et tierra muy abondada, en quanto duran los montes.[136] Lo otro es toda Zahara desabitada. Et los dos montes que dichos son llegan al Rio del Oro de que ya conté de suso, et alli cogen los dientes de los marfiles que crian rribera del rrio, et cogen oro en los formigueros que fazen las formigas rribera del rrio. Et las formigas son grandes como gatos et sacan mucha tierra.[137] Et con este rreynado confina el rreynado

---

[132] This river seems to be Oued Draa, that crosses the Atlas Mountains from Morocco to Algeria. Tocoron is probably Tamgrout, a city on this river.

[133] Tabelbala is now in Algeria. Jiménez de la Espada (253) conjectures that Sidan and Dan might refer to the Sudan, while Markham (69) simply identifies Sidan as an oasis. According to Jiménez de la Espada (185) Buda was the capital of a region called Tuat, south of the Atlas.

[134] Jiménez de la Espada (142) reports that there seems to be no other historical reference to such a king.

[135] Ghana, the capital of Guinea, which can be identified with Senegal.

[136] On several of the maps of this period, the area around Guinea is labeled with reference to seven mountains (Jiménez de la Espada 142–43). Hyde agrees, and adds that the information about them originally came from Solinus (145).

[137] In his translation of Le Canarien, Major (100, n.2) informs us that this legend goes back to Herodotus, who wrote that ants (smaller than dogs but larger than foxes) dug up gold with sand as they dug out their homes.

people are black. And the king of this Tocoron has as his insignia a white flag and in the center a black mountain, like the King of Guynoa. [LXX]

And from there I went to Tibalbert, which is a city that is in some very high sierras. And from there I went to another mountain they call Sydon, in which there are two cities. One they call Sidan, the other Dan, [and] they belong to the King of Guinoa. And from there I passed on to Buda, another very abundant city that is seated on top of a mountain. And know that a king of Tremeçen founded this city because he was evil and did evil deeds and angered the people. They tried to kill him, and he fled with his treasures to this place, and founded this city of Buda. And his insignia is a white flag with a vermilion moon, like this one. [LXXI]

Afterward I departed Buda and went through the Zahara to another mountain that they called Ganaht, in which there is a rich city abundant in all things, and they call it Ganaht. It is the capital of the Kingdom of Guinoa. And the king of this Guinoa has as his insignia a gold flag with a black mountain in the center. [LXXII]

I departed Ganaht and went to Crima, another city that is in the Zahara, and from there to Mesça, a rich city. And through it runs a river that originates in the White Mountains. And note that in this river ends the River Guynoa, which is very wide and very long, [and] in which there are many barren and inhabited lands, so that it is a sixty-five-day journey long and forty wide. And Guinoa means "seven mountains," because in Guynoa there are seven very populated mountains and very abundant land where the mountains are. The rest is all uninhabited Zahara. And the two aforementioned mountains extend to the River of Gold of which I have already told above, and there they collect ivory teeth that they raise along the river, and they collect gold from the anthills that the ants make on the shores of the river. And the ants are as big as cats and dig up a lot of earth. And this kingdom borders on the Kingdom of Organa, in which there are also many

de Organa, en que ay otrosy muchas tierras desabitadas toda Zahara, et confina todo de la una parte con el Rio del Oro que dizen Nilo. Et fuera en la Zahara tiene tres montes muy altos, et son poblados de muchas gentes. Al primero monte dizen Mons Orgando, et es la cabeça del rreyno et do coronan los rreyes. Al otro dizen Mons Tamar, por que ay en el muchas palmas. Al terçero dizen Mons Tamir, por que en él cogen mucho oro.[138] Los pueblos que son rribera del rrio non los pude asumar por que son muchos. Et el rrey desta Organa ha por señales un pendon blanco con una palma verde et dos llaves desta manera. [LXXIII]

Dende parti del rreinado de Organa et pasé al rreinado de Tauser, que tiene otro si muy grandes tierras yermas, desabitadas, todo Zaara muerta, pero que ay seys montes que son poblados de gentes de los negros como la pez. El primero monte, do mora sienpre el rrey et do coronan los rreyes, dizen Almena. Al otro monte dizen Albertara, al otro Merma, et al otro Catifi el Quibir, et al otro dizen Saploya.[139] El rrey deste rreynado Tauser está sienpre en guerra con los moros alarabes que biven en la Zahara, et a por señales un pendon de oro con un monte prieto como el Rey de Guynoa. [LXXIV]

Parti de Tauser et andude muy gran camino por la Zaara en camellos, et llegué a otro rreinado que dizen Tremisin, et confina con el flumen Nilus et sienpre bive en guerra con los cristianos de Nubia et de Etiopia. Et fallé en este rreynado çinco grandes logares poblados de gentes negras. Al primero dizen Trimisin, al otro Oadat, al otro dizen Manola, al otro Orzia, et al otro Palola.[140] Et sabet que las gentes deste rreynado poblaron a Tremeçen la de Berberia. Et el rrey deste rreynado a por señales un pendon cardeno con una luna blanca atal. [LXXV]

Dende fuy a otro rreinado que dizen Dongola. Este parte con los desiertos de Egipto et faze se do se parte el rrio del Nilo dos partes. La una dellas, la mayor, viene contra el poniente que dizen el Rio del Oro, rribera del qual son los rreinados de Guynoa. Et la otra parte va por los desiertos de Egipto et entra en el Mar Medio Terreno en la çibdat de Damiaca.[141]

---

[138] The legendary kingdom of Organa was supposedly in the north of Senegal. It figures on the Catalan Atlas, with a miniature of its king.

[139] The kingdom of Tauser apparently bordered on Organa, and is surely just as legendary.

[140] Markham (31–32) places the Kingdom of Tremecen on the north coast of Africa between Melilla and the Algerian city of Bejaia. The first king began his reign in 633, and during the time that this book was written, Tremecen was ruled by the Beni Zeian dynasty.

[141] Old Dongola was just south of the present-day city of the same name on the Nile. Damiaca refers to modern Damietta (Egypt).

inhabited lands, completely Zahara, and one side borders entirely on the River of Gold that they call Nilo. And further out in the Zahara there are three very high mountains, and they are inhabited by many people. They call the first mountain Mons Orgando, and it is the capital of the kingdom, and where they crown their kings. They call the other Mons Tamar because there are many palm trees in it. They call the third Mons Timer because they collect a lot of gold there. I could not count all the towns on the river because they are many. And the king of this Organa has as his insignia a white flag with a green palm tree and two keys, in this manner. [LXXIII]

From there I departed the Kingdom of Organa and went to the Kingdom of Tauser, which also has many barren, uninhabited lands, all Zahara, but there are six mountains inhabited by people as black as pitch. The first mountain, where the the king always resides and where they crown their kings, they call Almena. They call the other Albertara, the other Merma, and the other Catifi el Quibir, and the other they call Saploya. The king of this kingdom Tauser is always at war with the Arabs that live in the Zahara, and has as his insignia a gold flag with a black mountain, like the King of Guynoa. [LXXIV]

I departed Tauser and traveled a long way through the Zaara on camels, and arrived at another kingdom they call Tremisin, and it borders on the River Nilus and is always at war with the Christians of Nubia and Etiopia. And I found in this kingdom five great towns inhabited by black people. They call the first Trimisin, the other Oadat, they call the other Manola, the other Orzia, and the other Palola. And know that the people of the kingdom founded the Tremeçen in Berberia. And the king of this kingdom has as his insignia a cardinal red flag with a white moon, like this. [LXXV]

From there I went to another kingdom that they call Dongola. This borders on the deserts of Egipto where the Nilus River separates into two parts. One of them, the greater part, comes toward the west [and] they call it the River of Gold, on the shores of which are the kingdoms of Guynoa. And the other part goes through the deserts of Egipto and enters the Medio Terreno Sea in the city of Damiaca. Between these two branches of the

Entre estos dos braços del dicho rrio es este rreynado de Dongola, et es tierra muy poblada de cristianos de Nubia, pero que son negros. Et es tierra muy abondada et rrica de todos los bienes del mundo, de muchos ganados et de todas naturas, et de muchos frutos de arboles, commo quyer que es tierra muy caliente. Et el rrey della a por señales un pendon blanco con una cruz prieta asy.[142] [LXXVI]

En este rreynado de Dongola fallé cristianos ginoveses mercaderes et fuyme con ellos, et tomamos camino el rrio del Nilo ayusso. Et andodimos sesenta jornadas por los desiertos de Egipto fasta que llegamos a la çibdat de Alcaara que es cabeça del rreynado de Egipto et a do coronan los rreyes, et segund que ya conté de suso. Et parti de Alcaara et fuy me para Damieta et fallé una nao de cristianos et entré en ella. Et andude un tienpo en esta nao fasta que descargaron en la çibdat de Çepta, de que ya conté de suso. Et parti de Çepta por tierra et fuyme para Marruecos otra vez, et travesé los Montes Claros et fuyme para Gazula, et moré ay un tienpo por que es viçiosa et esenta. Et unos moros armaron una galeota para yr al Rio del Oro de que ya conté de suso, por que fazen allá grandes gananças, et fuy con ellos por algo que me dixeron. Et party de la Gazula en la dicha galea et levamos sienpre la rribera del Mar del Poniente, fasta que llegamos al Cabo de No, et dende al Cabo de Sant Bin, et dende al Cabo de Buyder de que ya conté de suso, que es toda la rribera desabitada. Et llegamos al Rio del Oro de que ya conté de suso, que se parte del Nilo, el qual nasçe de las altas sierras del polo Antartico do dizen que es el Paraisso Terrenal,[143] et atraviesa toda Nubia, et toda Etiopia, et a la sallida de Etiopia partese en dos braços. El uno va contra el desierto de Egipto por Damieta. El otro braço mayor viene al poniente et metese en la Mar Oçidental, et dizenle el Rio del Oro. Et andodimos despues que partimos del Rio del Oro muy grand camino, guardando sienpre la rribera. Et dexamos atras las Islas Perdidas, et fallamos una isla muy grande poblada et de muchas gentes et dezianle Ynsola Gropis,[144] et era tierra abondada de todos los bienes salvo que las gentes eran ydolatrias. Et llevaron nos a todos ante su rrey et maravillose mucho de nos, et de nuestra fabla, et de nuestras costunbres. Et los mercaderes que armaron la galea fezieron mucho de su provecho. Et el rrey dende a por señales un pendon blanco con la figura de su idolo tal. [LXXVII]

---

[142] *R* and *S* show a cross with two horizontal bars. In *N*, the lower bar traverses the whole banner, completely changing its appearance.

[143] On the various "locations" of Earthly Paradise, see Wright 261–63. Like the *Conoscimiento*, the Dalorto map of 1339 places it south of Ethiopia.

[144] This is probably one of the Bisagots Islands off the coast of Senegal (see Jiménez de la Espada 151).

aforementioned river is this kingdom of Dongola, and it is a land very populated with Christians from Nubia, but they are black. And it is a very abundant and rich land, with all the material wealth in the world, and much cattle of all kinds and many fruits from trees, although it is a very hot land. And its king has as his insignia a white flag with a black cross, like this. [LXXVI]

In the kingdom of Dongola I encountered some Genoese Christian merchants and went with them, and we went off down the Nilo River. And we traveled sixty days through the deserts of Egipto until we reached the city of Alcaara which is the capital of the kingdom of Egipto and where they crown their kings, of which I have already told above. And I departed Alcaara and went to Damieta and I encountered a ship of Christians and embarked it. And I traveled a time in this ship until they unloaded in the city of Çepta, which I have already told of above. And I departed Çepta on land and went to Marruecos once again, and crossed the White Mountains and went to Gazula, and there I lived for a time because it is rich and comfortable. And some Moors supplied a galley to go to the River of Gold of which I already told above, because there they make great profits, and I went with them because of something they told me. And I departed Gazula in the said galley and we always followed the coast of the Western Sea until we reached Cape No, and from there the Cape of Sant Bin, and from there Cape Buyder of which I have already told above; it is entirely uninhabited coastline. And we arrived at the River of Gold which I told of above, which originates in the Nilo, which originates in the high sierras of the Antarctic Pole where they say Earthly Paradise is, and it crosses all of Nubia and all Etiopia, and at the end of Etiopia it divides into two branches. One goes through the desert of Egipto to Damieta. The other branch comes west and enters the Western Sea, and they call it the River of Gold. And after we departed the River of Gold we traveled a long way, keeping always to the coast. And we left behind us the Lost Islands, and we found a very large populated island with a lot of people, and they called it the Insula Gropis, and it was a land abundant in all things, except that the people were idolaters. And they took all of us to their king and he marveled at us and at our speech, and at our customs. And the merchants that supplied the galley made a great profit. And its king has as his insignia a white flag with the figure of their idol, like this. [LXXVII]

E partimos de la Insola de Gropis et tomamos camino contra el levante por el Mar de India, et fallamos otra isla que dizen Quible.[145] Et dexamos la a man derecha et tomamos çerca de la rribera, et paresçio un monte muy alto que dezian Alboch. Et fuemos alla, et era todo poblado de muchas gentes, et nasçia del un rrio muy grande, et era tierra muy abondada. Et de aquy se tornó la galea. Et yo finqué alli un tienpo et despues party de Alboch con gentes, et fuy a otro monte que dizen Lirry. Et nasçia del un rrio que dizen Enalco.[146] Et parti deste monte que dizen Lirri et fuy al rreynado de Gotonie, que tiene muy grandes tierras pobladas et yermas. Et en este rreynado Gotonie son unos montes mucho altos, que dizen que non son otros tan altos en el mundo. Et dizenles los Montes de la Luna. Otros les dizen los Montes del Oro.[147] Et nasçen destos montes çinco rrios, los mayores del mundo, et van todos caer en el Rio del Oro, et esta es su figura.[148]

Et faze y un lago tan grande de veynte jornadas en luengo et diez en ancho. Et faze en medio una grand isla que dizen Palola, et es poblada de gentes negras. Pero la mas desta tierra es desabitada por la muy grand calentura et por que es toda arenas muertas. Pero son en este rreynado seys montes poblados de gentes. Los mayores son los Montes del Oro, et el otro monte es el Monte de Lirri, et el otro Monte Alboch, al otro monte dizen Burga, al otro Monte de Elbahat, et al otro Monte de Elmolar. Et sabet que deste rreinado Gotonye non es el mas poblado que destos montes que dichos son, pero que tiene muy grandes tierras, ca parte del un cabo con el Rio del Oro, et del otro cabo con el Mar Oçiano,[149] et del otro cabo con un golfo que entra en el Mar Ocçidental quinze jornadas. Asy que es uno de los grandes rreinos del mundo. Et sus señales son unos tovajones de oro atados en una lança. [LXXVIII]

Sabet que esta tierra de que ya contamos como quyer que es tierra muy caliente pero es tierra muy abondada de muchos datiles et muchos camellos. Et rribera deste rrio Nilo crian los grandes marfiles, et de aquy lievan los mercadores los dientes et los huesos dellos. Et rribera deste rrio cogen el oro en los formigueros, et cogen el alanbar, et por esso esta tierra es muy rrica.

---

[145] Perhaps this refers to the Sherbro Islands, near the coast of Sierra Leone.

[146] Jiménez de la Espada (175) and Markham (69) believe that Alboch might be Sierra Leone and that the Enalco River is the Kamaranka. Lirri is more difficult to identify: Markham refers to it simply as an oasis in Central Africa.

[147] For Jiménez de la Espada (207), Gotonie was a large area of Equatorial Africa, and the mountains mentioned are Kilimanjaro and Mount Kenya.

[148] In N and R appears a drawing of a mountain with five rivers coming from it and emptying into another, larger river.

[149] The Atlantic.

And we departed Insula Gropis and took the route eastward to the Sea of India, and we found another island they call Quible. And we left it on the right side and traveled near the coast, and there appeared a very high mountain that they called Alboch. And we went there, and it was totally inhabited by many people, and a very large river originated there, and it was a very abundant land. And from here the galley turned away. And I remained there for a time and afterward I departed Alboch with some people and went to another mountain they call Lirry. And a river they call Enalco originated in it. And I departed this mountain they call Lirri and went to the Kingdom Gotonie, which has many great inhabited and barren lands. And in this Kingdom Gotonie there are many high mountains, for they say that there are none higher in the world. And they call them the Mountains of the Moon. Others call them the Mountains of Gold. And five rivers originate in these mountains, the largest in the world, and all flow to the River of Gold, and this is its image.

And a very large lake is formed there, a twenty-days' journey in length and ten wide. And there is in the middle a great island that they call Palola, and it is inhabited by black people. But most of this land is uninhabited because of the great heat and because it is all dead sand. But there are in this kingdom six mountains inhabited by people. The largest are the Mountains of Gold, and the other mountain is Mount Lirri, and the other Mount Alboch, the other mountain they call Burga, the other Mount Elbahat, and the other Mount Elmolar. And note that this kingdom Gotonie is not the most populated other than in these aforementioned mountains, but it has many great lands since it borders on one end with the River of Gold and on the other end with the Ocean Sea, and on the other end with a gulf that enters fifteen-days' journey in the Western Sea. Therefore it is one of the largest kingdoms in the world. And its insignia are gold sashes tied on a lance. [LXXVIII]

Know that this land of which we have told, although it is a very hot land, is nevertheless a land abundant in many dates and many camels. And on the shore of this Nilo River they cultivate great ivories, and from there the merchants collect the teeth and the bones of them. And on the shore of this river they take gold from the anthills, and collect amber, and that is why this land is very rich. And I departed this kingdom Gotonie and

Et parti deste rreynado Gotonie et llegué a un golfo que faze y el Mar Oçiano. Et avia en este golfo tres islas. A la una dizen Zanno, a la otra Açevean, et a la otra Malicun.[150] Et travesé el dicho golfo et aporté a una grand çibdat que dizen Amenuan, et es otrosi un rreyno muy grande, et de muchas gentes, et es tierra muy abondada de todos los bienes, salvo que las gentes eran ydolatrias et creyan en los idolos. Et avia en este rreynado ocho çibdades grandes. Son: la mayor, Amenuan, do moran sienpre los rreyes et do los coronan, otra Goran, otra Asçida, otra Cologane, otra Benateo, otra Unda, otra Gaona, otra Canben.[151] Et el rrey dende a por señales un pendon blanco con una idola tal. [LXXIX]

En este rreynado de Amenuan entra un braço del rrio Eufrates, el qual rrio nasçe de las altas sierras del Polo Antarico do diz que es el Paraiso Terrenal.[152] Et este rrio Eufrates faze se tres braços: el un braço entra por medio del rreino de Amenuan, et los otros braços çircunrrodean todo el rreyno que ha en ancho en algunos lugares dos jornadas. Asi es el rreyno muy grande. Et dende travesé el dicho rrio et andove muy grand camino por su rribera, que es mucho poblada. Et llegué a una grand çibdat que dizen Graçiona, que es cabeça del ynperio de Abdeselib, que quiere dezir siervo de la cruz. Et este Abdeselib es defendedor de la iglesia de Nubia et de Etiopia, et éste defiende al Preste Juan, que es patriarca de Nubia et de Etiopia et señorea muy grandes tierras et muchas çibdades de cristianos.[153] Pero que son negros como la pez et quemanse con fuego en las fruentes en señal de cruz et en rreconosçimiento de bautismo. Et como quier que estas gentes son negras, pero son omes de buen entendimiento et de buen seso, et an saberes et çiençias, et an tierra muy abondada de todos los bienes, por que ay muchas aguas et muy buenas de las que salen del Polo Antarico do dizen que es el Paraiso Terrenal. Et dixeron me en esta çibdat de Grançiona que fueron y traidos los ginoveses que escaparon de la galea que se quebró

---

[150] Markham (69) places these islands in the Gulf of Guinea.

[151] Apparently an area in western Equatorial Africa.

[152] The narrator later demonstrates that he knows that this river is not the same Euphrates as the one in the Near East. Since he believed that Earthly Paradise was located in Africa, he must have thought it necessary to place a Euphrates River here also.

[153] According to Conti Rossini (673), the name Graçiona might be derived from Civitas Syone of the 1325 Dalorto map; or "hagara Siòn" (Sion City), probably Aksum (Ethiopia).

On the Pizigani brothers' map and on the metallic planisphere in the Borgiano Museum there exists in the south of Africa a region governed by a king "Ebini Chilebi" or "Ebinichibel" who, along with his vassals, had the head of a dog.

Prester John was a legendary and very wealthy priest-emperor sought out by Europeans in the fourteenth and fifteenth centuries. See Beckingham's article on the quest for this imaginary figure. Markham (38, n.1) states that the author of this book was the first to locate Prester John in the area of Ethiopia.

arrived at a gulf that the Ocean Sea forms there. And there were three islands in this gulf. They call one Zanno, the other Açevean, and the other Malicun. And I crossed the said gulf and took port in a great city they call Amenuan, and it is also a very large kingdom, and with many people, and it is a land abundant in all things, except that the people were idolaters and believed in idols. And there were in this kingdom eight large cities. They are: the largest, Amenuan, where the kings always reside and where they crown them, another [is] Goran, another Asçida, another Cologane, another Benateo, another Unda, another Gaona, another Canben. And its king has as his insignia a white flag with an idol, like this. [LXXIX]

Into this kingdom of Amenuan enters a branch of the River Eufrates, which [river] originates in the high sierras of the Antarctic Pole where they say Earthly Paradise is. And this River Eufrates divides into three branches: one branch enters through the middle of the kingdom of Amenuan, and the other branches surround all the kingdom, which is two-days' journey in width in some places. Therefore the kingdom is very large. And from there I crossed the aforementioned river and traveled a long way near the coast, which is very populated. And I reached a great city they call Graçiona, which is the capital of the empire of Abdeselib, which means "servant of the cross." And this Abdeselib is the defender of the Church of Nubia and of Etiopia, and he defends Prester John, who is the Patriarch of Nubia and of Etiopia and governs many great lands and many cities of Christians. But they are as black as pitch and they burn themselves with fire on their foreheads with the sign of the cross in recognition of their baptism. And although these people are black, they are men of good understanding and good mind, and they have knowledge and science, and they have a land that is very abundant in all things because there are many and very good waters that come from the Antarctic Pole where they say Earthly Paradise is. And they told me in this city of Graçiona that the Genoese men that

en Amenuan, et de la otra galea que escapó nunca sopieron qué se fizo.[154] Et este enperador Abdeselib a por señales un pendon de plata con una cruz prieta desta manera. [LXXX]

Parti de la çibdat de Graçiona por que las çibdades deste inperio non pude asumar, et andude por muchas tierras et çibdades et llegué a la çibdat de Malsa, do mora sienpre'l Preste Iohn, patriarca de Nubia et de Etiopia.[155] Et a la ida yva sienpre rribera del rrio Eufrates, que es una tierra muy poblada et abondada. Et desque fuy en Malsa folgué y un tienpo por que via et oya cada dia cosas maravillosas. Et pregunté por el Parayso Terrenal que cosa era et que dezian del. Et dixeron me omes sabios que eran unos montes tan altos que confinan con el çirculo de la luna et que los non podia ver todo ome, ca de veynte omes que fuesen non los verian los tres dellos, et que nunca oyeran dezir de ome que alla subiese. Et omes ay que dizen que los vieron a la parte de oriente, et otros a la parte de medio dia. Et dizen que quando el sol es en Geminis veen los a medio dia, et quando el sol es en Capricornio veen los a la parte de oriente. Et dixeron me que estos montes eran todos çercados de pielagos muy fondos del agua que dellos desçiende, de los quales pielagos salen quatro rrios muy grandes que son los mayores del mundo, que les dizen Tigris, Eufrates, Gion, et Ficxion.[156] Et estos quatro rrios rriegan toda Nubia et Etiopia, et las aguas que delos dichos montes desçienden fazen tan grand rruydo, que a dos jornadas suena el son de las aguas. Et todos los omes que çerca moran son todos sordos que non se oyen unos a otros del grand rroydo de las aguas. Et en todo tienpo da el sol en aquellos montes, quier de noche quier de dia, quando del un cabo, quando del otro. Esto es por que la meitad destos montes son sobre el orizonte et la otra so el orizonte, en tal manera que ençima de los montes nunca faze noche, nin tiniebra, nin faze frio, nin calentura, nin sequedat, nin umidat, mas mucho egual tenplamiento. Et todas las cosas asi vigitables como sentibles et animales que alli son, non pueden jamas conrronper nin morir. Et dixeron me otros secretos muchos de las virtudes de las estrellas, asi en los juyzios como en la magica, et

---

[154] It is said that in 1281, two ships originating in Genoa were headed for India; one stopped in an Ethiopian city called Menam, where all the Genoese aboard were taken prisoner. No one returned from this expedition. See Rogers, "The Vivaldi Expedition," for details.

[155] Conti Rossini (673) affirms that it is difficult to identify the supposed city of Malsa, and it does not appear in any Ethiopian historical documents or maps.

[156] Genesis (2:10) first mentions the four rivers of Paradise: the Pison, the Gihon (Nile), the Hiddekel (Tigris), and the Euphrates (see also n.152). Benjamin de Tudela calls Fison the Nile that emptied into the Mediterranean.

escaped the galley that broke up in Amenuan were taken there, and they never knew what happened to the other galley that escaped. And this Emperor Abdeselib has as his insignia a silver flag with a black cross in this manner. [LXXX]

I departed the city of Graçiona because the cities of this empire cannot be counted, and I traveled through many lands and cities and reached the city of Malsa, where Prester John, the Patriarch of Nubia and of Etiopia, always resides. On my way I always kept to the shore of the River Eufrates, which is a very inhabited and abundant land. And when I arrived in Malsa I stayed there for a time because I saw and heard marvelous things every day. And I asked what Earthly Paradise was, and what they said about it. And some wise men told me that it was some very high mountains that border on the circle of the Moon and that not every man could see them, since of twenty men who might go, only three of them would see it, and they never heard of any man climbing them. And there are men that say that they saw them on the eastern side, and others on the south. And they say that when the Sun is in Gemini they see them to the south, and when the Sun is in Capricorn they see them to the west. And they told me that these mountains were completely surrounded by seas deep with the water that descends from them, from which [seas] flow four very large rivers that are the greatest in the world, which they call Tigris, Eufrates, Gion and Ficxion. And these four rivers irrigate all of Nubia and Etiopia, and the waters of the aforementioned mountains that descend make such a great noise, that the sound can be heard two-days' journey away. And all the men that live near are totally deaf, since they cannot hear each other because of the great noise of the waters. And the Sun always shines in those mountains, be it night or day, whether on one side or the other. This is because half of these mountains are above the horizon and the other under the horizon, so that atop the mountain it is never night, nor dark, nor cold, nor hot, nor dry, nor wet, but a great even temperature. And all things that are there, vegetable as well as sentient and animal, can never decay nor die. And they told me many other secrets of the virtues of the stars, concerning predictions as well as magic, and also the virtues of the herbs and plants and

virtudes otrosi de las yervas, et plantas, et mineras. Et vy ende cossas mara-villosas. Et los griegos dizen a este logar Ortodoxis, et los abraicos dizen le Ganheden,[157] et los latinos Paraiso Terrenal por que sienpre ally es grand tenpramiento. Et las señales del Preste Iohn son un pendon de plata con una cruz prieta, et de amas partes dos blagos desta manera, por que en tierra de Nubia et de Etiopia son dos enperadores, el uno el Enperador de Graçiona et el otro el Enperador de Magdasor.[158] [LXXXI]

Salli de la çibdat de Malsa do mora el Preste Ihon, et tomé camino contra el levante et travesé el rrio Nilo, et fallé muchas çibdades en su rri-bera. A la primera dizen Amo, et a la otra Araot, et a la otra Sarma, et a la otra Ocçidela, et a la otra Moraina, et a la otra Vyma, et a la otra Gabencol-it, et a la otra Glaot, et otros muchos pueblos. Et travesé dos vezes el rrio Gion, que lo non pude escusar, fasta que llegué a una grand çibdat que dizen Magdasor.[159] Et es un inperio muy grande en que ay muchas çib-dades, et villas, et castillos, et logares, et es tierra muy poblada de cristianos de Nubia. Este ynperio de Magdasor es todo çercado de los dos rrios que sallen de los grandes pielagos que se fazen derredor del Paraiso Terrenal. Al un rrio dizen Gion, et al otro Fison, et del otro cabo confinan con un golfo del Mar de India que entra por la tierra quarenta jornadas. En esta çibdat de Magdasor me dixeron de un ginoves que dezian Sorleonis que fuera y en busca de su padre que fuera en una de las galeas de que ya conté de suso. Et fizieronle toda onrra. Et este Sorleonis quysiera traspasar al inperio de Gra-çiona a buscar a su padre, et este Enperador de Magdasor non le consintio yr por que la yda era dubdosa por que el camino es peligroso.[160] Et sabet que en esta tierra de Nubia et de Etyopia son çiento et çinquenta et quatro rregiones que tienen muy grandes tierras yermas et pobladas, en tal manera

---

[157] Gan Ha'Eden is Hebrew for the Garden of Eden.

[158] Each manuscript treats Prester John's coat of arms in a different manner. In S, in its center is a long cross flanked by a bishop's crook on either side. N provides two banners: the first contains a cross with four equal branches between two bishop's crosses; the other has only what appears to be an orthodox cross, with its three, successively larger cross bars. In R, the shield is traversed completely by a simple cross.

Markham (plate 15, facing p. 35) attributes the orthodox cross banner to S, the flag that actually is found in S to N, and the other arms drawn in N to R. He does not provide the coat of arms that appears in R.

[159] Conti Rossini (674) finds these place-names inexplicably altered from their counterparts on the Dalorto map. He tentatively identifies them as cities along the Ethiopian and Somalian coast down to Mogadishu (here, Magdasor). In their order of appearance in the text: Amhara, Roha, Sarmat, Uag, (Moraina is left unidentified), Urma, and Galloc.

Conti Rossini also remarks that this is the first time that a Western text mentions Moga-dishu (675, n.1).

[160] See n.154.

minerals. And I saw there marvellous things. And the Greeks call this place
Ortodoxis, and the Hebrews call it Ganheden, and the Latins Paraiso Terrenal because it is always a wonderful temperature there. And the insignia
of Prester John is a silver flag with a black cross, and on both sides two
crooks in this manner, because in the land of Nubia and of Etiopia there are
two emperors: one is the Emperor of Graçiona and the other is the Emperor of Magdasor. [LXXXI]

I left the city of Malsa where Prester John resides and took the road east
and crossed the Nilo River, and I found many cities on its shores. They call
the first Amo, and the other Araot, and the other Sarma, and the other Ocçidela, and the other Moraina, and the other Vyma, and the other Gaben-
colit, and the other Glaot, and many other towns. And I twice crossed the
river Gion, which I could not avoid, until I reached a great city they call
Magdasor. It is a very large empire in which there are many cities and
towns and castles and villages, and it is a land quite populated by Christians
from Nubia. This empire of Magdasor is totally surrounded by two rivers
that come out of the great seas that are formed around Earthly Paradise.
They call one river Gion, and the other Fison, and on the other end they
border on a gulf of the Sea of India that enters into land a distance of a
forty-days' journey. In this city of Magdasor they told me of a Genoese man
that they called Sorleonis who had gone there in search of his father who
had gone there in one of the galleys that I told of above. And they did him
every honor. And this Sorleonis had wanted to cross the empire of Graçiona to look for his father, and this Emperor of Magdasor did not consent
that he go because the journey was dubious because the way is dangerous.
And note that in this land of Nubia and of Etiopia there are 154 regions
that have many great barren and inhabited lands, so that it forms one fourth

que es la quarta parte de toda la faz de la tierra. El Enperador de Magdasor a por señales un pendon blanco con una cruz prieta atal.[161] [LXXXII]

Parti del inperio de Magdasor et fuyme contra el levante por el Gion ayuso. Et a la salida deste inperio este rrio Gion partese en dos braços. El uno va contra medio dia et metese en el Mar de Yndia. Este braço dexé yo a man derecha et fuy por el otro braço muy grand camino, et fallé gentes de muchas creençias et de estrañas maneras et costunbres, que seria luengo de contar, fasta que llegué a un golfo del Mar de Yndia que entra por la tierra çinquenta jornadas. Et en este golfo son tres islas muy grandes. A la una dizen Zinzibar, a la otra Alcubil, et a la terçera Insola Aden, que es la mayor et la mas poblada et es contra Arabia.[162] Et desta comiença el Mare Rubro et salle por la tierra contra el poniente quarenta jornadas, et rriberas del son muchas çibdades et villas et logares. Et quando vienen las naos de India llegan a la Isla Aden et pagan y el diezmo de las mercadurias que traen, por que entre esta Isla Aden et la punta de Aravia es una rrica çibdat. Faze se muy grand angostura que mala vez cabe una nao, et entran luego en el Mar Rubro et descargan en una çibdat que llaman Sacam, que es del Rey de Caldea. Ribera deste Mar Rubro es una çibdat que dizen Albaçio,[163] que antigua mente era cabeça de rreynado, et de alli derraman para Egipto et a Damasco et lievan las mercadurias por tierras en camellos. Et sabet que este Mar Rubro confina con Arabia et con Caldea, et llega fasta los desiertos de Egipto. Ribera del son muchas çibdades et señorios, pero diré los mayores. Al primero dizen Chos, al otro Lidebo, al otro Made, al otro Exion Gabel, al otro Gide, al otro Serayn, al otro Sacan, al otro Yude, al otro Adromar, al otro Rasaquipal, et al otro Meça.[164] Et a este Mare Rubro dizen asi por que el suelo del es todo almagra et tierra bermeja, et faze el agua rruvia. Et por este mar pasaron los judios quando salieron de Egipto del cautiverio del Rey Faraon. Et dende entré luego por Caldea, que es toda çercada de dos rrios muy grandes que naçen de los Montes del Toro. Al uno dizen el

---

[161] All three manuscripts depict a patriarchal cross with two horizontal branches.

[162] For information on Zinzibar, see Jiménez de la Espada, n.xlvi. The narrator now heads into the Arabian Sea and the Arabian Peninsula.

[163] Sacam refers to the port city of Suakin, now in Sudan on the Red Sea. Both Markham (39) and Jiménez de la Espada (174–75) believe that Albaçio is a corruption of Abyssinia.

[164] All are cities on either side of the Red Sea, ending with Mecca. Conti Rossini establishes the identity of several of them: on the Egyptian side are Quseir, Aidhâb, and the port Bâtse; Exion Gabel is Ezeongeber (Gulf of Aqaba); Gide is surely Jedda, followed by the port Sirrein to its south; Yude might be Zebid, an important city at the time, followed perhaps by Uadi Rima (677).

of the entire face of the earth. The Emperor of Magdasor has as his insignia a white flag with a black cross, like this. [LXXXII]

I departed the empire of Magdasor and went eastward down the Gion. And at the exit to this empire this river Gion divides into two branches. One goes south and enters the Sea of India. I left this branch to my right and went along the other branch a long way, and found people of many beliefs and of strange manners and customs that would take long to relate, until I reached a gulf of the Sea of India that enters into land a distance of fifty-days' journey. And in this gulf there are three very large islands. They call one Zinzibar, the other Alcubil, and the third Insula Aden, which is the largest and most populated and faces Arabia. And here the Red Sea begins and penetrates the land in a westward direction the distance of a forty-days' journey, and on its shores there are many cities and towns and villages. And when the ships from India come, they arrive at the island Aden and there they pay the tax for the merchandise they are carrying because between this island Aden and the tip of Arabia there is a rich city. It becomes so narrow there that a ship hardly fits, and they enter the Red Sea and unload in a city they call Sacam, which belongs to the King of Caldea. On the shores of this Red Sea is a city they call Albaçio, which in ancient times was the capital of the kingdom, and from there they leave for Egipto and Damasco and take their merchandise by land on camels. And note that this Red Sea borders on Arabia and Caldea, and extends to the deserts of Egipto. On its shores are many cities and lordships, but I will mention [only] the largest. They call the first Chos, the other Lidebo, the other Made, the other Exion Gabel, the other Gide, the other Serayn, the other Sacan, the other Yude, the other Adromar, the other Rasaquipal, and the other Meça. And they call it the Red Sea because its bottom is all red ochre and red earth, and it makes the water red. And over this sea the Jews passed when they left Egipto from the captivity of the Pharaoh King. And from there I then entered Caldea, which is surrounded entirely by two very large rivers that originate in the Toro Mountains. They call one the River Cur and the

flumen Cur et al otro Eufratres, mas non el de Nubia.[165] Et anbos dos estos rrios entran en el Mar de Yndia en un golfo que dizen el Mar Negro, et los judios le dizen Mare Porticun.[166] Esta Caldea es una tierra mucho poblada et rrica et muy abondada de todos los bienes et de todas las cosas. Et sabet que en este rreyno de Caldea es la muy grande Torre de Bavel que fezieron los gigantes en medio de un gran canpo que dizen el Agro de Senabar. Et aqui fue la grand çibdat de Bavilonia, que agora es ya destruida, de que fue señor Nabucodonusor. Et las gentes desta Babilonia se partieron en dos partes. Los unos poblaron a Bandacha, una noble çibdat que es en la provinçia de Baldaque, et los otros poblaron a Mistrayn en Egipto.[167] Et esta es la figura de Babilonia con la torre asy commo esta que se sigue.

Et en este Mestrayn estudieron los judios captivos en el tienpo de Moysen. Et despues fue destroydo este Mestrayn por el Rio de Nilo, et los que escaparon poblaron a la çibdat de Alcahara do agora mora el Soldan de Egipto. Et pasé un braço del rrio Eufrates et entré en la provinçia de Baldaque, en que ay una grand çibdat que dizen Bandacho, de que fue otrosy señor Nabucodonusor. El rrey destas dos provinçias a por señales un pendon de plata con una tal señal commo ésta.[168] [LXXXIII]

Parti de Bandacha et fuy a Mesopotania, una grant çibdat et muy abondada de muchos bienes, en la qual fue coronado el Enperador Merlinus Tartarus, Señor de Armenia la Mayor.[169] Et parti de Mesopotania et fuy a una çibdat que dizen Mon Falcon, et alli faze una grand isla el rrio Cur que llaman Ansera, en la qual ysla está una grand çibdat. Et pasado este rrio es el logar do fue la çibdat de Ninive, que fue destruyda por el pecado de Sodomia que fazian los omes.[170] Et sabet que esta rregion tiene muy grandes tierras et çibdades et logares, et es toda çercada de dos rrios muy grandes. Al uno dizen el flumen Eufrates et al otro el flumen Cur. Et de la otra parte el Mar Rubro et de la otra el Mar Parçicun fasta Aqyusio,[171] et

---

[165] The Tigris and Euphrates Rivers. It is here that the author distinguishes between this and the Euphrates River on the African continent.

[166] The Persian Gulf.

[167] Bandacha and Baldaque both refer to Baghdad. Jiménez de la Espada (227) identifies Mistrayn simply as Egypt.

[168] The object in the center of this flag is an inverted triangle. Only the outline of the banner appears in S. Markham (and thus Pasch) does not supply an illustration.

[169] Markham (40, n.5) and Jiménez de la Espada (158) conjecture that this might be Holagou Khan, a grandson of Genghis, who conquered Baghdad in 1258.

[170] Might Mon Falcon be Al Mawsil, a city on the left bank of the Tigris? Across from it is the site of ancient Ninive, and the name Ansera could refer to an islet in the river itself.

[171] Qeshm, the island and city of this name that are now part of Iran, in the Persian Gulf.

other the Eufrates, but not the one in Nubia. And both of these rivers enter the Sea of India in a gulf that they call the Black Sea, and the Jews call it the Porticun Sea. This Caldea is a very populated and rich land and is very abundant in all things. And note that in this kingdom of Caldea is the great Tower of Babel that giants built in the middle of a great field that they call the Agro de Senabar. And here was the great city of Babilonia, which is now destroyed, which belonged to the lord Nebuchadnezzar. And the people of this Babilonia split into two parts. Some of them founded Banda-cha, a noble city that is in the province of Baldaque, and the others found-ed Mistrayn in Egipto. And this is the image of Babilonia with the tower, like the one that follows.

And in this Mestrayn the Jews were captive in the time of Moses. And later this Mestrayn was destroyed by the River Nilo, and those who escaped inhabited the city of Alcahara where the Sultan of Egipto now resides. And I passed a branch of the River Eufrates and entered the province of Balda-que, in which there is a great city they call Bandacho, which also belonged to the lord Nebuchadnezzar. The king of these two provinces has as his insignia a silver flag with an emblem like this one. [LXXXIII]

I departed Bandacha and went to Mesopotania, a great city abundant in many things, in which the Emperor Merlinus Tartarus, Lord of Armenia Major, was crowned. And I departed Mesopotania and went to a city that they call Mon Falcon, and there the River Cur forms a large island they call Ansera, on which there is a great city. And beyond this river is the place where the city of Ninive used to be, which was destroyed for the sin of Sodomia that men committed. And know that this region has many great lands and cities and villages, and is surrounded totally by two very large rivers. They call one the River Eufrates and the other the River Cur. And from the other side of the Red Sea and the other of the Parçicun Sea up to

non posimos aqui señales por que Caldea et Baldaque todo es un señorio et toda es una rregion.[172]

Party de la isla de Ansera et fuyme por el rrio de Cur ayuso muy grand camino, fasta que llegué a la provinçia de Arabia. Et travesé muy grand tierra fasta que llegué a la çibdat de Almedina donde nasçio Mahomat, et dende fuy a Meca donde está la ley et el testamento de Mahomat, que está en una arca de fierro en una casa de piedra calamita. Et por eso esta en el ayre, que nin desçiende ayuso nin sube arriba. Et sabet que esta Meca es la cabeça del ynperio de los alarabes, et sus señales son un pendon bermejo et en medio letras de oro aravigas. [LXXXIV]

Parti de Meca et fuy por el rreyno de Arabia adelante, et llegué a una çibdat muy grande et muy rica et de muchos bienes abondada que dizen Fadal, que es ribera del Mar de India, et alli folgué un tienpo. Et entré en un navio en la mar et pasé a una ysla que dizen Sicroca, muy grande et mucho poblada. Et avia en ella una grand ciudad que dezian otrosi Sicroca,[173] et es del rrey de Aravia et trae esas mesmas señales que son tales commo las de Meca, et es un pendon bermejo con letras aravigas. Et sabed que a esta mesma ysla aportan las naves que vienen de India cargadas de especias. [LXXXV]

Parti de la ysla de Sicroca et fuy a otra ysla que dizen Enrro,[174] et fazese a la entrada del golfo del Mar Perticun, quiere dezir el mar negro. E en este golfo cojen el aljofar. E esta ysla Enrro es del Rey de Arabia. E fuymos por el dicho golfo adelante contra la transmontana, que fallamos dos mares que era el agua della bermeja commo la sangre. E fuemos mas adelante fasta la tierra, e fallamos otras dos yslas. A la una dezian Aquisio, apres de la qual está una grand ciudad que dizen Aquisio, et a la otra dizen Hormixio, apres de la qual está otrosi una grand ciudad que dizen Hormixio.[175] E sabed que fasta estas dos ciudades llega el imperio del Persia et el señorio del grand soldan Benaçayt. E parti del dicho golfo et entré por la provincia de Sabba do cojen encienso, e llegué a una grand ciudad que dizen Golfathan, et dende a Gepta, et dende a otra que dizen Cabat,[176] que son muy grandes ciudades et muy ricas et muy abondadas, pero que son pobladas de tartaros et

---

[172] Both N and R repeat the previous coat of arms (that of Baghdad) here.

[173] Perhaps Fadal is Ra's Fartak, on the southern coast of the Arabian peninsula. From there the traveler crosses the Gulf of Aden to the Island of Socotra.

[174] Both Jiménez de la Espada (200) and Markham (70) identify this as Suto, at the entrance to the Persian Gulf.

[175] Once again Qeshm, and Hormuz.

[176] The province named here seems to correspond to the part of present-day Oman that faces the gulf of the same name.

Aquysio, we did not put down the insignia because Caldea and Baldaque belong to the same lordship, and it is all one region.

I departed the island of Ansera and went down the River Cur a long way until I reached the province of Arabia. And I crossed a great expanse of land until I arrived at the city of Almedina where Mohammed was born, and from there I went to Meca where the law and testament of Mohammed is found, which is in an iron chest in a house of lodestone. And for this reason it is in the air, and does not descend nor ascend. And note that this Meca is the capital of the Empire of the Arabs, and its insignia is a vermilion flag, and in the center gold Arabic letters. [LXXXIV]

I departed Meca and went onward through the kingdom of Arabia, and arrived at a very large and rich city abundant in many things that they call Fadal, which is on the shore of the Sea of India, and I remained there for a time. And I embarked a ship in the sea and went to an island they call Sicroca, very large and very populated. And on it there was a city that they also call Sicroca, and it belongs to the King of Arabia and has the same insignia as Meca, and it is a vermilion flag with Arabic letters. And know that on this same island the ships that come from India laden with spices take port. [LXXXV]

I departed the island of Sicocra and went to another island that they call Enrro, which is at the entrance to the Perticun Sea, and it means black sea. And in this gulf they collect pearls. And on the island Enrro is the King of Arabia. And we went onward through the aforementioned gulf to the north and found two seas whose waters were as red as blood. And we went onward toward land and found two other islands. They call one Aquisio, beyond which is a great city they call Aquisio, and they call the other Hormixio, beyond which is also a great city they call Hormixio. And know that the empire of Persia and the lordship of the great Sultan Benascayt extend to these two cities. And I departed the aformentioned gulf and entered the province of Sabba where they get incense, and I arrived at a great city that they call Golfathan, and from there Gepta, and from there to another that they call Cabat, which are very great and rich and abundant cities, but they are inhabited by Tartars and people without religion who do not keep one

de gentes sin ley que non guardan ningund mandamiento de Dios, salvo que non fazen mal a otro. Et parti de Sabba et torné me a la ciudad de Hormixo de que ya conté de suso, et moré un tienpo. Et fuy dende con mercadores muy grand camino et llegamos a un rreynado que dizen Delini, et es de los reyes de India et tiene muy grandes tierras et muy pobladas et muy ricas. Las que yo andude son nueve ciudades muy grandes, que les dizen Noncla, et Chequimo, et Demonela, et Coximocha, et Granbaet, et Ganabrat, et Mahobar, et Gomar, et Colon.[177] E sabed que en este reynado de Lini fructifica la pimienta et el gengibre et la gualoc et otras muchas especies, et cojen dellas grand muchedunbre que lievan por todo el mundo. E a esta provincia llaman India la arenosa. Et las gentes deste reynado son negros de color et usan todos traer arcos turques. Et son gentes de buenas memorias et sabios en todos los saberes. E las señales deste rrey es un pendon de plata con un baston de oro tal. [LXXXVI]

E parti del reynado de Dilini et entré en el regnado de Viguy, que es otrosi ribera del Mar de India. Et es tierra muy rica et abondada de todos los bienes. Las ciudades que yo andude en el reynado de Viguy son estas: Panora, Frumisia, et Tusi, Artillo, et Corsa, et Rusna, et Armonea, et Androvar, et Moncaspi, et Pascar.[178] Apres deste reynado es una ysla en el Mar de India que dizen Sagela en que ay una grand ciudad et rica.[179] E en esta ysla ay almadenes donde sacan oro et plata et otros metales, et sacan piedras rubiis muy gordas et otras pequeñas, et otras. En este reynado es otrosy un grand monte en que es una rica ciudad que dizen Baxaja. E en este monte otrosy ay almadenes de todos los metales, et prinçipal mente sacan muy gordas esmeraldas. Este reynado parte con el imperio de Armalet,[180] et con el reyno de Lini, et con el Mar de India. E sabed que este Mar de India es un braço que entra del grand Mar Oriental,[181] e dizen algunos que atraviesa toda la tierra fasta el Mar Occidental. E los sabios dizen le el Mar Meridional. E deste mar fasta el Polo Antartico es una grand tierra que es la deçima parte de la faz de la tierra, e quando el sol es en Tropico de Capricornio pasa el sol sobre las cabeças de los pobladores, a los

---

[177] The traveler crosses the Arabian Sea to India, and treks to Delhi (here, Delini) and other cities of the kingdom.

[178] Jiménez de la Espada (245) conjectures that the Kingdom of Viguy was between Delhi and the Bay of Bengal.

[179] The present-day island of Sri Lanka.

[180] The identity of this kingdom is difficult to determine.

[181] The Pacific.

of God's commandments, except that they do not do harm to one another. And I departed Sabba and headed for the city of Hormixio of which I told above, and I stayed there for a time. And from there I went with merchants a long way and we reached a kingdom they call Delini, and it belongs to the kings of India and has many great inhabited and rich lands. The ones I traveled are nine very large cities that they call Noncla, and Chequimo and Demonela and Coximocha and Granbaet and Ganabrat and Mahobar and Gomar and Colon. And know that in this kingdom of Lini pepper and ginger and *gualoc* and many other spices grow, and they harvest a great amount of them that they take all over the world. And they call this province India the Sandy. And the people of this kingdom are black in color and they all use Turkish bows. And they are people of good memory and are wise in all kinds of knowledge. And the insignia of this king is a silver flag with a gold pale, like this. [LXXXVI]

And I departed the kingdom of Dilini and entered the kingdom of Viguy, which is also on the shores of the Sea of India. And it is a rich land abundant in all things. The cities in which I was in the kingdom of Viguy are these: Panora, Frumisia, and Tusi, Artillo, and Corsa and Rusna and Armonea and Androvar and Moncaspi and Pascar. Beyond this kingdom is an island in the Sea of India that they call Sagela on which there is a great and rich city. And on this island there are mines where they get gold and silver and other metals, and they mine very large and some smaller rubies and other stones. And in this kingdom is also a great mountain in which there is a rich city they call Baxaja. And in this mountain there are also mines of all metals, and they principally mine very large emeralds. This kingdom borders on the Empire of Armalet and with the kingdom of Lini, and with the Sea of India. And note that this Sea of India is a branch that enters the great Eastern Sea, and some say that it crosses the whole Earth up to the Western Sea. And the wise men call it the South Sea. And from this sea to the Antarctic Pole there is a great expanse of land that is one tenth of the face of the Earth, and when the Sun is in the Tropic of Capricorn it passes over the heads of the inhabitants, which the wise men call the

quales llaman los sabios antipodas.[182] Et son gentes negras quemadas de la grand calentura del sol, pero que es tierra en que son muchas aguas que salen del Polo Antartico. Et llaman los sabios a esta tierra Trapovana,[183] et confina con la ysla de Java et llega fasta el poniente, pero que traviesa por medio de un braço del mar grande que çircunrrodea toda la tierra et metese en el Mar de India. E sabed que en la ysla de Java et Trapovana son quarenta et çinco regiones muy grandes, et lo mas destas tierras es deshabitado por la muy grand calentura del sol, pero que en lo que es poblado cojen mucha pimienta et muchas otras espeçias. Et aqui son los grandes grifos et las grandes cocatrizes. E el rey dende ha por señales un pendon de plata con un baston de oro tal. [LXXXVII]

Dende parti del reynado de Viguy et pasé un golfo del Mar de India que dizen el Golfo de Bangalia, por que en la ribera del es una rica ciudad que dizen Bangala del imperio de Armelet, et es cabeça de rreynado. E dende pasé al reynado de Oxanap que es otrosy ribera del Mar de India. E son en este reynado quatro ciudades grandes. La primera es Moroa, et Cortomar, et Sorfaxa, et Xaloat.[184] E esta Xaloat confina con el imperio de Catayo, e en su ribera deste Xaloat es el Mar Verde,[185] que es un golfo que entra del Mar de India entre este Oxanap et la ysla de Java. El Rey de Oxanap ha por señales un pendon de plata con un baston de oro tal. [LXXXVIII]

D'alli parti del reynado de Oxanap et entré en una nao con mercadores, et travesamos el Mar Verde. Et aportamos a la insula de Java que es dentro en el Mar de India, et es muy grand ysla que ha en luengo quarenta jornadas. E son en esta ysla tres rreynos muy grandes. Al uno dizen Mogoles, et al otro Javales, et al otro Manbrot.[186] E es tierra muy poblada, pero que no ay ciudades por que todos los moradores biven en los canpos, et cogen muchas especias, et mucha pimienta, et muchas gomas odoriferas. Como quier que es tierra muy caliente. Et las gentes son negras et adoran al Enperador de Catayo, cuyos vasallos son. Et traen su ymagen en los pendones desta manera.[187] [LXXXIX]

---

[182] The antipodeans, other creatures of medieval lore, resided at the other extreme of the Earth and were black from over-exposure to the sun.

[183] According to Jiménez de la Espada (261), Trapovana is Australia; Markham (43, n.2) is probably correct in his assertion that it is Sumatra; he states that the name Taprobana originally referred to Sri Lanka, but during the Middle Ages is was applied to Sumatra.

[184] The Kingdom of Oxanap is probably Burma.

[185] The sea referred to could be the South China, which is in the area described here.

[186] Mogoles is probably named for the race of people who inhabited it.

[187] N and R show the Emperor seated, with a sword in his right hand and a sphere in his left. The outlined, horizontal flag is left blank in S, but Markham (plate 16, facing p. 40) illustrates a vertical banner with the Emperor as just described, and it labels it with S.

antipodeans. And they are black people, burnt from the great heat of the sun, but it is a land in which there are many waters that come from the Antarctic Pole. And the wise men call this land Trapovana, and it borders on the island of Java and extends westward, but it crosses through a branch of the great sea that surrounds all the land and flows into the Sea of India. And note that in this island of Java and Trapovana there are forty-five very large regions, and the largest of these lands is uninhabited because of the great heat of the sun, but in the inhabited part they harvest a lot of pepper and many other spices. And here can be found large griffins and crocodiles. And the king has as his insignia a silver flag with a gold pale, like this. [LXXXVII]

From there I departed the kingdom of Viguy and passed a gulf of the Sea of India that they call the Gulf of Bangalia because on its shore is a rich city that they call Bangala of the Empire of Armelet, and it is the capital of the kingdom. And from there I went to the kingdom of Oxanap that is also on the shores of the Sea of India. And in this kingdom there are four large cities. The first is Moroa, and Cortomar and Sorfaxa and Xaloat. And this Xaloat borders on the Empire of Catayo, and on the shores of the Xaloat is the Green Sea, which is a gulf that enters the Sea of India between this Oxanap and the island of Java. The King of Oxanap has as his insignia a silver flag with a gold pale, like this. [LXXXVIII]

From there I departed the kingdom of Oxanap and embarked a ship with merchants, and we crossed the Green Sea. And we took port at the island of Java that is in the Sea of India, and it is a great island that is forty-days' journey long. And there are three great kingdoms on this island. They call one Mogoles, and the other Javales, and the other Manbrot. And it is an inhabited land, but there are no cities because all the inhabitants live in the countryside and harvest many spices, and a lot of pepper and fragrant gums. Nevertheless it is a very hot land. And the people are black and worship the Emperor of Catayo, whose vassals they are. And they have his image on their flags, in this manner. [LXXXIX]

Sali de la ysla de Java et tornéme al rreyno de Oxanap, et tomé camino por la tierra al imperio de Armalet, que tiene muy grandes provincias et muchas çibdades. Las çibdades que yo andude son estas: la primera et la mayor do coronan los reyes es Canbalech, que es cabeça del inperio, et es una de las grandes çibdades del mundo; e otra que dizen Orga, et otra que dizen Balaxia donde es un almaden donde sacan los balaxes, et otra que dizen Menoar, et Almodasi, et Laçeria, et Noranda, et Rafama.[188] E este imperio parte con el rreyno de Lini, et con el rreyno de Viguy, et con el Golfo de Vangala, et con el imperio de Catayo. Et las señales deste imperio son un pendon de plata con un baston de oro tal. [XC]

Parti del imperio de Armalet et fuy me por la tierra muy grand camino, e como quier que es muy poblado de gentes et de ganados, pero que no ay çibdades nin villas por que todos biven en los canpos. Et llegué al imperio de Catayo, et todas las mas de sus çibdades son ribera del Mar Oriental que se tiene con el Mar de India. E este Mar Oriental es todo baxios et yslas, et dende en adelante contra el levante non ay nuevas de ningunas tierras salvo aguas como en el poniente. E sabed que Catayo es el cabo de la faz de la tierra en la liña de España, et parte con el imperio de Armalet a la parte del poniente, et al levante con el Mar Oriental, e a la parte del nort parte con los Montes Caspios que tienen la Tartaria çercada.[189] E las çibdades que yo ay andude del imperio de Catayo son estas: Solin, et Godiana, et Mago-diana, et Morrosia, et Facolisia, et Dardasan, et Tordaor, et Bocarda, et As-tania, et Longavisa.[190] E rriega se este imperio de tres rrios muy grandes que nascen de los Montes Caspios, que se parten en muchas partidas. El mayor destos rrios dizen el flumen Magot por que nasce apres del castillo de Magot, que es una de las puertas de la Tartaria cercada. Este flumen Magot entra en el Mar Verde, et los otros dos rrios en el Mar de Java. Llaman a este emperador Gosnian Imperator Morroy, Grand Can, Señor de la parte de oriente.[191] E sus señales son un pendon de oro et en medio un em-perador asentado con paños blancos, et tiene corona imperial en la cabeça, et en la mano un arco torque, et en la otra mano una mançana de oro desta manera. [XCI]

---

[188] The first city named is perhaps the present-day Beijing; the rest are difficult to identify.

[189] The Caspians here described refer to a mountain range in Central Asia which include the Himalayas and the Caucasus.

[190] Solin was the capital of this empire, either Beijing or near it in the estimation of Markham (71).

[191] Jiménez de la Espada (162–63) guesses that the title could mean "Great Emperor of Muren" (a Tartar region) but offers no further identification of the person.

I left the island of Java and turned to the kingdom of Oxanap, and followed the land route to the empire of Armalet, which has many great provinces and many cities. The cities that I traveled are these: the first and largest, where they crown their kings, is Canbalech, which is the capital of the empire, and it is one of the greatest cities in the world; they call the other Orga, and the other they call Balaxia, where there is a mine where they get rubies, and another they call Menoar, and Almodasi and Laçeria and Noranda and Rafama. And this empire borders the Kingdom of Lini and the Kingdom of Viguy and the Gulf of Bangalia, and the Empire of Catayo. And the insignia of this empire is a silver flag with a gold pale, like this. [XC]

I departed the Empire of Armalet and went by land a great distance, and although it is very populated with people and cattle, there are nevertheless no cities or towns because everyone lives in the countryside. And I reached the Empire of Catayo, and most of its cities are on the shores of the Eastern Sea that borders the Sea of India. And this Eastern Sea is all sandbanks and islands, and from there on eastward there is no news of any lands, only waters as in the west. And know that Catayo is the end of the face of the Earth in the line of España, and it borders on the empire of Armalet on the western side, and in the east with the Eastern Sea, and in the north with the Caspios Mountains that have Tartaria surrounded. And the cities that I traveled in the Empire of Catayo are these: Solin and Godiana and Magodiana and Morrosia and Facolisia and Dardasan and Tordaor and Bocarda, and Astania and Longavisa. And three very large rivers, which originate in the Caspios Mountains, irrigate this empire, and they branch into many parts. The largest of these rivers they call the River Magot because it originates beyond the castle of Magot, which is one of the entrances to encircled Tartaria. This River Magot enters the Green Sea, and the other two rivers [enter] the Java Sea. They call this emperor Gosnian Imperator Morroy, Great Can, Lord of the East. And his insignia is a gold flag and in its center an emperor seated with white clothing, and he has an imperial crown on his head, and in his hand a Turkish bow, and in the other hand a gold apple, in this manner. [XCI]

Los caminos çiertos para Catayo son dos. El uno es por Costantinopla et travesar el Mar Mayor, et entrar por el Mar de Letana, et entrar por tierra de Avegazia, et dende entrar por tierra del Rey David, et pasar apres de Armenia la Mayor, et atravesar todo el rreyno de Armenia la Mayor, et yr al Puerto del Fierro, et desi entrar en el Mar de Sara, et yr a la Ysla de Janula por el Golfo de Monimenti, et salir en la çibdad de Trastago, et dende tomar camino para Norgançia, et dende travesar los Montes Caspios, et desi a la çibdad de Cato, et dende al rreynado de Bocarin, et atravesar toda Asia que non fallara çibdades nin villas fasta el imperio de Catayo.[192] El otro camino es entrar en el Mar Mediterraneo et yr a la ysla de Chipre, et dende a Armenia la Mayor, et dende a la çibdad de Savasco que es en la Turquia, et yr camino fasta el rrio Eufrates et travesallo en la çibdad de Argot, et travesar el imperio de Mesopotania, et desi llegar al rrio de Cur et travesarlo por el rreyno de la Eglesia, que es el imperio de Persia, et travesar toda Persia et yr por la çibdad de Toris, et dexar el Mar de Sara a la parte siniestra, et travesar todo el rreyno de Siras, que no ay çibdad nin villas, et travesar otrosi el rreynado de Sarmagant, et yr siempre contra el levante por el rreynado de Sçim. Esta Sçim no es de la que de suso fablamos, por que la otra Sçim es en India la alta et confina con el Mar Oriental, el qual confina con el imperio de Catayo. Pero que Sçim fasta Catayo non ay çibdad nin villa por que los moradores biven todos en los canpos.[193]

Parti del imperio de Catayo contra el nort et el flumen Magot arriba, et andude sesenta et çinco jornadas et non fallé villa nin çibdad, pero que la tierra es toda poblada de gentes et de ganados, et es toda la tierra llana et non ay piedras, nin arbores, nin las gentes comen pan nin fructos, salvo tan sola mente carne et leche, pero siembran una semiente que dizen monos et es asi como ajonjoli. Et siembranla en qual quier parte del año et nasce luego et cojenla fasta treinta dias. La cojen grand muchedunbre della. E desta monos lançan en la leche et cuezenla et fazen sabrosos manjares que comen todos, et dan a los viandantes. E estas gentes han muchos cavallos sin cuenta, et no comen çevada por que la no ay, mas comen yerva verde et seca. E ay grand muchedunbre por que es la tierra muy tenplada. Desi llegué a los Montes Caspios al castillo de Magot. E sabed que estos montes

---

[192] The first route to Cathay begins in Constantinople, crosses the Black Sea, passes the Sea of Azov (the old Sea of Tana) and Armenia, enters the Caspian Sea (Jiménez de la Espada, n.L), heads for the Island of Kulaly in the Caspian, then arrives in China, where it crosses the Himalayas and continues by traversing the rest of Asia to Cathay.

[193] The other route to Cathay passes Cyprus, Armenia, and Turkey on the way to the banks of the Euphrates, crosses Iraq to the Tigris River, passes through Iran and its old capital Tabriz, continues through Samarkand (Uzbekistan), then heads east, finally reaching Cathay.

There are two certain routes to Catayo. One is through Constantinopla, crossing the Great Sea, and entering the Letana Sea, and entering the land of Avegazia, and from there entering the land of King David, and then passing Armenia Major and crossing the whole kingdom of Armenia Major, and going to the Port Fierro, and from there entering the Sea of Sara, then going to the island of Janula through the Gulf of Monimenti, and ending up in the city of Trastago, and then taking the road to Norgançia, and then crossing the Caspios Mountains, and from there to the city of Cato, and from there to the kingdom of Bocarin, and crossing all of Asia where you will not find cities nor towns until the Empire of Catayo. The other route is entering the Mediterraneo Sea and going to the island of Chipre, and from there to Armenia Major, and from there to the city of Savasco that is in Turquia, and going along until the River Eufrates and crossing it in the city of Argot, and crossing the empire of Mesopotania, and from there reaching the River Cur and crossing it in the kingdom of Eglesia, which is in the empire of Persia, and crossing all of Persia and going through the city of Toris, and leaving the Sea of Sara on your left, and crossing the whole kingdom of Siras, where there are no cities or towns, and also crossing the Kingdom of Sarmagant, and going always eastward through the Kingdom of Sçim. This Sçim is not the one we mentioned above, because the other Sçim is in High India and borders on the Eastern Sea, which borders on the Empire of Catayo. But from Sçim to Catayo there is no city nor town because the inhabitants live in the country.

I departed the Empire of Catayo going north, up the River Magot, and I traveled sixty-five days and did not find a town nor city, but the land is inhabited with people and cattle, and it is all flat land and there are no stones, nor trees, nor do the people eat bread or fruit, except only meat and milk, but they sow a seed they call *monos*, and it is like sesame. And they sow it at any time of the year and it then grows and they reap it after thirty days. They harvest a great amount of it. And they put this *monos* in milk and cook it and make delicious dishes that everyone eats, and they give it to travelers. And these people have numerous horses, and they do not eat barley because there is none, but they eat green and dry grass. And there is abundance because it is a very temperate land. From there I reached the Caspios Mountains and the castle of Magot. And know that these

son muy altos sin mesura et çircunrrodean la Tartaria de mar a mar, et asy que no ay mas de una sola entrada muy angosta. E de una parte desta entrada es un castillo todo de piedra magnita ferrea, todo entero, que lo fizo desta manera la natura, et confina con las nuves. E del pie del sale el flumen Magoti. E luego de la otra parte es otro castillo que dizen Got, desa mesma piedra et tan alto commo el otro que dizen Magot. E son estos castillos en çima muy altos et muy anchos, de manera que en cada uno pueden morar diez mill omes. E entre el un castillo et el otro estan las puertas del fierro, que es la entrada de la Tartaria çercada. Et esta su figura de Got et Magot.[194]

E dentro de aquellos montes es toda la tierra llana sin piedras et sin arbores, et tierra muy tenplada et abondada de muchos ganados. Et ay en luengo çient jornadas et en ancho setenta, et es todo çercado destos Montes Caspios. Et de la parte oriental çerca la toda la mar, et otrosi muy grandes roquedales. Dentro desta Tartaria son muchedunbre de gentes sin cuenta, et non guardan ningund mandamiento de Dios salvo non fazer mal a otro. Et son gentes muy esentas et fuertes lidiadores de pie et de cavallo, en tal manera que el Grant Alexandre no los pudo conquerir nin les pudo entrar aquellos montes, pero que los ençerró et atapóles las puertas del fierro con grandes peñas, en tal manera que estodieron gran tienpo en aquel ençerramiento. E despues desto delibraron se de aquel ençerramiento et salieron et conquirieron muy gran partida del mundo.[195] Por que de aquel linaje salieron todos los del imperio de Catayo, maguer agora son contrarios. E dese linaje salieron los del imperio de Armalet, et del imperio de Aravia, et de Mesopotania, et todos los persianos, et los del imperio de Sara, asi turcos commo tartaros, et saraynos, et godos, como quier que algunos dellos se tornaron a la ley de Abraham et otros se tornaron moros. E dizen los sabios de la Tartaria que quando se conplieren los siete mil años de la era de Adam serán señores de toda la faz de la tierra, et que farán tornar todas las gentes del mundo a su ley et a su libertad. E çierto ellos non han ley ninguna, nin guardan ningund mandamiento de Dios salvo non fazer mal a otro. E esta Tartaria çerrada es la quarta parte de la faz de toda la tierra. Et en medio desta tierra es una laguna de mar que dizen Mare Tabasur.[196] Et las gentes

---

[194] In *R* only, there is a sketch of the castle described here.

[195] Gog and Magog, two tribes led by Satan, were thought to be in the north of Asia. The Bible mentions them in several places, warning that on Judgement Day they would bring about the destruction of the world. Legend has it that Alexander the Great built walls of bronze, pitch, and brimstone to enclose these people, and medieval maps generally show Gog and Magog behind such walls. In the Middle Ages many different versions of this apocryphal story appear, including one which has Alexander enclosing these people behind the walls (Wright 72–73, 287–88; Markham 45, n.2).

[196] Markham (48) identifies this body of water as "Lake Lob."

mountains are very high, without measure, and they surround Tartaria from sea to sea, so that there is no more than one narrow entrance. And on one side of this entrance is a castle all of magnet iron stone, all of it entirely, since nature made it that way, and it reaches to the clouds. And from its foot the River Magoti flows. And then on the other side is another castle they call Got, made of that same stone and as high as the other that they call Magot. And these castles are very high and narrow on the top, so that on each one 10,000 men can live. And between one and the other castle there are iron gates, which are the entrance to encircled Tartaria. And this is the image of Got and Magot.

And within those mountains there is just flat land without stones and without trees, and [it is] a very temperate and abundant land with many cattle. And it is in length a 100-days' journey and in width sixty, and it is totally surrounded by these Caspios Mountains. And on the eastern side the sea surrounds all of it, and also many great rocky places. Within this Tartaria there are innumerable persons, and they do not keep any of God's commandments except not to harm one another. And they are very free and strong fighters on foot and on horse, so that Alexander the Great could not conquer them nor enter those mountains, but he enclosed them and shut the iron gates with large rocks so that they were enclosed for a long time. And after this they freed themselves from this enclosure and got out and conquered a great part of the world. Despite the fact that from that lineage came all of the empire of Catayo, they are now hostile to one another. And from this lineage came all of the Empire of Armalet, and the Empire of Arabia, and of Mesopotania, and all the Persians, and those of the Empire of Sara, Turks as well as Tartars, and Saracens and Goths, although some of them converted to the law of Abraham and others became Moors. And the wise men of Tartaria say that when 7000 years of the era of Adam are completed, they will be lords of the whole face of the Earth and they will make all the people in the world convert to their law and their freedom. And it is true that they have no religion at all, nor do they keep any of God's commandments, except not to harm others. And this encircled Tartaria is one fourth of the face of the Earth. And in the middle of this land is a great lagoon they call the Tabasur Sea. And the people of this land they call

desta tierra llaman mogoles et a la tierra dizen Tierra de Mogolin, et Tierra de Tagojar, et Tierra de Got et Magot. E con estos montes confina el imperio de Catayo. Et en este castillo de Magot moré un tienpo por que veya et oya cada dia cosas maravillosas. E ala parte del nort confinan con la Tartaria çerrada las tierras de Albizibi,[197] que son tierras yermas et deshabitadas, pero que en algunos lugares habitan gentes, et son omes viles et comen la carne et los pescados crudos et han los rostros luengos como canes, pero que son blancos et fazen todas las cosas que veen fazer, et llamanlos sinofalos.[198] Et yo vi uno dellos en la çibdad de Norgançio. En el imperio de Catayo ay un rreynado que dizen Sçim que confina con el rreyno de Sarmagant, et con el rreyno de Bocarin, et con el rreyno de Trimit.[199] E este rreyno de Sçim es en India la alta, que confina con el Mar Oriental que es fin de la tierra. E deste rreyno de Sçim sale el grand monte Cancasum que traviesa desde'l Mar Oriental fasta el Mar de India la Baxa. E el rreyno de Trimit es todo çercado de montes de que nasçen muchas fuentes et rios. Et es tierra muy tenplada et muy egualada, de manera que los omes que alli biven et nasçen son de grand vida que biven mas de dozientos años. Et son omes de buenos entendimientos, et sanas memorias, et han profundas sçiençias, et biven por ley. Et dizen que los omes del mundo que primera mente ovieron sçientias et saberes que fueron estos, et de aqui los ovieron los persianos, et por eso meresçieron la nobleza mas que todos los otros omes. Por que no se egualaron a estos en sçientia nin en saberes, et por esto meresçieron la nobleza sobre todos. E esto es por que son en el comienço del oriente de lo poblado, et las mas de sus villas et sus grandes çibdades, et la rayz deste rreynado es en la clima de medio, onde son las naturas tenpladas. Et tiempran se y los cuerpos et los elementos, et alegranse y et estiendense y los spiritus. Et por ende han mejores entendimientos et mas sanas memorias, et por esto meresçieron la mayor nobleza. En pos estos son los de India que son sola liña equinoçial. E maguer la su tierra es de grand calentura, pero las mas de sus villas son rribera del mar et son muchas yslas, et por eso el ayre resçibe humidad del mar con que se tiempra la sequedad et la calentura. Et con esto se fezieron de fermosos

---

[197] Jiménez de la Espada (259) asks whether this might be Siberia, while Markham (71) thinks it could be part of Mongolia.

[198] The cynocephali were reputed to have the heads and paws of dogs, and to bark as well. They were mentioned by Pliny and Solinus, and drawings of them often appeared on mappae-mundi. *R* includes an illustration of two of these creatures.

[199] Trimit is Tibet. According to Markham (49, n.3) this is the earliest European account of the Tibetans that exists.

Mogols and they call the land Land of Mogolin, and Land of Tagojar, and Land of Got and Magot. And these mountains border the Empire of Catayo. And in this castle of Magot I lived for a time because every day I saw and heard marvelous things. And to the north the lands of Albizibi border on encircled Tartaria, which are barren and uninhabited lands, but people live in some places, and they are vile men and they eat raw meat and fish and have long faces like dogs, but they are white and do everything they see done, and they call them cynocephali. And I saw one of them in the capital of Norgançio. In the Empire of Catayo there is a kingdom they call Sçim that borders on the Kingdom of Sarmagant and the Kingdom of Bocarin and the Kingdom of Trimit. And this Kingdom of Sçim is in Upper India, that borders on the Eastern Sea, which is the end of the earth. And from the Kingdom of Sçim there emerges the great mountain Cancasum that crosses from the Eastern Sea to the Sea of Lower India. And this Kingdom of Trimit is totally surrounded by mountains from which many springs and rivers originate. And it is a very temperate and healthy land, so that the men that live and are born here have a long life and live more than 200 years. And they are men of good understanding and healthy memory, and they are very learned in science, and live by the law of religion. And they say that these were the first men in the world to have science and knowledge, and the Persians got them here, and for that reason they merited nobility more than any other men because they were not equalled in science nor in other knowledge, and for that reason they merited nobility above all others. And this is because they are at the beginning of the east of populated lands, and the majority of their towns and their great cities, and the root of this kingdom is in the temperate climate, where nature is temperate. And their bodies and elements are tempered there and they are happy there and it has extended to their spirits. And therefore they have better understanding and healthier memories, and for this reason they merited greater nobility. After them are those from India, that are below the celestial equator. And although their land is very hot, the majority of their towns are on the shores of the sea and there are many islands, and for this reason the air receives moisture from the sea with which the dryness and the heat are tempered. And in this way they derived beautiful bodies and

cuerpos et de apuestas formas et de leznes cabellos, et non les faze al la calentura salvo que los faze baços de color. India la Alta confina con el Mar Oriental et es llamado Mare Sericun o Mare Cancasur por los Montes Caucasos.[200] E en este mar es una grand ysla que dizen Insula Manzie, e despues desta es fallada otra que dizen Insula Paradisa.[201] Et de aqui se departe un grand golfo que entra por la tierra et traviésala toda fasta que entra en el poniente. Et llaman lo el Mar de India. E rribera deste mar es India la alta et India la arenosa et todas las çibdades de Nubia. E sabed que el agua deste mar es caliente commo agua de baño, et crian se en él muy grandes pescados. E los otros dos rreynados son en la partida oçidental del poblado. El primero dellos es la tierra de Babilonia et de Persia, que son tenprada gente por que son en medio de las climas en el lugar do son las naturas et las conplisiones tenpladas ca son en el comienço del medio oçidental del poblado. E por eso son otrosi sotiles et de buenas memorias, et entremeten se en las sçiençias et de los saberes et han señorio et setas et leyes. Et por esto meresçieron la nobleza, mas por que son en la partida occidental menguales la calentura ya quanto. E por esto son en el segundo grado de la nobleza de los orientales. E por esto los rromanos que son en la clima quinta et toman de la sexta ya quanto, et han señorio et ley et sçiençias et saberes, como quier que menos que los otros. E por eso son ufanosos et orgullosos et libradores et guerreros et soberbios. Mas los de Sçim meresçieron la nobleza sobre todos. Et en este rreyno de Sçim fallé quatro çibdades grandes. A la una dizen Catigora, et a la otra Çebia, et a la otra Cuçi, et Baçerta.[202] E las señales del rrey de Sçim son un pendon de plata et en medio la figura del sol tal. [XCII]

Çiertas despues desto parti me del castillo de Magot, donde moré un tienpo, et vine con otras conpañas contra el poniente treynta et çinco jornadas al rreynado de Bocarin, a do mora siempre el rrey. Et es una çibdad muy grande, et corre por ella un rrio que nasçe de los Montes Caspios. E en todo este rreyno non ay mas çibdades por que los pobladores del moran en los canpos con sus ganados. Aqui fallé mercadores cristianos que venian de Catayo, et vyn con ellos treynta et çinco jornadas a otra çibdad que dizen Cato, que es cabeça del rreynado que tiene muy grandes tierras, pero todos los moradores biven en los campos salvo una çibdad sola, do mora el

---

[200] This body of water seems to be the South China Sea.

[201] The first is Manji, followed by Taiwan.

[202] Markham (50, n.1) believes that Sçim might be a legendary kingdom or perhaps the old realm of Siam.

elegant forms and fine hair, and the heat does nothing else to them except make them brown in color. High India borders on the Eastern Sea and is called Mare Sericun or Mare Cancasur for the Caucasos Mountains. And in this sea there is a large island they call Insula Manzie, and after this one is found another they call Insula Paradisa. And from here flows a great gulf that penetrates the land and crosses it completely until it enters the west. And they call it the Sea of India. And on the shores of the sea is High India and India the Sandy and all the cities of Nubia. And know that the water of this sea is as hot as bath water, and many large fish are bred there. And the other two kingdoms are on the western side of the land. The first of these is the land of Babilonia and of Persia, [in] which [there] are temperate people because they are in the middle of the climates in the place where their natures and dispositions are temperate, for they are at the entrance to the middle west of the land. And for this reason they are also keen-minded and of good memory, and they study the sciences and other knowledge and they have government and sects and religions. And for this reason they merited nobility, because they are on the western side, suffering a bit less heat. And for this reason they are in the second grade of eastern nobility. And for this reason the Romans, that are in the fifth climate and even the sixth somewhat, have government and religion and sciences and knowledge, although less than others. And for that reason they are arrogant and proud and free and warlike and haughty. But those from Sçim merited nobility above all others. And in this kingdom of Sçim I found four large cities. They call one Catigora, and the other Çebia, and the other Cuçi, and Baçerta. And the insignia of the King of Sçim is a silver flag with a figure of the sun in the center. [XCII]

After this I departed the castle of Magot, where I resided for a time, and came westward with some companions thirty-five days to the Kingdom of Bocarin, where the king always resides. And it is a very large city, and through it runs a river that originates in the Caspios Mountains. And in all this kingdom there are no other cities because its inhabitants live in the countryside with their cattle. There I encountered some Christian merchants who were coming to Catayo, and I came with them thirty-six days to another city they call Cato, which is the capital of the kingdom and has many great lands, but all the inhabitants live in the countryside except for one city where the king resides. And this kingdom of Cato borders the

rrey. Et este rreynado de Cato confina con el inperio de Medio que es
entre Nori et Levante, que dizen Inperio Medorun. Estos dos reyes han por
señales sendos pendones amarillos con estrellas blancas muchas. [XCIII]

Desi partimos del rreynado de Cato et andodimos muy grand camino
que no fallamos villa nin çibdad, pero que es la tierra poblada de gentes et
de ganados. Et fallamos un monte muy alto que se aparta de los Montes
Caspios et llega fasta el Mar de Sara. Este monte es en luengo çiento et
veynte çinco jornadas, que atraviesa Asia fasta el Mar de Sara. Et atrave-
samos el dicho monte por un puerto muy alto et andodimos muy gran camino por una tierra muy abondada, maguer non ay çibdades nin villas, fasta
que llegamos a una grand çibdad que dizen Norgançio, que es del imperio
de Uxbeco.[203] Et corre por esta çibdad un grand rrio que dizen Organçio
que nasçe de aquel monte que se aparta de los Montes Caspios. E el rrey
desta Norgançia ha por señales un pendon blanco con estas señales bermejas,
Uxbeco Enperador de Sara atal.[204] [XCIV]

Partimos de Norgançio et andudimos treynta jornadas que non ay villa
nin çibdad, pero que ay abondo de leche et carnes et de monos. Et llegamos
al Mar de Sara a una çibdad que dizen Raansinlia, que es çerca del Golfo de
Monimenti.[205] Et alli moré un tienpo. E despues entré en la Mar de Sara
en una nave de comaneses cristianos et travesamos todo el mar et aportamos
en una çibdad que dizen Godaspi, que es del imperio de Benascayt, Emperador de Persia.[206] E apres della entra en la mar un grand rrio que dizen
Tigris, que nasçe de los Montes del Toro. Et entré por aquel rrio arriba por
la rribera fasta que llegué a los Montes del Toro, que son en medio de la faz
de la tierra et son en el imperio de Persia. De los quales montes nasçen
quatro rrios muy grandes. Al uno dizen el flumen Tigris, que entra en el
Mar de Sara entre dos çibdades que dizen Godaspi et Sarmagante, que son

---

[203] The Kingdom of Shah Usbek (1292–1341) figures on the Catalan Atlas, where it covers
the territory between the Caspian Sea and the Ural Mountains. Nearby is the river Amu Dar'ya;
on its shores is a city called Urgench, which resolves the identity of the river Organçio and the
city Norgançio or Norgançia.

[204] According to Pasch (29), the sign on this banner, as depicted in all three codices, is that
of the Uzbek emperors.

[205] Markham (51) says that this city might be the present-day Astrakhan and the gulf in
which it is situated may be Mertvoy, which is just across the Caspian.

[206] Benascayt is Abu Said Jan Bahadur, Sultan of Persia from 1317 to 1335 (Markham 51,
n.8, and Jiménez de la Espada 166–67). The city referred to was apparently somewhere on the
Caspian.

On the plains of Russia lived a tribe called the Komans (Cumans) who dwelled in tents and
ate a diet of raw meat, rice, and milk. They are mentioned in several places, including Benjamin
of Tudela's travel account (Wright 331–14).

Empire of Medio which is between Nori and Levante, which they call the Medorun Empire. These two kings have as their insignia each a yellow flag with many white stars. [XCIII]

From there we departed the kingdom of Cato and traveled a long way and did not find a town or city, but it is a land very populated by people and cattle. And we found very high mountains that juts off the Caspios Mountains and extend to the Sea of Sara. This mountain is in length a 125-days' journey and crosses Asia all the way to the Sea of Sara. And we crossed the aformentioned mountain by a very high pass and traveled a long way through a very abundant land, although there are no cities or towns, until we reached a great city that they call Norgançio, which is in the Empire of Uxbeco. And a great river they call Organçio runs through this city and originates in that mountain that juts from the Caspios Mountains. And the king of this Norgançio has as his insignia a white flag with these vermilion signs, Uxbeco Emperor of Sara, like this. [XCIV]

We departed Norgançio and traveled thirty days without a town or city, but there is an abundance of milk and meats and monkeys. And we reached the Sea of Sara and a city they call Raansinlia, which is near the Gulf of Monimenti. And I stayed there for a time. And later I entered the Sea of Sara in a boat of Christian Komans and we crossed the whole sea and took port in a city they call Godaspi, which belongs to the empire of Benascayt, Emperor of Persia. And beyond it a great river they call the Tigris, which originates in the Toro Mountains, enters the sea. And I went up that river on the shore until I arrived at the Toro Mountains, which are in the center of the face of the Earth and belong to the Empire of Persia. From these mountains originate four very large rivers. They call one the River Tigris, which enters the Sea of Sara between two cities they call Godaspi and

en el imperio de Persia. Al otro dizen Cur,[207] que va por medio de Persia, rribera del qual rrio son muchas çibdades. La primera, que dizen Çensor, es çerca de los Montes del Toro que llaman el rreyno de Eglesia, el qual es poblado de cristianos armenios. Et otra çibdad que dizen Malascort, et otra Masol, otra Orbe, Esustar, et Maxate, et Mahumen, et Brasara, et Aquisio, que es rribera del Mar Negro.[208] E en esta Aquisio fenesçe el imperio de Persia. Al terçero rrio dizen Eufrates, rribera del qual son estas çibdades: Argor, et Nega, et Camar, et Alargeo, et Malaxia Bira. E este rrio se faze tres partes. La una entra en el Mar Rubro, la otra parte va por Aravia et entra en el Mar Negro, e la otra parte va por Damasco et por la tierra de Jafet, et entra en el Mar Medio Terraneo apres de Armenia la Menor. Al quarto rio dizen Surmena, que va por la grand çibdad de Toris et por la Jorgania et entra en el Mar Mayor apres de Trapesonda.[209] Et esta es la figura de los Montes del Toro, et tiene en somo una gran cruz por que sean conosçidos.[210]

Despues desto parti de los Montes del Toro et fuy veer los Montes de Armenia la Mayor, do arribó el arca de Noe quando escapó del general diluvio. Aquel monte es todo de piedra de sal tan blanca como el cristal.[211] E sabed que es una de las montañas altas del mundo et es medio de la faz de la tierra, e ningund omme puede alla sobir maguer fue provado por muchas vezes. E son en el imperio de Persia. E toda en derredor es poblada de cristianos armenios que son la guarda del emperador et fia mucho dellos, ca ellos lo guardan. Et por ellos es el enperador mucho honrado, et ellos son mas validos por él. E sabed que es tierra mucho rica et muy abondada de todas las riquezas que todas las tierras pueden aver. Et deven aver en sy para ser abondados todos los ommes et riquezas que todas las tierras han. E esta es la figura de las montañas de Armenia, ado es el arca de Noe que yo vy, mas es toda desbaratada.[212]

E parti de la Armenia et fuy a la grand çibdad de Toris, que es cabeça del imperio de los persianos. E es una de las grandes çibdades del mundo,

---

[207] Samarkand, in Uzbekistan. The Kura River empties into the Caspian, although it does not cross Persia, as the narrator claims.

[208] Some of the cities named here are apparently along the Tigris River: Masol was probably Al Mawsil (Mosul) in Iraq; Brasara could be Al Basrah. The list ends to the east in Qeshm (Iran) on the Persian Gulf.

[209] A tributary of the Euphrates.

[210] N and R contain illustrations of these mountains.

[211] Medieval accounts differ on whether Mount Ararat was reachable or not, but our narrator now claims to have seen the remains of Noah's ark. John Mandeville also refers to a mountain of rock salt close to this place. See Jiménez de la Espada (167).

[212] In N and R the artists have drawn the mountains mentioned here, atop which is a chest. Apparently the word "arca" was taken quite literally by the illuminators.

Sarmagante, which are in the empire of Persia. They call the other, that goes through the middle of Persia, the Cur, on the shores of which there are many cities. The first, that they call Çensor, is near the Toro Mountains that they call the Kingdom of Eglesia, which is inhabited by Armenian Christians. And another city they call Malascort, and another Masol, another Orbe, Esustar, and Maxate, and Mahumen, and Brasara, and Aquisio, which is on the shores of the Black Sea. And in this Aquisio the Empire of Persia ends. They call the third river Eufrates, on the shores of which are these cities: Argor and Nega and Camar, and Alargeo, and Malaxia Bira. And this river divides into three parts. One enters the Red Sea, the other part goes through Arabia and enters the Black Sea, and the other part goes through Damasco and through the land of Jafet and enters the Medio Terraneo Sea beyond Armenia Minor. They call the fourth river Surmena, which goes through the great city of Toris and through Jorgania and enters the Great Sea beyond Trapesonda. And this is the image of the Toro Mountains, and it has on top a great cross so they can be recognized.

After this I departed the Toro Mountains and went to see the mountain of Armenia Major, where Noah's ark reached when it escaped the general flood. That mountain is all rock salt as white as glass. And know that it is one of the highest mountains in the world and is in the middle of the face of the Earth, and no man can ascend there, although it has been tried many times. And they belong to the Emperor of Persia. And all around it is populated by Armenian Christians that are the Emperor's guards, and he trusts them very much because they guard him. And the Emperor is very honored by them, and they are appreciated by him. And know that it is a rich land and abundant in all things that any land can have. And in order to be so abundant they must have all the men and riches that all lands have. And this is the image of the mountains of Armenia, where Noah's ark is, which I saw, but it is totally destroyed.

And I departed Armenia and went to the great city of Toris, which is the capital of the empire of the Persians. And it is one of the great cities of

et mucho abondada et rica, et es tierra muy tenplada. E por eso los omes de Persia son muy sabios et entendidos en todas las sçientias, e han saberes muy profundos en los juyzios de las estrellas. E el Emperador de Persia ha por señales un pendon de oro et en medio una quadra bermeja tal. [XCV]

Sabed que en Persia nasçen dos fuentes, et cada una dellas faze un grand lago de agua de doze millas en ancho, et sale de cada un lago destos un grand rrio que cada uno dellos traviesa toda Persia. A la una fuente dizen Mar Sargis, et a la otra dizen Mare Argis.[213] Et ayuntan se estos dos rrios et entran en el Mar de India en el Mar Negro. Et a las çibdades que son rriberas destas dos fuentes son Argis, et Caperti, et Salamoda, et Orinorde, et Buxila, et Pastello.[214] Et travesé el dicho rrio de Argis et andude muy grand partida de Persia, et fuy al rreynado de Saldania, que es noble çibdad et rica. E el rrey della ha por señales un pendon de oro et en medio una quadra bermeja tal. [XCVI]

Parti de Saldania et fuy contra el levante con mercadores, et fuy a otra çibdad que dizen Premua del Rey de Persia, et desi a otra que dizen Aba. Et fuy muy grand camino fasta que llegué a la çibdad de Syras, que los tartaros dizen Sarax, a do fenesçe el imperio de Persia.[215] Et es çibdad muy rica et abondada et muy antigua. Et dizen que en esta çibdad fue fallada primera mente la astronomia, que quiere dezir ley de las estrellas, por que esta çibdad es en la liña de la meytad de lo poblado.[216] E las çibdades que yo andude en Persia son estas: Casar, et Seranes, et Thesi, et Spaor, et Jorjaman, et Spalonero, et Saldania, et Toris.[217] E en esta Toris fue coronado Benascayt emperador de Persia. E el su imperio llega desde el Mar de Sara fasta el Mar de India, do es la çibdad de Hormixio, e desde el Mar Mayor fasta Aquisio, que es otrosi el Mar Negro que es en longura veynte çinco jornadas et en ancho desde el rrio Cur fasta la çibdad de Siras, que ay çient jornadas. Benascayt emperador de Persia allegó muy grand hueste et fue a pelear con Uxbeco emperador de Sara. Aqui fueron llegados mas de un cuento et medio de cavallerias. E Benascayt prometio a unos monjes armenios con quien se consejava que si la batalla vençiese, que se tornaria cristiano. Et los cristianos armenios que con el yvan llevaron la cruz en la

---

[213] The first is Lake Oroumieh (in northwest Iran), and the other is Van Gölü (Lake Van), just to the west in present-day Turkey.

[214] Argis (the origin of the name Mare Argis) is today the city of Van. It is difficult to identify the other towns that are said to surround these lakes.

[215] Premua del Rey might be Tehran. From there the traveler would head south for a long way before arriving at Shiraz.

[216] The Catalan Atlas makes the same observation next to the site of this city.

[217] This random selection of cities in Iran seems to include Kazerun, Esfahan, and Tabriz, among others.

the world and it is very abundant and rich and the land is very temperate. And for this reason the men of Persia are very wise and knowledgeable about all the sciences, and they have very profound knowledge about the predictions of the stars. And the Emperor of Persia has as his insignia a gold flag with a vermilion square in the center, like this. [XCV]

Note that two springs originate in Persia, and each one of then forms a great lake of water twelve miles wide, and out of each of these lakes a great river flows and each one crosses all of Persia. They call one spring Mar Sargis, and the other Mar Argis. And these two rivers converge and enter the Sea of India in the Black Sea. And the cities that are on the shore of these two springs are Argis, and Caperti, and Salamoda, and Orinorde, and Buxila, and Pastello. And I crossed the aforementioned River Argis and traveled a great part of Persia, and went to the kingdom of Saldania, which is a noble and rich city. And its king has as his insignia a gold flag with a vermilion square in the center, like this. [XCVI]

I departed Saldania and went eastward with merchants, and I went to another city they call Premua of the King of Persia, and from there to another they call Alba. And I went a long way until I reached the city of Syras, that the Tartars call Sarax, where the Empire of Persia ends. And it is a very rich and abundant and ancient city. And they say that in the city astronomy, which means the law of the stars, was first discovered, because this city is in the line of the middle of the populated land. And the cities I traveled in Persia are these: Casar, and Seranes, and Thesi, and Spaor, and Jorjamen, and Spalonero, and Saldania, and Toris. And in this Toris Benascayt, Emperor of Persia, was crowned. And his empire extends from the Sea of Sara to the Sea of India, where the city of Hormixio is, and from the Great Sea to Aquisio, which is also the Black Sea, that is twenty-five days' journey in length and in width from the River Cur to the city of Siras, which is 100 days. Benascayt the Emperor of Persia assembled a great army and went to do battle with Uxbeco, Emperor of Sara. More than 1,000,000 soldiers came here. And Benascayt promised some Armenian monks from whom he took advice that if he won the battle, he would become a Christian. And the Armenian Christians who went with him carried the

delantera. Et ayudólos Dios et vençieron la batalla, et Uxbeco fue vençido et sus cavallerias, et fuxo, et fueron muertos muchos dellos et captivos, et todos sus reales robados et sus mugeres captivas. Et entróle muy grand partida de la tierra que avia rribera del Mar Mayor. Despues desto unos alhages moros que predicavan cada dia a Benascayt dieron le yervas, et morio.[218] Pero los rreyes de Persia siempre fezieron mucho bien a los cristianos de Armenia et fiaron dellos. Despues desto parti de Persia con mercadores cristianos que venian de Catayo. Et travesamos el rrio Cur por la ysla de Ansera et venimos a la çibdad de Mesopotania, que es del imperio de Baldat. Et parti dende et vine contra el poniente grande camino que non fallé villa nin çibdad, por que los pobladores dende moran todos en los canpos, fasta que llegué al rrio Eufrates. Et travesélo en una çibdad que dizen Malaxia.[219] Et alli se parte un braço deste rrio que viene por Damasco et por la tierra de Jafet et entra en el Mar Mediterraneo apres de Armenia la Menor. Et dende vyn me por el rrio ayuso fasta que llegué a una çibdad que dizen Tripul de la Suria,[220] que es rribera del Mar Mediterraneo. Et entré en una nao de cristianos et vin me para Chipre, et de Chipre vine me a las yslas perdidas de la Romania, que son Ancandia, et dende a la Morea, et de si a Creta, et dende a Negro Ponte. Et dende fuy a un rreynado de griegos que dizen Salonico que parte con Maçedonia, donde fue el Grand Alexandre, et con la montaña de Pirus. E el rrey desta Salonico ha por señales un pendon bermejo con una cruz de oro et quatro eslabones de oro desta manera. [XCVII]

Dende fuy a una çibdad que dizen Galipoli, que es rribera del golfo que entra del Mar Mediterraneo al Mar Mayor. Et por aqui pasaron los françeses quando conquirieron la Suria. E dende fuy por la marisma a una çibdad que dizen Reçira[221] del imperio de Costantinopla. E parti de Reçira et fuy a Costantinopla, una rica çibdad cabeça del imperio do se coronan los rreyes, en la qual es una grande eglesia de Dios que dizen Santa Sofia. Et es muy alta et muy ancha et fermosa, en que ay trezientas et sesenta et seys puertas. Apres della es una torre de piedra que no ha sobida ninguna. En çima desta torre está un cavallero fecho de metal en su cavallo muy grande, et tiene en

---

[218] Markham (54, n.1) states that Abu Said died while bathing in the River Kur, but allows that others believe he was poisoned by his favorite wife. Jiménez de la Espada (168–69) dates the events in the years 1334–35, stating that Abu Said went out to fight against invaders of his realm, but was taken ill because of heat and died while bathing; he also mentions that some writers refer to the poisoning episode, which could be legend.

[219] Malatya is a Turkish city just north of the Euphrates.

[220] Jiménez de la Espada (169) observes that this supposed tributary of the Euphrates is non-existent, and that the traveler could not possibly have arrived at "Tripul de la Suria" (now Tarabulus in Lebanon) in this way.

[221] Heraclea, now only ruins in southwest Turkey.

cross in the front line. And God helped them and they won the battle, and Uxbeco and his soldiers were defeated and he fled, and many of them were killed and taken captive, and all of his military camps were taken and his women taken captive. And [Benascayt] penetrated a long way into the land on the shores of the Great Sea. After this some Moorish Hajjis who preached every day to Benascayt gave him some herbs, and he died. But the kings of Persia always treated the Christians of Armenia well and trusted them. After this I departed Persia with Christian merchants who were coming from Catayo. And we crossed the River Cur near the island of Ansera and came to the city of Mesopotania, which is in the Empire of Baldat. And I departed from there and came westward for a long way and did not find a town or city, because the inhabitants from there live in the countryside, until I arrived at the River Eufrates. And I crossed it in a city they call Malaxia. And there a branch of the river that comes through Damasco and the land of Jafet and enters the Mediterraneo beyond Armenia Minor. And from there I came downriver until I reached a city they call Tripul de la Suria, which is on the shores of the Mediterraneo Sea. And I embarked a boat of Christians and came to Chipre, and from Chipre I came to the lost islands of Romania, which are Ancandia, and from there to Morea, and from there to Creta, and from there to Negro Ponte. And from there I went to the kingdom of the Greeks they call Salonico that borders on Maçedonia, where Alexander the Great was from, and [it also borders] on the mountain Pirus. And the king of this Salonico has as his insignia a vermilion flag with a gold cross and four gold links in this manner. [XCVII]

From there I went to a city they call Galipoli, which is on the shores of the gulf that enters the Mediterraneo Sea and the Great Sea. And the French passed here when they conquered Suria. And from there I went along the coast to a city they call Reçira, of the Empire of Constaninopla. And I departed Reçira and went to Constaninopla, a rich city [which is] the capital where they crown their kings, in which there is a great church of God they call Santa Sophia. It is very tall and very wide and beautiful, and there are 366 doors. Beyond it there is a stone tower that is impossible to climb. On top of this tower is a knight made of metal on his very large horse, and he has on his head an episcopal hat in honor of the Emperor

la cabeça sombrero obispal a honrra del Enperador Costantino. Et tiene la mano derecha tendida demostrando la Turquia, que antigua mente dezian Asia la Menor que es allende de aquel golfo de la mar.[222] E esta es la figura del enperador cavallero en su cavallo et de la torre, como esta que se sigue.[223]

Este Enperador de Constantinopla es muy rico et muy abondado et de muy grandes poderes et de muy grandes gentes et muchas. E el Emperador de Costantinopla ha por señales un pendon a quarterones, los dos quartos blancos con cruzes bermejas, et los otros dos quarterones son bermejos con sendas cruzes de oro et con quatro eslabones de oro desta manera. [XCVIII]

Parti de Costantinopla et entré en la Mar Mayor, et tomé la parte esquierda por la marisma et llegué a un rreynado que dizen Lodomago.[224] Et es tierra muy rrica et abondada. E el rrey dende ha por señales un pendon bermejo con una cruz de oro et quatro eslabones de oro desta manera.[225] [XCIX]

Parti de Lodomago et fuy me para Meseber, et dende a Burna.[226] Aqui es la vera Greçia. Et el imperio de los griegos en Greçia son muchas provinçias departidas, convien a saber: Archadia, Achia, Boeçia, Maçedonia, Cahonia, Leçedomonia, Asalonica, Para, otra Maçedonia, fasta Costantinopla et Tierra de Sufragia et Tierra de Macali. E çerca todas estas tierras un rrio que dizen flumen Pirus, que nasçe de los Montes de Çerva.[227] E el rrey ha por señales un pendon bermejo con una cruz de oro con quatro eslabones de oro tales. [C]

De si parti del rreyno de Meseber et fuy me por la rribera del Mar Mayor a una grand çibdad que dizen Veçina, que confina con la Ungria. En esta Veçina se ayuntan nueve rrios que todos entran en el Mar Mayor. Al primero dizen Turbo, al segundo Danubio, al terçero dizen Orinçinçia, al

---

[222] The statue of Constantine fell during a storm in 1201. Afterwards, a statue of Theodosius was placed there, on a column of silver, which was later used to coin currency. During the fourteenth century, a statue of Justinian occupied this place (Markham 55; Jiménez de la Espada 169–70).

[223] N and R contain drawings of the column, upon which the Emperor on his horse can be seen.

[224] Markham (72) places this kingdom northwest of Constantinople, on the Black Sea.

[225] The flag is divided into four parts. In S, two of the quarters are traversed completely by a cross; in N and R, the crosses are smaller and centered.

[226] The narrator travels north along the west coast of the Black Sea, first to Mesemvria (now Nesebur) and then Varna (both in Bulgaria).

[227] The old provinces of Greece included Arcadia, Achaia, Boeotia, Macedonia, Laconia, Lacedaemonia, Thessaly, and Epirus. Para might be the island Paros. The "other" Macedonia could be the islands in the Aegean and the Turkish coast, land of Mount Mycale, near the island of Samos. The Pirus River is now the Drin (or Drina) between Albania and Herzegovina.

Constantine. And he has his right hand extended pointing to Turquia, which was in ancient times called Asia Minor, which is beyond that gulf of the sea. And this is the image of the knight emperor on his horse and of the tower, like this one that follows.

This Emperor of Constantinopla is very rich and very endowed and has many great powers and very many and very great people. And the Emperor of Constantinopla has as his insignia a quarterly flag, two quarters white with vermilion crosses, and the other two quarters are vermilion, each with a cross of gold and four gold links, in this manner. [XCVIII]

I departed Constantinopla and entered the Great Sea, and went on the left side of the coast and reached a kingdom they call Lodomago. And it is a rich and abundant land. And its king has as his insignia a red flag with a gold cross and four gold links, in this manner. [XCIX]

I departed Lodomago and went to Meseber and from there to Burna. Here is true Greçia. And the empire of the Greeks in Greçia has many scattered provinces, to wit, Archadia, Achia, Boeçia, Maçedonia, Cahonia, Leçedomonia, Asalonica, Para, another Maçedonia, extending to Constan- inopla and the Land of Sufragia and the Land of Macali. And a river they call Pirus, which originates in the Mountains of Çerva, surrounds all these lands. And the king has as his insignia a vermilion flag with a gold cross and four gold links, like this. [C]

I departed from the Kingdom of Meseber and went along the shores of the Great Sea to a city they call Veçina, which borders on Ungria. In this Veçina nine rivers converge and all of them enter the Great Sea. They call the first Turbo, the second Danubio, the third they call Orinçinçia, the

quarto Drinago, al quinto Pinga, al sexto Raba, al seteno Rabeza, al octavo
Ur, al noveno Veçine.[228] Estos nueve rrios fazen ante esta çibdad Veçina
muy grandes tremadales. Esta çibdad Veçina es cabeça del rreynado et ha
por señales un pendon blanco con estas señales bermejas. [CI]

Parti de Veçina por la marisma et fuy a Manro Castro et dende al
Puerto de Lobo, que es una sierra muy alta, et çerca la toda un rrio que
dizen Lusur que nasçe de los Montes Rexos. E apres deste puerto es una
çibdad que dizen Pidea, et es cabeça del rreynado. Et trae tales señales como
Uxbeto por que es su vasallo. E dende fuy al Puerto de Nigropila, que es
un golfo muy grande del Mar Mayor.[229] E dende fuy al cabo de Gotia
que lo çerca del un cabo el Mar Mayor, et del otro el Mar de Letana. Este
cabo conquirieron los godos quando salieron del ençerramiento de Alexandre. Con esta Gotia confinan dos provinçias muy grandes: son tierra del
Rey David et la provinçia de Avogasia, et confina con Tana. E dende entré
en el Mar de Tana por una angostura que es entre esta Gotia et el Cabo de
Tus, do es una çibdad que dizen Materga.[230] E rribera deste Mar de Letana son tres rreynados muy grandes que obedesçen a Uxbeto. Son Comania, que es de cristianos, et Tana, que es de turcos et de tartaros et el rreyno
de Canardi. Et partelos un grand rrio que dizen Tanay, et por este rrio dizen
a la çibdad Tana.[231] E las señales destos rreynados son pendones blancos con
señales bermejas como las de Uxbeto, por que son sus vasallos. [CII]

De si parti del Mar de Letana et torné me al Mar Mayor, et tomé la
marisma del levante muy grand camino. Et pasé por Arvasaxia et por Pesonta del imperio de Uxbeto, et llegué al rreynado de Sant Estopoli, que es
de cristianos comanes.[232] Et son muchas gentes que han nombres de judios, pero que todos fazen obras de cristianos en los sacrifiçios, llegan se mas
a los griegos que a los latinos. El rrey dende ha por señales un pendon bermejo con una mano blanca tal. [CIII]

---

[228] These are probably the Rivers Dniester, Danube and one of its tributaries, Drina, Pinka,
and the Raab and several of its tributaries.

[229] All are apparently port cities around the Black Sea.

[230] Gotia is the Crimea, with the Black Sea on one side and the Azov (here, Letana) on the
other. The provinces mentioned are apparently to the north of the Crimea, in the area south of
the Don River. The traveler enters a strait connecting the Black Sea with the Azov, where he
comes upon a city that could be the present-day Kerch.

[231] These three kingdoms are between the Azov and the Don (Tanay) River. According to
Newton (*Travels and Travellers*, 142) Tana was on the caravan silk route across Central Asia. Also
traded there were the furs of Russia and the merchandise of the Far East and India. Newton also
informs us that contemporary travelers found this area safe day or night, and that there was a
Franciscan mission station at Tana (145).

[232] The narrator follows the east coast of the Black Sea to Pitsunda, then seems to find
himself in Sevastopol, although this would take him once again to the Crimea.

fourth Drinago, the fifth Pinga, the sixth Raba, the seventh Rabeza, the eighth Ur, the ninth Veçine. These nine rivers make a great swamp before the city of Veçina. This city Veçina is the capital of the kingdom and has as its insignia a white flag with these vermilion emblems. [CI]

I departed Veçina along the coast and went to Manro Castro and from there to the Puerto de Lobo, which is a very high sierra, and a river they call Lusur, which originates in the Rexos Mountains, surrounds it all. And beyond this port is a city they call Pidea, and it is the capital of the kingdom. And it has the same insignia as Uxbeto because it is his vassal. And from there I went to the Port of Nigropila, which is a very large gulf of the Great Sea. And from there to the Cape of Gotia which is surrounded on one end by the Great Sea and the other end by the Sea of Letana. The Goths conquered this cape when they escaped from the imprisonment of Alexander. Gotia borders on two very large provinces: they are the land of King David and the province of Avogasia, and it borders on Tana. And from there I entered the Sea of Tana through a strait that is between this Gotia and the Cape of Tus, where there is a city they call Materga. And on the shores of this Sea of Letana there are three very large kingdoms that obey Uxbeto. They are Comania, which belongs to the Christians, and Tana, which belongs to the Turks and the Tartars, and the Kingdom of Canardi. And they are separated by a great river they call Tanay, and after this river they named the city Tana. And the insignia of these kingdoms are white flags with vermilion emblems, like the one for Uxbeto, because they are his vassals. [CII]

I departed the Sea of Letana and turned to the Great Sea, and took the eastern shore for a long way. And I passed through Arvasaxia and through Pesonta in the empire of Uxbeto, and I reached the kingdom of Sant Estopoli, which belongs to Koman Christians. And there are many people that have Jewish names, but all do Christian works in the sacrifices, more like Greeks than Latins. Its king has as his insignia a vermilion flag with a white hand, like this. [CIII]

E parti de Sant Estopoli et fuy a la Gorgania, que es entre el Mar Mayor et el Mar de Sara, muy grand tierra del imperio de Uxbeto, et fuyme por la marisma contra el poniente, et pasé por Faxa et por Conisa a la çibdad de Trapesonda, et moré ay un tienpo.[233] Este imperio parte con la Turquia pero que son cristianos griegos. E el Emperador de Trapesonda ha por señales un pendon bermejo con un aguila de oro con dos cabeças desta manera.[234] [CIV]

De si parti de Trapesonda et fuy por Quinisonda, et llegué al rreynado de Semiso[235] que confina con el Mar Mayor et con la Turquia, un rreynado grande de muchas gentes. El rrey dende ha por señales un pendon blanco con un signo tal como este, et son cristianos griegos.[236] [CV]

Parti de Semiso et fuy me por la marisma a un rreynado que dizen Castelle,[237] que es de cristianos griegos que guerrean con los turcos. Et es un rreynado fuerte et bien poblado. Et sus señales son un pendon bermejo con una cruz de oro et quatro eslavones de oro tales. [CVI]

De si parti de Castelle et fuy a Samasco, de si a Punta Rancha, de sy a Carpi. Et llegué a un rreynado que dizen Palolimen[238] que confina con la provinçia de Troya et con el Mar Mayor. Et es una tierra muy viçiosa et muy poblada et muy abondada de todas las cosas que son menester et es de cristianos griegos. E el rrey dende ha por señales otras tales commo las de Castelle.[239] [CVII]

Parti de Palolimen et vine a Diaschilo et a Veda, et dende a Ferandelfia de que ya conté de suso, e dende fuy a Faya,[240] una rica çibdad et abondada. Todas estas çibdades son en la Turquia et antigua mente dezian la Asia Menor. El rrey destas çibdades ha por señales un pendon con vandas blancas et cardenas, et çerca de la vara una cruz bermeja et el canpo blanco tal. [CVIII]

---

[233] From Georgia, between the Black and the Caspian Seas, the traveler arrives in Trebizond (now Trabzon), an empire in north Turkey that bordered on the Black Sea. It was located on the trade route linking East and West and therefore frequented by the Genoese and Venetians during the Middle Ages.

[234] The double-headed eagle is the last coat of arms in R.

[235] Continuing west on the south shores of the Black Sea, the next stop is probably Semsun (also in Turkey).

[236] A six-point star, in N it appears unadorned, while in S it is florid.

[237] The province of Sinop (a little farther west along the same coast) had as its capital a city named Casteli (Jiménez de la Espada 189–90).

[238] Continuing in a westerly direction, the traveler reaches Scutari (Palominen, according to Markham, 58).

[239] In N, the previous arms are repeated. In S, the emblem of the Emperors of Uzbekistan appears.

[240] Across the Marmara Sea from Scutari was the city of Dascylium, from where the narrator headed south to Philadelphia, now called Alasehir.

And I departed Sant Estopoli and went to Gorgania, which is between the Great Sea and the Sea of Sara, a great land in the empire of Uxbeto, and I went westward along the shore and passed by Faxa and by Conisa to the city of Trapesonda, and there I stayed for a time. This empire borders on Turquia but they are Greek Christians. And the Emperor of Trapesonda has as his insignia a vermilion flag with a gold eagle with two heads, in this manner. [CIV]

From there I departed Trapesonda and went by Quinisonda and reached the Kingdom of Semiso, which borders the Great Sea and Turquia, a large kingdom with many people. Its king has as his insignia a white flag with an emblem like this one, and they are Greek Christians. [CV]

I departed Semiso and went along the coast to a kingdom they call Castelle, which belongs to Greek Christians who war with the Turks. And it is a strong and well populated kingdom. And its insignia is a vermilion flag with a gold cross and four gold links, like this. [CVI]

From there I departed Castelle and went to Samasco, from there to Punta Rancha, from there to Carpi. And I reached a kingdom they call Palolimen that borders on the province of Troya and on the Great Sea. And it is a very rich and very populated land and abundant in all things that are necessary, and it belongs to Greek Christians. And its king has as his insignia like one that is Castelle's. [CVII]

I departed Palolimen and came to Diaschilo and to Veda, and from there to Ferandelfia which I already told of above, and from there to Faya, a rich and abundant city. All these cities are in Turquia and in ancient times they called it Asia Minor. The king of these cities has as his insignia a flag with white and cardinal red bands, and near the bar a vermilion cross and the field is white, like this. [CVIII]

Parti del rreynado de Feradelfia et fuy a otro rreynado que dizen Atologo,[241] que tiene muy grandes tierras en la Turquia rribera del Mar Mayor. E el rrey dende ha por señales un pendon bermejo et en medio una rueda prieta desta manera. [CIX]

De si parti de Atologo con mercadores por la tierra et travesé toda la Turquia et fuy a la çibdad de Savasco, e parti dende et travesé el rrio Sur que nasçe de los Montes del Toro. Et travesé toda la Jorgania fasta que llegué al Mar de Sara a una çibdad que dizen Dernent,[242] que tiene muy grandes tierras et tierra muy abondada, como quier que es tierra fria. E el rrey dende ha por señales asi como Uxbeto por que es su vasallo. [CX]

Entré aqui en esta Derebent en el Mar de Sara en un panfil, et llegué a una çibdad que dizen Caraol,[243] et es un rreynado muy grande et muy abondada del imperio de Persia. E el rrey dende ha por señales un pendon amarillo con quadra bermeja tal. [CXI]

Entre estas dos çibdades, es a saber Derbent et Caraol, es el puerto que dizen Januas Ferri.[244] E sobre este puerto son avidas muchas peleas por que Derbent es del imperio de Uxbeto et Caraol es del imperio de Persia. E parti de Caraol et fuy Axanbran, et dende a Barnachu, et dende a la Punta de Bacu,[245] que es toda çercada del Mar de Sara pero que ay una entrada por tierra firme. Et alli entra en el Mar de Sara un grand rrio que dizen Tigres, que nasçe de las altas Sierras del Toro et corre por Armenia la Mayor. A la entrada desta punta es una rica çibdad que dizen Bacu, et al mar dizen Sara de Bacu. Este nonbre ha por rrey de aquella tierra que dezian don Bacus, el qual era muy poderoso. Et fazia creer a la gentes de aquella tierra que el era Dios, et que lo adorassen asi como a Dios, et dezian le el Dios de Bacu. Et pobló aquesta çibdad de Bacu. Este Mar de Sara llamanle los tartaros por muchos nonbres, ca le dizen el Mar Caspio por los Montes Caspios que y llegan, et dizen le el Mar de la Jorgania por que la ha por vezina, et dizen le el Mar de Quillan por una provinçia que es en su ribera que dizen Quillan, e dizen le el Mar de Sara por la prerogatura del imperio de Sarra, e dizen le el Mar Bacu por la çibdad de Bacu. E parti de

---

[241] Jiménez de la Espada (180) and Markham (73) believe that this was Hypsili in Asia Minor.

[242] The narrator travels through the interior of Turkey this time, passing the city of Sivas and crossing its river, the Kizil. He then traverses Georgia and arrives in Derbent, on the Caspian.

[243] Caraol seems to have been a city on the west coast of the Caspian.

[244] The Iron Gates, according to Markham (73).

[245] Here he goes south along the west coast of the Caspian to Baku.

I departed the kingdom of Feradelfia and went to another kingdom they call Atologo that has many great lands in Turquia on the shores of the Great Sea. And the king has as his insignia a vermilion flag and in the center a black wheel, in this manner. [CIX]

From there I departed Atologo by land with merchants and crossed all of Turquia and went to the city of Savasco, and departed there and crossed the river Sur that originates in the Toro Mountains. And I crossed all of Jorgania until I reached the Sea of Sara at a city they call Dernent, which has many great lands and very abundant land, although it is a cold land. And its king has as his insignia an emblem like Uxbeto because he is his vassal. [CX]

Here in this Derebent I entered the Sea of Sara in a *panfilo*, and arrived at a city they call Caraol, and it is a very large and very abundant kingdom in the Empire of Persia. And its king has as his insignia a yellow flag with a vermilion square, like this. [CXI]

Between these two cities, that is Derbent and Caraol, is the port they call Januas Ferri. And near this port there are many battles because Derbent belongs to the Empire of Uxbeto and Caraol is of the Empire of Persia. And I departed Caraol and went to Axanbran, and from there to Barnachu, and from there to the Punta de Bacu, which is totally surrounded by the Sea of Sara, but there is an entrance on firm soil. And there a great river they call Tigris enters the Sea of Sara, [a river] that originates in the high Sierras of Toro and runs through Armenia Minor. At the entrance to this point is a rich city they call Bacu, and they call the sea Sara de Bacu. It has this name for a king of that land that they called Don Bacus, who was very powerful. And he made the people of that land believe that he was God, and that they should worship him like God, and they called him the God of Bacu. And he founded that city of Bacu. The Tartars call this Sea of Sara by many names, for they call it the Caspio Sea for the Caspios Mountains that are found there, and they call it the Sea of Jorgania because it is near [that place], and they call it the Sea of Quillan for a province that is on its shore that they call Quillan, and they call it the Sea of Sara for the Empire of Sarra, and they call it the Bacu Sea for the city of Bacu. And I departed

la çibdad de Bacu et fuy a Godaspi, et dende a Reversa, et a Var, et a Maumet, et a Sangui, et a Musaur, et a Espanor,[246] et a Quillan, que son todas estas çibdades ribera del Mar de Sara contra la parte del medio dia, et son del imperio de Persia. E dende fuy me por la rribera a la otra parte que es contra la trasmontana al Golfo de Monimenti, et dende a Trescargo et a Contulicanchi, et dende a la gran çibdad de Sara[247] do fue coronado Ux-beto, emperador de los tartaros. Esta çibdad está asentada entre el Golfo de Monimenti et el rrio de Tanay, rribera del qual son muchas ricas çibdades et abondadas, como quier que es tierra muy fria. Et las señales del Empera-dor de Sara son un pendon blanco con una señal bermeja tal.[248] [CXII]

Parti de la çibdad de Sara et fuy me el rrio de Tirus adelante, fasta do se ayuntan con el rrio de Tanay. Et las çibdades que yo andude rribera de Tanay son Baltachinca, et Escluerza, et Tifer, et Coranchi,[249] et son cabe-ças de rreynados que cada una tiene muy grandes terminos, et son del im-perio de Sara. Et son tierras muy ricas et abondadas et mayor mente de muchos ganados, que son camellos, vacas, ovejas, et bufanos. Et andude tanto fasta el levante, fasta que llegué a do se ayunta el rrio Tir (otros dizen Caspio), et nasçe de los Montes Caspios. E este rrio Tir sale del grand Lago Tanays[250] et ayuntanse ambos a dos, et fazese muy grand rrio que va con-tra la trasmontana. Et non pude saber do fenesçen por que van contra las tierras del Albizibi que son yermas et desabitadas, pero que en algunos lu-gares dellas ay gentes viles que comen carne cruda et los pescados crudos et beven agua de la mar et han rostros luengos commo canes, et dizen les sig-nosalos. E torné me contra el poniente el rrio de Tir arriba por que lo non pude pasar, que lieva dos jornadas en ancho, et llegué a una provinçia que dizen Sebur. Et es en ella una grand çibdad que dizen Castrama, et es ca-beça del rreyno de Sabur.[251] E este rreyno es todo çercado de los dos rrios que dizen el flumen Tyr et el flumen Tanay. E el rrey dende ha por señales un pendon blanco et señales bermejas como el Emperador de Sara. [CXIII]

Desi parti del rreyno de Sebur et llegué a una çibdad que dizen Rastaor et a otra que dizen Pidea. Et por aqui pasé el rrio Tanay et entré en una grand provinçia que dizen Roxia, que es en ella una grand çibdad que dizen

---

[246] All of these cities were apparently located along the west coast of the Caspian Sea.

[247] The narrator is now on the other side of the Caspian, heading north. Here the Tanay seems to refer to the Volga River, and the Monimenti Gulf is probably the Mertvoy.

[248] Again, the emblem of the Emperors of Uzbekistan appears.

[249] Cities along the Volga River, near the Caspian.

[250] This imaginary lake was the supposed origin of the Volga, Don, and Dvina Rivers. It figured on the Catalan Atlas as well as on the map prepared by the Pizigani brothers.

[251] The capital of this kingdom was Kostroma, in Russia.

the city of Bacu and went to Godaspi, and from there to Reversa, and to Var, and to Maumet, and to Sangui, and to Musuar, and to Espanor, and to Quillan, all of which are cities are on the shores of the Sea of Sara near the south, and they belong to the Empire of Persia. And from there I went along the shore to the other side that is on the north to the Gulf of Monimenti, and from there to Trescargo and to Contulicanchi, and from there to the great city of Sara where Uxbeto, Emperor of the Tartars, was crowned. This city is seated between the Gulf of Monimenti and the River Tanay, on the shores of which there are many rich and abundant cities, although the land is very cold. And the insignia of the Emperor of Sara is a white flag with a vermilion emblem, like this. [CXII]

I departed the city of Sara and went along the River Tirus to where it converges with the River Tanay. And the cities [to which] I traveled on the shores of the Tanay are Baltachinca, and Escluerza, and Tifer, and Coranchi, and they are capitals of kingdoms and each one is very large, and they belong to the Empire of Sara. And the lands are very rich and abundant and generally have many cattle, which are camels, cows, sheep, and buffalo. And I traveled a long way going eastward until I reached the place where the River Tir (others call it Caspio) converges, and it originates in the Caspios Mountains. And this River Tir comes out of Lake Tanays and both converge, and there a great river is formed which flows north. And I could not find out where they end because they go near the lands of Albizibi that are barren and uninhabited, but in some places there are vile people that eat raw meat and raw fish and drink sea water and have long faces like dogs, and they call them the cynocephali. And I turned west, going up the River Tir because I could not cross it, because it is a two-day journey wide, and I reached a province they call Sebur. And in it there is a great city they call Castrama, and it is the capital of the Kingdom of Sabur. And this kingdom is totally surrounded by two rivers they call the River Tyr and the River Tanay. And its king has as his insignia a white flag with vermilion emblems like the Emperor of Sara. [CXIII]

From there I departed the Kingdom of Sebur and reached a city they call Rastaor and another they call Pidea. And near here I crossed the River Tanay and entered a great province they call Roxia, and in it is a great city

Xorman,[252] et es cabeça del rreynado et confina con el grand lago de Tanay. Et sus señales son un pendon roxo et un castillo en medio, atal commo este que se sigue. [CXIV]

El grand lago de Tanay es en luengo tres jornadas et en ancho dos, et nasçen dende tres rrios muy grandes. Al uno dizen Tanay, que entra en el Mar Mayor apres de la çibdad de Tana.[253] Al otro rrio dizen Tir et va se contra las tierras del Albirzibi por tierras deshabitadas. Al otro dizen Nu[254] et va contra el poniente et mete se en el Mar de Alemaña apres de una çibdad que dizen Virona, de que ya conté de suso. Con este rrio Nu confina una grand provinçia que dizen Sicçia, et es tierra muy fria. E en esta Sicçia es una grand çibdad que es cabeça del rreynado que dizen Nogarado.[255] E son las gentes muy ricas et muy abondadas de todas cosas. E el rey dende ha por señales un pendon roxo con un castillo blanco tal. [CXV]

Parti de Sicçia et entré luego en otro rreynado que dizen Xorman. Et es en el una grand çibdad que dizen Xorman, que es cabeça del rreynado.[256] E el rrey dende ha por señales un pendon verde con una estrella de oro, atal commo esta. [CXVI]

E parti de Xorman et entré luego en otro rreynado que dizen Maxar en que son tres çibdades grandes. A la una dizen Casama, et a la otra Lasat, et a la otra Monsaior.[257] Este rreynado confina con el rreynado de Nogarado et con el rreyno de Silvana,[258] de que ya conté de suso. E el rrey deste Maxar ha por señales un pendon cardeno con estrellas blancas de plata tal. [CXVII]

Sali del rreynado de Maxar et entré luego en el rreyno de Silvana, que dizen Septen Castra et los griegos dizen le Horgimil, que es todo çercado de dos rrios muy grandes, et dizen al uno flumen Turbo et al otro flumen Lusim. En este rreynado es una gran çibdad que dizen Sarax.[259] E el rrey dende ha por señales un pendon con un alfanje bermejo. Et son cristianos sçismaticos et ya conté dellos de suso. [CXVIII]

---

[252] Not far from Moscow can be found the cities of Rostov and Kholm (here, Xorman).

[253] Although this lake was imaginary, many geographers of the Middle Ages believed in its existence. Tana is the present-day city of Azov.

[254] The River Dvina.

[255] Scythia was a large region lying north and east of the Black and Caspian Seas. The narrator identifies its capital as Novgorod.

[256] Kholm.

[257] Markham (75) claims that this kingdom was named Moxia, and that it reached between Orenburg and Moscow. The cities mentioned here are probably Kazan, Lyskovo, and Moscow.

[258] Eastern Novgorod and Transylvania (Ukraine), according to Jiménez de la Espada (250).

[259] The narrator is now between the Dniester and the Dnieper Rivers in Ukraine. Perhaps the city of Saras is Odessa.

they call Xorman, and it is the capital of the kingdom and borders on the great lake of Tanay. And its insignia is a red flag with a castle in the center, like the one that follows. [CXIV]

The great lake of Tanay is three-days' journey long and two wide, and three very large rivers originate in it. They call one Tanay, which enters the Great Sea beyond the city of Tana. They call the other river Tir, and it goes near the lands of Albizibi through uninhabited lands. They call the other Nu, and it goes eastward and flows into the Sea of Alemaña beyond a city they call Virona, which I have already told of above. This River Nu borders on a great province they call Sicçia, and it is a very cold land. And in this Sicçia there is a great city that is the capital of the kingdom, which they call Nogarado. And the people are very rich and well-supplied with all things. And its king has as his insignia a red flag with a white castle, like this. [CXV]

I departed Sicçia and then entered another kingdom they call Xorman. And in it is a great city they call Xorman, which is the capital of the kingdom. And its king has as his insignia a green flag with a gold star, like this one. [CXVI]

And I departed Xorman and then entered another kingdom they call Maxar, in which there are three great cities. They call one Casama, and the other Lasat, and the other Monsaior. This kingdom borders the kingdom of Nogarado and the Kingdom of Silvana, which I already told of above. And the king of this Maxar has as his insignia a cardinal red flag with white stars of silver, like this. [CXVII]

I left the kingdom of Maxar and then entered the kingdom of Silvana, which they call Septen Castra and the Greeks call Horgimil, which is totally surrounded by two very large rivers; and they call one the River Turbo and the other River Lusim. In this kingdom is a great city they call Sarax. And its king has as his insignia a flag with a vermilion scimitar. And they ar schismatic Christians and I have already told of them above. [CXVIII]

Allende del rrio Tir contra la trasmontana son dos provinçias muy grandes. Et dizen a la una Yrcania et a la otra dizen Gotia, donde salieron los godos que conquirieron a toda España et fueron señores della muy grand tienpo. Et es llamada Tierra de Nogulaus.[260] Et son gentes fuertes et lidiadores, pero que es tierra muy fria. Et el rrey desta Siria otrosi el de Arcania han por señales.[261] [CXIX]

Esta Gotia et esta Yrcania parten con las altas sierras de la trasmontana. En estas sierras veen la estrella del norte en el medio çielo, et faze todo el año un dia seys meses dura el dia, et seys meses dura la noche. Et es tierra desabitada pero que dizen que son fallados en esta tierra ommes que han las cabeças pegadas sobre los ombros, que non han cuellos ningunos, et la barva tienen sobre los pechos, et las orejas dellas llegados a los ombros. Et esta es su figura, commo estos dos ommes que están en este monte desnudos.[262]

Otrosi son fallados en esta tierra muy grandes osos et puercos javalis blancos, segund que ya conté de suso. Estas dos provinçias de Yrcania et de Gotia poblaron los godos que salieron de la Tartaria çerrada de los castillos de Got et Magot quando se delibraron del ençerramiento de Alexandre, e conquirieron la mayor parte del mundo. Con esta Gotia confina otra grand provinçia que dizen Paschar,[263] que confina con Suevia, la que de suso reconté. En esta Suevia es una grand çibdad que dizen Roderin. Otrosi en esta Suevia son dos lagos muy grandes, que cada uno dellos es de ancho una jornada. Al uno dizen Lacus Stocol, et al otro dizen Lacus Estarse. Et dende nasçen dos rrios muy grandes que çircunrrodean una gran tierra que es entre los montes de la trasmontana et el Mar de Alemaña. Et es tierra muy fria sin mesura. E despues estos dos rrios metense en el Mar de Alemaña, en un golfo de mar que dizen Golfus Stocol. Este golfo el mas tienpo es todo elado et quajado de los grande frios que y faze. En esta mar es la ysla Godlandia que de suso reconté. E parti de Suevia et torné me a la rribera del mar a una çibdad que dizen Sordepinche, e de si a otra que dizen Calman, e de si a otra que dizen Estocol, et a otra que dizen Sormençes, e otra que dizen Ystat, et a otra que dizen Londis que confina con la Noruega.[264] En esta çibdad Londis entré en una quinta de alemanes et venimos por el Mar

---

[260] Ukraine and a land called Gotia, for the Goths who inhabited it.

[261] This emblem looks like a cross with two legs. According to Pasch (29) it might represent a cross planted upon a hill, an emblem not unlike some found on old Russian banners.

[262] In N there is an illustration of two nude men in a wood, pointing at one another; neither has a neck.

[263] On the banks of the Volga.

[264] Sördeköping, Kalmar, Stockholm, Ystad, and Lund, all in Sweden. It is unclear what Sormences might be.

Beyond the River Tir near the north are two very large provinces. And they call one Yrcania and the other Gotia, where the Goths that conquered all of España came from, and they were lords of it for a long time. And it is called the Land of Nogulaus. And the people are strong and warlike, but the land is very cold. And the king of Siria and also the one from Arcania have this insignia.

This Gotia and this Yrcania border on the high sierras of the north. In these sierras they see the North Star in the center of the sky, and in the whole year a day lasts six months, and a night lasts six months. And it is an uninhabited land but they say that in this land men are found that have their heads attached to their shoulders, who have no necks, and their beard is on their chests, and their ears go down to their shoulders. And this is their image, like these two men that are naked on this mountain.

In this land also are found many great bears and white boars, according to what I have already told above. These two provinces of Yrcania and of Gotia were populated by the Goths who came out of encircled Tartaria from the castles of Got and Magot when they freed themselves from the imprisonment of Alexander, and they conquered the better part of the world. Gotia borders on another great province they call Paschar, which borders on Suevia, of which I told above. In this Suevia is a great city they call Roderin. In this Suevia there are also two very large lakes, for each of them is a day's journey wide. They call one Lacus Stocol, and they other they call Lacus Estarse. And from there originate two very large rivers that surround a great land that is between the mountains of the north and the Sea of Alemaña. And it is a very cold land, without measure. And later these two rivers flow into the Sea of Alemaña in a gulf of the sea they call the Stocol Gulf. This gulf is most of the time frozen and immobilized from the great cold that is there. In this sea is the island Godlandia I told of above. And I departed Suevia and turned to the shores of the sea to a city they call Surdepinche, and from there to another they call Calman, and from there to another they call Estocol, and to another they call Sormençes, and another they call Ystat, and to another they call Londis which borders on Noruega. In this city Londis I entered the boat of some Germans and

de Alemaña contra el poniente. Et fallamos en esta mar çinco yslas de que ya conté de suso. A la una dellas dizen Godlandia, a la otra Cola, a la otra Lister, a la otra Bondelet, a la otra Salandia.[265] E aqui entra un grand golfo del Mar de Alemaña que çircunrrodea toda la punta del rreyno de Daçia de Danes, de que ya conté de suso. E a la entrada deste golfo son dos yslas, que dizen a la una Insula Janglant et a la otra Finonia.[266] E dende vin me para Flandes, e dende vin me para Sevilla donde sali primera mente.

[265] Gotland, Öland, the Swedish peninsula Listerlandet, then Bornholm and Åland.
[266] These are the Danish islands of Lolland and Fyn.

we came westward on the Sea of Alemaña. And we found in this sea five islands that I already told of above. They call one Godlandia, the other Cola, the other Lister, the other Bondelet, the other Salandia. And a great gulf of the Sea of Alemaña enters here and surrounds the whole tip of the kingdom of Daçia de Danes, of which I have already told above. And at the entrance of this gulf there are two islands; they call one Insula Janglant and the other Finonia. And from there I came to Flandes, and from there I came to Sevilla, from where I first left.

Bibliography

Anderson, A. R. *Alexander's Gate, Gog and Magog, and the Inclosed Nations.* Cambridge, Mass.: Harvard University Press, 1932.

Atlas catalán de Abraham Cresques: Primera edición con su traducción en el sexto centenario de su realización. Barcelona: Diáfora, 1975.

Bagrow, Leo. *History of Cartography.* Chicago: Precedent, 1985.

Barraclough, E. M. C., and W. G. Crampton. *Flags of the World.* London: Warne, 1978.

Battuta, Ibn. *Travels, A.D. 1325–54.* Cambridge: Cambridge University Press, 1958.

Beazley, Raymond C. *The Dawn of Modern Geography.* 3 vols. London: H. Frowde, 1906.

Beckingham, C. F. "The Quest for Prester John." *Bulletin of the John Rylands Library of Manchester* 62 (1979–80): 290–304.

Béthencourt, Jean de. *The Canarien or Book of the Conquest and Conversion of the Canarians in the year 1402.* London: Hakluyt Society, 1872.

Bonnet, Buenaventura. "Las Canarias y el primer libro de geografía medieval, escrito por un fraile español en 1350." *Revista de Historia* 67 (1944): 205–27.

Ceballos-Escalera y Gila, Alfonso de, Marqués de la Floresta. *Heraldos y reyes de armas en la corte de España.* Madrid: Colección El Perservante Borgoña, 1993.

Chandos Herald. *Life of the Black Prince.* Ed. Milfred K. Pope. Oxford: Clarendon Press, 1910.

Conti Rossini, Carlo. "Il *Libro del Conocimiento* e le sue notizie sull'Etiopie." *Bollettino della Reale Società Geografica Italiana* Series 5, 6:9–10 (1917): 656–79.

Cortesão, Armando. *Historia da cartografia portuguesa.* 2 vols. Lisbon: Junta de Investigacões do Ultramar, 1969.

Deyermond, Alan. *A History of Spanish Literature: The Middle Ages.* New York: Barnes and Noble, 1971.

Díaz Martín, Luis Vicente. *Los oficiales de Pedro I de Castilla*. Valladolid: Universidad de Valladolid, 1987.

Dormer, Diego José. *Progresos de la historia en el reino de Aragón*. Zaragoza, 1680.

Fernández Armesto, Felipe. *Before Columbus: Exploration and Civilization from the Mediterranean to the Atlantic, 1229–1492*. Philadelphia: University of Pennsylvania Press, 1987.

Fick, Barbara. *El libro de viajes en la España medieval*. Santiago de Chile: Editorial Universitaria, 1976.

Flint, Valerie I. J. *Ideas in the Medieval West: Texts and Their Contexts*. London: Variorum Reprints, 1988.

———. *The Imaginative Landscape of Christopher Columbus*. Princeton: Princeton University Press, 1992.

Foulché-Delbosc, R. "Bibliographie des voyages en Espagne et Portugal." *Revue Hispanique* 3 (1896): 88–112.

Freidman, John Block. *The Monstrous Races in Medieval Art and Thought*. Cambridge, Mass.: Harvard University Press, 1981.

Freiesleben, Hans-Christian. *Der katalanische Weltatlas vom Jahre 1375*. Stuttgart: Brockhaus, 1977.

———. "Map of the World or Sea Chart? The Catalan Mappamundi of 1375." *Navigation: Journal of the Institute of Navigation* 26 (1979): 85–89.

Grosjean, Georges, ed. *The Catalan Atlas of the Year 1375*. Dietikon-Zurich: Urs Graf, 1978.

Harley, J. B. and David Woodward. *The History of Cartography*. 2 vols. Chicago: University of Chicago Press, 1987.

Harvey, P. D. A. *Medieval Maps*. Toronto: University of Toronto Press, 1991.

Hyde, J. K. "Real and Imaginary Journeys in the Later Middle Ages." *Bulletin of the John Rylands University Library of Manchester* 65:1 (1982): 125–47.

Juan Manuel. *Libro de las armas*. Ed. José Manuel Blecua. Vol. I of *Obras completas*. Madrid, 1982.

Kimble, George H. T. *Geography in the Middle Ages*. London: Methuen, 1938.

———. Foreword to *Catalan World Map of the R. Biblioteca Estense at Modena*. London: Royal Geographical Society, 1934.

Labarge, Margaret Wade. *Viajeros medievales: Los ricos y los insatisfechos*. Madrid: Nerea, 1992.

Ladero Quesada, Miguel Angel. *El mundo de los viajeros medievales*. Madrid: Anaya, 1992.

LaRoncière, Charles de. *La découverte de l'Afrique au Moyen Age: Cartographes et explorateurs.* Mémoires de la Société Royale de Géographie d'Egypte. Vols. 5, 6, 13. Cairo: Institut Français d'Archéologie Orientale, 1924–27.

LaRoncière, Monique and Michel Mollat du Jourdin. *Les portulans: Cartes marines du XIIIe au XVIIe siècle.* Fribourg: Nathan, 1984.

Lasso de la Vega, Angel. "Viajeros españoles de la Edad Media." *Boletín de la Sociedad Geográfica de Madrid* 12 (1882): 227–57.

Libro del conosçimiento. Ed. Marcos Jiménez de la Espada. Madrid, 1877. Reprint with a foreword by Francisco López Estrada. Barcelona: El Albir, 1980.

Libro del conosçimiento. (Microfiche of MSS. *N, R,* and *S*) Ed. Nancy F. Marino. Madison: Hispanic Seminary of Medieval Studies, 1993.

López de Ayala, Pero. *Crónica del rey don Pedro.* Eds. Constance L. Wilkins and Heanon M. Wilkins. Madison: Hispanic Seminary of Medieval Studies, 1985.

Markham, Clements R., ed. and trans. *Knowledge of the World.* London: Hakluyt Society, 1912.

Menéndez Pidal de Navascués, Faustino. *Heráldica medieval española I: La casa real de León y Castilla.* Madrid: Hidalguía, 1982.

Messía de la Cerda y Pita, Luis F. *Heráldica española: El diseño heráldico.* Madrid: Aldaba Ediciones, 1990.

Michael, Ian. "Topological Problems in Medieval Alexander Literature: The Enclosure of Gog and Magog." In *The Medieval Alexander Legend and Romance Epic. Essays in Honor of J. A. Ross,* eds. Peter Noble, Lucie Polak, and Claire Isoz, 131–47. New York and London: Kraus, 1982.

Mollat, M. *Grands voyages et connaissance du monde du milieu du XIII siècle à la fin du XV siècle.* Paris, 1966.

Morel-Fatio, Alfred. Review of *Andanças e viajes de Pero Tafur por diversas partes del mundo avidos, 1435–1439.* Ed. Marcos Jiménez de la Espada. *Revue Critique d'Histoire et de Littérature* 9 (1875): 135–41.

Newton, Arthur P. *Travels and Travellers of the Middle Ages.* London: Routledge & Kegan Paul, Ltd., 1949.

Ohler, Norbert. *The Medieval Traveller.* Trans. Caroline Hillier. Suffolk: Boydell Press, 1989.

Pasch, Georges. "Les drapeaux des cartes-portulans: L'atlas dit de Charles V (1375)." *Vexillologia: Bulletin de l'Association Française d'Etudes Internationales de Vexillologie* 1, nos. 2–3 (1967): 38–60.

———. "Les drapeaux des cartes-portulans: Drapeaux du *Libro de Conoscimiento.*" *Vexillologia: Bulletin de l'Association Française d'Etudes Internationales de Vexillologie* 2, nos. 1–2 (1969): 8–32.

————. "Drapeaux des Canariens: Témoignage des portulans." *Vexillologia: Bulletin de l'Association Française d'Etudes Internationales de Vexillologie* 3, no. 2 (1973): 51–76.

————. "Les drapeaux des cartes-portulans [portulans du groupe Vesconte]." *Vexillologia: Bulletin de l'Association Française d'Etudes Internationales de Vexillologie* 3, no. 2 (1973): 52–62.

Pastoureau, Michel. "L'heraldique imaginaire." *Perpectives médiévales* 10 (1984): 98–102.

Pérez Embid, Florentino. *Los descubrimientos en el Atlántico y la rivalidad castellano-portuguesa hasta el Tratado de Tordesillas.* Seville, 1948.

Pérez Priego, Miguel Angel. "Estudio literario de los libros de viajes medievales." *Epos* 1 (1984): 217–39.

Peschel, O. *Geschichte der Erdkunde.* Amsterdam: Meridian, 1961.

Richard, Jean. *Les récits de voyages et de pèlerinages.* Turnhout: Brepols, 1981.

Riquer, Martín de. *Heráldica castellana en tiempos de los Reyes Católicos.* Barcelona: Biblioteca Filológica, Quaderns Crema, 1986.

————. "La heráldica en el *LdC* y el problema de su datación." In *Dicenda: Cuadernos de Filología Hispánica.* Vol. 6 of *Estudios y textos dedicados a Francisco López Estrada.* Madrid: Universidad Complutense, 1987.

————. "La heráldica en el *LdC* por tercera vez." In *Letters and Society in Fifteenth-Century Spain: Studies Presented to P. E. Russell on His Eightieth Birthday.* London: Dolphin, 1993.

Rogers, Francis M. "The Vivaldi Expedition." *Annual Report of the Dante Society of America* 73 (1955): 31–45.

Rubio Tovar, Joaquín, ed. *Libros españoles de viajes medievales (Selección).* Temas de España 167. Madrid: Taurus, 1986.

Russell, Peter E. "La heráldica en el *Libro del conosçimiento.*" In *Studia Riquer,* vol. 2, 687–97. Barcelona: Quaderns Crema, 1987.

————. "The Infante Dom Henrique and the Libro del conoscimiento del mundo." In *In memoriam Ruben Andresen Leitão,* vol 2, 259–67. Lisbon, 1981.

Santarém, Manuel Francisco de Barros e Sousa, Viscount of. *Atlas composé de mappemondes, de portulans et de artes hydrographiques depuis le VIe jusqu'au XVIIe siècle.* Paris, 1849. Facsimile reprint. Amsterdam: R. Muller, 1985.

Santiago, Miguel. "Las dos ediciones (¿o dos modalidades de una misma?) de 'Le Canarien' por Bergeron, en 1630." *Revista de Bibliografía Nacional* 7 (1946): 364–75.

Schiff, Mario. *La bibliothèque du Marquis de Santillane.* Paris: Emile Bouillon, 1905.

Serrano y Sanz, M. *Autobiografía y memorias*. Nueva Biblioteca de Autores Españoles 2. Madrid: Bailly-Bailliére e hijos, 1925.

Tafur, Pero. *Andanças e viajes de Pero Tafur por diversas partes del mundo avidos, 1435–1439*. Ed. Marcos Jiménez de la Espada. *Revista Europea* May 2, 1875.

Taylor, E. G. R. "Pactolus: River of Gold." *Scottish Geographical Magazine* 44 (1928): 129–44.

Valera, Diego de. *Espejo de la verdadera nobleza y Tratado de las armas*. Ed. M. Penna. Biblioteca de Autores Españoles 116. Madrid: Real Academia, 1959.

Viera y Clavijo, José de. *Noticias de la historia general de las islas de Canaria*. Madrid, 1772–83.

Voyages, quêtes, pèlerinages dans la littérature et la civilization médiévale. Actes du colloque du CUERMA, 5–7 March, 1976. Aix, 1976.

Wagner, Anthony Richard. *Heralds and Heraldry in the Middle Ages*. London: Oxford University Press, 1946.

Winter, Heinrich. "Catalan Portolan Maps and Their Place in the Total View of Cartographic Development." *Imago Mundi* 11 (1954): 1–12.

Wolfel, D. J. "La falsificación del Canarien." *Revista de Historia* (La Laguna), 100 (1952): 495–508.

Woodcock, Thomas and John Martin Robinson. *The Oxford Guide to Heraldry*. Oxford: Oxford University Press, 1988.

Wright, John K. *The Geographical Lore of the Time of the Crusades*. New York: Dover, 1965.

Index to the Introduction

Names and Places in the Text/Translation

MRTS

MEDIEVAL AND RENAISSANCE TEXTS AND STUDIES
is the major publishing program of the
Arizona Center for Medieval and Renaissance Studies
at Arizona State University, Tempe, Arizona.

MRTS emphasizes books that are needed —
texts, translations, and major research tools.

MRTS aims to publish the highest quality scholarship
in attractive and durable format at modest cost.

Current scholarship regards the *El libro del conoscimiento de todos los reinos* **(The Book of Knowledge of All Kingdoms)**, an anonymous work of some 20,000 words composed in the last quarter of the fourteenth century, as a pseudo-travel book that does not describe an authentic voyage throughout the known world as it claims. It is rather a geographical novel probably composed with the aid of a portolan chart or *mappamundi*. In the fourteenth and fifteenth centuries, it was regarded as a reliable travel account and was therefore used as a geographical textbook and may have been used in the production of the important Este World Map.

The facing-page translation presented here is based on the four known manuscripts of the *Conoscimiento*. The edition also includes 110 heraldic devices that identify each kingdom mentioned.

Nancy F. Marino is Professor of Spanish at Michigan State University.